SWIMMING AGAINST THE TIDE

Since 1985 the International Center for Economic Growth, a nonprofit organization, has contributed to economic growth and human development in developing and post-socialist countries by strengthening the capacity of indigenous research institutes to provide leadership in policy debates. To accomplish this the Center sponsors a wide range of programs—including research, publications, conferences, seminars, and special projects advising governments—through a network of more than 230 correspondent institutes worldwide. The Center's research and publications program is organized around five series: Sector Studies; Country Studies; Studies in Human Development and Social Welfare; Occasional Papers; and Working Papers.

The Center is affiliated with the Institute for Contemporary Studies, and is headquartered in Panama with the administrative office in San Francisco, California.

For further information, please contact the International Center for Economic Growth, 243 Kearny Street, San Francisco, California, 94108, USA. Phone (415) 981-5353; Fax (415) 986-4878.

ICEG Board of Overseers

SWIMMING AGAINST THE TIDE

Turkish Trade Reform in the 1980s

Anne O. Krueger and Okan H. Aktan

An International Center for Economic Growth Publication

ICS PRESS

San Francisco, California

Inquiries, book orders, and catalog requests should be addressed to ICS Press, 243 Kearny Street, San Francisco, California 94108, USA. Telephone: (415) 981-5353; Fax: (415) 986-4878; book orders within the contiguous United States: (800) 326-0263.

Distributed to the trade by National Book Network, Lanham, Maryland.

Cover designer: Herman + Company
Copyeditor: Gertrude Kaplan
Production editor: Tracy Clagett
Indexer: Linda Gregonis

10   9   8   7   6   5   4   3   2   1

Library of Congress Cataloging-in-Publication Data

Krueger, Anne O.
    Swimming against the tide : Turkish trade reform in the 1980s / Anne O. Krueger and Okan H. Aktan.
        p.   cm.
    "An International Center for Economic Growth publication."
    ISBN 1-55815-178-8
    1. Commercial policy—Turkey.   2. Balance of payments—Turkey. 3. Turkey—Economic policy.   I. Aktan, Okan H.   II. International Center for Economic Growth.   III. Title.
    HF1583.4.K78   1992
    382'.3'09561'09048—dc20   91-45069
                                                                        CIP

Contents

List of Tables

Preface

As the 1980s began, the government of Turkey undertook substantial changes in economic policy. *Swimming against the Tide* analyzes those changes, with emphasis on the trade and payments regime, and examines the Turkish economy's response to the new policies.

Even though the early 1980s were a time of worldwide recession, Turkey persevered—against the tide—in its trade reform strategy, implementing a series of generally successful measures throughout the decade. Supporting their analysis with a wealth of economic data, the authors show how Turkey was able to dismantle a long-standing system of protective barriers and effectively liberalize foreign trade. Improved export performance kept Turkey creditworthy at a time when most other heavily indebted countries faced severe borrowing constraints. Thus, Turkey's experience offers a counterexample to the view that the debt crisis of the 1980s was entirely the result of recession in the world economy.

The senior author of this volume is a former vice president of the World Bank and is one of the most respected economists writing today. She has made significant contributions to advanced international trade theory and policy. Her coauthor is a Turkish economist with a doctorate from Oxford University. The International Center for Economic Growth is pleased to publish their authoritative study, the result of extensive investigations they carried out in Istanbul.

This account of successful trade reform, with the insight it provides into the functioning of the Turkish economy, will be useful to development economists, policy makers and scholars in developing countries, and all those who ponder the relationship of Turkey to the European Community and a changing world economy.

Nicolás Ardito-Barletta
General Director
International Center for Economic Growth

January 1992
Panama City, Panama

Authors' Preface

Starting in 1980 Turkey embarked on major economic policy changes. Although 1980 was several years before the start of the debt crisis, the timing coincided closely with the onset of the severe worldwide recession that lasted until 1983. Despite that, the Turkish government continued with its reform strategy, implementing still further measures throughout the 1980s. There is great interest in Turkey's experience, because Turkey is itself important and also because other countries found themselves confronted with the need to alter policies at later points in the decade.

We were therefore more than willing to undertake an analysis of the policy reforms affecting Turkish international trade when it was suggested to us by Arnold Harberger. We are indebted to him for suggesting the undertaking and to the International Center for Economic Growth for funding much of the research. Support for research assistance in Turkey was generously provided by the Central Bank of Turkey. We are indebted to Hasan Ersel, director general of the Research, Planning, and Education Department of the Central Bank for his willingness to assist us in locating needed data and by providing access to others at the Central Bank.

In the course of the project, a large number of individuals contributed. We are especially indebted to Professor Osman Okyar, who read and commented on an earlier draft of the manuscript. In the fall of 1989 we visited Istanbul and sought to interview exporters about their experience with the trade regime of the 1980s. We are especially indebted to Feyyaz Berker of the Turkish Businessmen's Association (TUSİAD) and Çelik Kurdoğlu of the Foreign Economic Relations Board (DEİK) for their assistance in making the interviews possible. We are also grateful to the many individuals who willingly gave their time and assistance in helping us to understand the trade regime. A list of all of those who were so generous is contained in the appendix to Chapter 5.

A major part of our effort was devoted to obtaining the basic data that appear in the various chapters of the study and in the Data Appendix. We are indebted to a large number of persons who assisted in providing data and in helping us understand the relationships between various data sets. They include the following:

at the Central Bank:
Ülkü Özgüler, assistant director general of the Research, Planning, and Education Department
Yalçın Altan, director of Export Credits
Tarık Sunkurlu, director of the Funds

at the Undersecretariat of Foreign Trade and Treasury:
Attila Duygan, head of the General Directorate of Economic Research and Evaluation
Ahmet Güresin, at the same department
Sami Dönmez, head of the Computer Department
Beratiye Öncü, head of the Research and Development Department, Export Promotion Center (IGEME)
Füsun Balıkçıoğlu, head of the EC Department, IGEME
Nusret Fırıncı, head of the Istanbul Office, IGEME, for planning and arranging the interviews in Istanbul

at the State Planning Organization:
Tumuçin Sanalan, head of the Investment Incentives Department
Nezih Kaynar, at the same department

at the State Institute of Statistics:
Gülsen Gümüşlü, director of the National Income Section
Yalçın Acuner, expert, Research Department
Ali Arca, director of the Foreign Trade Section

at the Ministry of Finance:
Kemal Kılıçlaroğlu, deputy general director of revenues
Münevver Kılıçkaya, section head, General Directorate of Revenues

at Hacettepe University:
Professor Dr. Sadık Kırbaş, head of the Department of Finance, for providing and discussing the legal documents
Mine Turhan, assistant, Department of Economics, for the tedious job of entering data into the computer and assisting in collecting data

at Duke University:
David Orsmond, graduate research assistant
Laura Osborne, graduate research assistant

David Orsmond also read and commented on the entire manuscript and did many other tasks to ensure consistency and reliability of the text and the data. We are both grateful to him. Finally, Tercan Baysan and Dani Rodrik both read and commented on the penultimate draft. Neither they nor any of the others who assisted us necessarily agree with our interpretations or conclusions. The manuscript is nonetheless improved thanks to their support.

In all analysis of recent economic events, there is a problem in cutting off the flow of new information. We met in Ankara in June 1990. Our data and analysis are current through that date.

1

Introduction

On January 24, 1980, the Turkish government announced a major economic reform program. Many of the policy changes—a change in the exchange rate, major increases in prices of goods and services sold by public sector enterprises, inauguration of a stabilization program backed by the International Monetary Fund—had also been components of earlier packages of measures in 1958 and 1970. Indeed, in 1977 and 1978 reform programs had been announced, although their effect had been minimal. What differed in 1980 from earlier programs was the government's statement that, in addition to the usual stabilization measures, it intended to liberalize the economy more generally. It made significant alterations in the Turkish trade and payments regime. In addition, the government announced that its role in economic activity would be diminished and that greater reliance would be placed on the private sector for economic growth. Further, the 1980 measures were said to be only the beginning of the reform program.

Before 1980 Turkish development strategies and economic policies had been based on the premise that industrialization was essential and could be effected only through policies that protected fledgling Turkish industries from foreign competition. Thus, once domestic production of particular items began, imports had been limited in quantity. Indeed, they had been prohibited once it was deemed that domestic production was sufficient to meet domestic demand. In other regards Turkish economic policies since the Second World War had varied, but at no time had the policy of protecting domestic industry been seriously questioned. As a consequence, by the late 1970s Turkish exports were only around 5 percent of gross national product, and imports were commensurately small. This was clearly an uneconomic situation for a country of Turkey's size, proximity to Europe, and resource endowment.

From the outset, therefore, the 1980 reform program differed significantly from earlier programs. Of course, it could be questioned whether the announced program would be sustained, but even the announcement constituted a significant break from the past. Moreover, despite twists and turns, the essential thrust of the program was continued from 1980 onward. Some analysts believe that there were two major waves of reform: one starting in 1980 and the other late in 1983. Either way, the central thrust of policy toward opening the economy and relying more on markets and less on government controls continued throughout the 1980s.

The reform program has not been successful in all its dimensions. One of its purposes was sharply to retard inflation, which had reached an annual rate of about 117 percent, as measured by the consumer price index, by the beginning of 1980. Although the rate of inflation subsequently fell to about 30 percent by 1983, it rose thereafter and stood at rates between 65 and 75 percent in the autumn of 1989 and the winter of 1990. The macroeconomic stabilization objectives announced in January 1980 were only partially and temporarily achieved, and inflation remains an economic and political problem of major magnitude.

Nonetheless, the achievements of the Turkish program of trade liberalization and switching to an outer-oriented trade regime are remarkable by any standard. The Turkish economy has been restructured from being inward looking and insulated to an outward orientation. Exports have been a major engine of growth. Turkey's exports measured in U.S. dollars grew at an average annual rate of 22.2 percent from 1980 to 1985 at a time when world trade was almost stagnant. They continued to grow rapidly in the latter half of the 1980s, reaching US$11.7 billion in 1989. Exports increased from 7.1 percent of GNP in 1980 to 21.0 percent in 1987.

Turkey had accumulated sizable debts to official and private creditors in the 1970s and faced a debt crisis in January 1980 as severe as the crises that were to confront Mexico, Brazil, Argentina, and other heavily indebted countries in 1982–1983. While other developing countries struggled and failed to resume growth and restore credit worthiness, Turkish economic growth accelerated, and Turkey was credit worthy throughout the worldwide recession of 1980–1983 and beyond.

The Turkish experience is therefore worthy of close analysis. Regardless of whether macroeconomic stabilization is achieved or whether current trends of accelerating inflation continue and finally force another wrenching adjustment, an examination of the Turkish policy changes and their effects is warranted. On one hand, Turkey experienced remarkable success in many dimensions of the economic program. It is therefore worthwhile to examine the policy reforms and their effects in an effort to understand what elements of the program may have lessons for other countries embarking on policy reforms. On the other hand, it is also worthwhile examining the Turkish program critically, and especially analyzing some of its less successful parts— such as the failure to contain inflation—that threaten the achievements of the trade and payments liberalization. Again, there may be lessons both for Turkish policy and for other policy makers contemplating serious reform efforts.

It is the purpose of this book to undertake such an analysis, with a focus on the trade and payments liberalization of the 1980s and its effects on the Turkish economy and its growth. Such an examination cannot be undertaken, however, without some understanding of the context in which the reforms took place. Such a context includes both the circumstances of the Turkish economy and Turkish economic policy before the January 1980 reform program and also the macroeconomic environment within which trade and exchange rate policy had its effects after the January 1980 reforms.

To that end the analysis starts with an account of Turkish economic policy and performance before the start of the reforms. Chapter 2 briefly chronicles Turkish economic policy and economic growth before 1980, with particular attention to those policies and factors that contributed to the economic crisis as well as to those features of the Turkish economy the understanding of which is important in interpreting later events. Chapter 3 provides an account of the policy reforms undertaken during the 1980s and the overall macroeconomic performance of the economy. Chapter 4 goes into greater depth in analyzing the changes in incentives confronting producers of exportables and import-competing goods and the evolution of the overall bias of the trade and payments regime.

A final chapter analyzes the response of the economy to the policy reform package, with special emphasis on export performance. It also gives attention to some of the less satisfactory aspects of Turkish economic performance in the 1980s. The chapter ends with an assessment of the ways in which the successes to date are to some degree threatened by the remaining problems and of the lessons that may be learned from the Turkish experience.

2

The Turkish Economy before 1980

Turkey is a country of 55 million people, straddling Europe and Asia. After the Second World War it could reasonably be claimed that Turkey was the poorest European country and the richest Asian one, if one ignored the Soviet Union and the relatively unpopulated oil exporters of the Middle East. Although Turkish economic growth was reasonably rapid from 1950 to 1980, averaging about 5.5 percent annually, a high rate of population growth (over 2.5 percent annually) resulted in per capita income growth of just under 3 percent annually. While this rate was far above that achieved by many countries, it was well below that of the East Asian countries and somewhat below that achieved by Thailand, Malaysia, and Indonesia. Thus by 1980 Turkey remained the poorest country in Europe (with the possible exception of Albania) but was in the middle ranks of Asian countries in per capita income.[1]

Turkey is unique in a number of ways. First, the Turkish Republic was formed in the aftermath of the First World War, some thirty years before many other developing countries attained independence. Earlier Turkey had been not a colony but rather the seat of the Ottoman Empire. Second, Turkey is strategically located between Europe, the Middle East, and the Soviet Union, with strong ties to both Europe and the Middle East and high economic costs of membership in the North Atlantic Treaty Organization because of the geographical proximity to the Soviet Union. Third, Turkey's geographic endowment is diversified from Black Sea forests to the Anatolian plateau, the Mediterranean coast, and the western Bosporus region. This diversification provides Turkey with a variety of comparative advantages in agriculture vis-à-vis both European and Middle Eastern neighbors. Turkey has no significant known oil deposits, however, and has only low-grade lignite deposits. It is therefore an oil importer.

Structure and Growth of the Turkish Economy, 1950 to 1980

Like most developing countries in the early years after the Second World War, Turkey was predominantly an agricultural country: 45 percent of gross domestic product and 79 percent of the population are estimated to have been in agriculture in the early 1950s. With its diversified climatic regions, Turkey was a major exporter of tobacco (the Aegean and Marmara regions), cotton (the Mediterranean coastal region), hazelnuts (the Black Sea coast), olive oil (the western coast), and wheat (the Anatolian plateau). Indeed, in the context of European postwar recovery, major emphasis had been placed on transforming pastureland into wheat land, and Turkey was a major wheat exporter (from the Anatolian plateau) in the early 1950s.

Table 1 provides data on the structural transformation of the Turkish economy from 1950 to 1980. Agriculture's share of GNP declined markedly; accompanying this, the fraction of the labor force engaged in agriculture fell steadily from 79 percent in 1950 to 63 percent in 1980.[2]

This structural transformation was the result of reasonably rapid economic growth. The government was committed to industrialization through import substitution and also increased investment rapidly.

Table 1

Sectoral Composition of GNP, 1950–1980
(percentages of GNP, 1968 prices)

	1950	1955	1960	1965	1970	1975	1980
Agriculture	45	42	41	34	29	25	24
Industry	12	13	15	18	20	22	22
Services	43	45	44	48	51	53	54

Source: State Institute of Statistics, *Statistical Yearbook*, various issues.

Infrastructure investment, financed in part by foreign aid, provided a basis for the rapid expansion of economic activity. Table 2 gives an overview of growth in real gross national product and in GNP per capita from 1950 to 1980. Annual data and greater detail about the changing structure and uses of output may be found in Tables 3 and 4.

Growth did not proceed evenly over the 1950–1980 period. The early 1950s were a period of very rapid growth, reflecting postwar recovery and large infrastructure investments financed in part by receipt of Point IV and then Marshall Plan aid. The heavy investment program, however, was also partly financed by government deficits, which resulted in inflationary pressures on the Turkish economy. When, after several good harvests, there was a massive crop failure in 1954, inflationary pressures accelerated rapidly. At that time the Turkish government still adhered to a fixed exchange rate that had been set in 1946 (see section "The 1975–1980 Period"); pressures resulting from excess demand associated with the sizable fiscal deficit and from the overvalued exchange rate in the face of domestic inflation led to a sharp deterioration in the balance of payments. The government responded by instituting and subsequently tightening exchange controls, imposing surcharges and additional duties on imports, and sharply restricting import licensing. Four years of decelerating growth followed as Turkish foreign creditors at first extended credit on increasingly

Table 2

Population and Real GNP, 1950–1980

	1950	1955	1960	1965	1970	1975	1980
Real GNP (bil.TL)	40.6	58.7	71.1	90.4	125.4	181.4	206.1
Population (mil.)	20.8	23.9	27.8	31.4	35.6	40.4	44.7
Real GNP per capita (TL)	1,952	2,459	2,560	2,879	3,522	4,495	4,606
Percentage annual average change over preceding five years:							
GNP		7.7	3.9	4.9	6.8	7.7	2.6
Population		2.8	3.1	2.5	2.5	2.6	2.0
Real GNP per capita		4.7	0.8	2.4	4.1	5.0	0.5

Note: Real and per capita GNP are in 1968 Turkish liras.
Source: OECD, *National Accounts: Main Aggregates 1960–87,* and earlier issues.

Table 3

GNP and Its Components, Current Prices, 1950–1980

	1950	1955	1960	1961	1962	1963	1964	1965	1966	1967	1968	1969
Level (billions of Turkish liras)												
Consumption	8.7	16.7	40.6	43.3	51.2	59.5	61.8	66.2	76.4	84.5	94.2	104.9
Private	7.6	14.2	35.6	37.3	44.8	52.1	53.2	56.7	65.4	72.0	80.1	89.2
Public	1.1	2.5	5.0	6.0	6.4	7.4	8.6	9.5	11.0	12.5	14.1	15.7
Investment	1.1	3.0	7.5	7.8	8.8	9.7	10.4	11.1	14.4	16.6	19.4	21.7
Private	0.6	1.6	3.9	4.1	6.1	5.0	4.8	5.3	6.7	7.8	8.4	9.7
Public	0.4	1.4	3.6	3.7	5.8	4.7	5.6	5.8	7.7	8.8	11.0	12.0
Stocks	—	—	—	—	—	0.6	0.5	0.2	1.7	1.1	0.8	0.1
Exports	0.6	1.2	2.9	3.1	3.6	4.1	4.4	4.7	5.6	5.9	6.0	6.4
Imports	0.7	1.7	4.0	4.4	5.7	7.0	5.7	5.8	7.3	6.8	8.2	8.5
Trade deficit	0.1	0.5	1.1	1.3	2.1	2.9	1.3	1.1	1.7	0.9	2.2	2.1
GDP, market prices	9.7	19.2	47.0	49.8	57.9	66.9	71.4	76.4	90.8	101.3	112.2	124.6
Net factor income from abroad	-0.1	-0.2	-0.3	-0.3	-0.3	-0.1	-0.2	0.3	0.6	0.3	0.3	0.4
GNP	9.6	19.0	46.7	49.5	57.6	66.8	71.2	76.7	91.4	101.6	112.5	125.0
Population (millions)	20.8	23.9	27.8	28.5	28.2	29.9	30.6	31.4	32.2	33.0	33.9	34.7
GNP/capita (TL)	463	796	1,681	1,740	2,045	2,236	2,325	2,443	2,839	3,078	3,323	3,600
Percentage change (average 50–55, 55–60, then annual)												
Consumption		13.9	19.5	6.7	18.2	16.2	3.9	7.1	15.4	10.6	11.5	11.4
Private		13.4	20.2	4.8	20.1	16.3	2.1	6.6	15.3	10.1	11.2	11.4
Public		16.7	15.1	20.0	6.7	15.6	16.2	10.5	15.8	13.6	12.8	11.3

(continued on next page)

Percentage change (average 50–55, 55–60, then annual) *(continued)*

Investment	23.3	19.8	4.0	12.8	10.2	7.2	6.7	29.7	15.3	16.9	11.9
Private	20.4	19.0	6.5	49.2	-18.4	-3.1	9.8	26.4	16.4	8.0	15.3
Public	27.3	20.7	1.3	56.4	-18.6	18.2	4.1	32.8	14.3	24.8	9.2
Exports	14.6	19.7	6.9	16.1	13.9	7.3	6.8	19.1	5.4	1.7	6.7
Imports	20.9	18.9	10.0	29.5	22.8	-18.6	1.8	25.9	-6.8	20.6	3.7
GDP, market prices	14.6	19.6	6.0	16.3	15.5	6.7	7.0	18.8	11.6	10.8	11.1
GNP	14.5	19.7	6.0	16.4	16.0	6.6	7.7	19.2	11.2	10.7	11.1
Population	2.8	3.1	2.5	-1.0	6.1	2.5	2.5	2.5	2.5	2.6	2.5
GNP/capita	11.4	16.1	3.5	17.6	9.3	4.0	5.1	16.2	8.4	7.9	8.4
Share of GNP:											
Consumption	90.3	87.0	87.5	88.9	89.1	86.8	86.3	83.6	83.2	83.7	83.9
Private	78.5	76.3	75.4	77.8	78.0	74.7	73.9	71.6	70.9	71.2	71.4
Public	11.9	10.7	12.1	11.1	11.1	12.1	12.4	12.0	12.3	12.5	12.6
Investment	11.0	16.1	15.8	15.3	14.5	14.6	14.5	15.8	16.3	17.2	17.4
Private	6.6	8.3	8.3	10.6	7.5	6.8	6.9	7.3	7.7	7.5	7.8
Public	4.4	7.8	7.5	10.0	7.0	7.8	7.5	8.4	8.6	9.7	9.6
Exports	6.2	6.2	6.3	6.3	6.1	6.2	6.1	6.1	5.8	5.3	5.1
Imports	6.8	8.6	8.9	9.9	10.5	8.0	7.6	8.0	6.7	7.3	6.8
Trade deficit	0.6	2.4	2.6	3.6	4.3	1.8	1.4	1.9	0.9	2.0	1.7

(continued on next page)

9

(continued)

Table 3

	1970	1971	1972	1973	1974	1975	1976	1977	1978	1979	1980
Level (billions of Turkish liras)											
Consumption	120.5	161.2	188.0	239.4	342.3	430.3	529.8	689.6	1,018.9	1,738.9	3,536.0
Private	101.8	136.1	160.0	202.6	295.3	366.4	445.2	573.3	846.2	1,444.9	2,991.9
Public	18.7	25.1	28.0	36.8	47.0	63.9	84.6	116.3	172.7	294.0	544.1
Investment	27.0	31.7	46.8	59.5	77.8	110.9	154.7	210.8	279.6	449.3	863.6
Private	13.5	15.8	23.5	31.6	40.4	53.0	82.6	103.7	144.9	234.9	424.0
Public	13.5	15.9	23.3	27.9	37.4	57.9	72.1	107.1	134.7	214.4	439.6
Stocks	1.8	1.6	7.0	4.4	16.9	21.5	27.0	32.9	26.3	57.7	279.6
Exports	8.6	13.1	16.6	26.0	30.0	30.8	48.4	45.5	74.8	125.6	317.1
Imports	12.5	20.3	26.3	33.8	57.3	74.3	96.0	115.8	124.8	215.6	668.3
Trade deficit	3.9	7.2	9.7	7.8	27.3	43.5	47.6	70.3	50.0	90.0	351.2
GDP, market prices	145.4	187.3	232.1	295.5	409.7	519.2	663.9	863.0	1,274.8	2,155.9	4,328.0
Net factor income from abroad	2.3	5.5	9.6	14.6	17.4	16.6	11.0	9.9	15.9	43.6	107.2
GNP	147.7	192.8	241.7	310.1	427.1	535.8	674.9	872.9	1,290.7	2,199.5	4,435.2
Population (millions)	35.6	36.6	37.5	38.5	39.4	40.4	40.9	41.8	42.8	43.7	44.7
GNP/capita (TL)	4,148	5,275	6,445	8,065	10,840	13,279	16,489	20,863	30,178	50,286	99,133
Percentage change (annual)											
Consumption	14.9	33.8	16.6	27.3	43.0	25.7	23.1	30.2	47.8	70.7	103.3
Private	14.1	33.7	17.6	26.6	45.8	24.1	21.5	28.8	47.6	70.8	107.1
Public	19.1	34.2	11.6	31.4	27.7	36.0	32.4	37.5	48.5	70.2	85.1

(continued on next page)

Investment	24.4	17.4	47.6	27.1	30.8	42.5	39.5	36.3	32.6	60.7	92.2
Private	38.3	17.1	49.2	34.3	28.1	31.1	55.8	25.5	39.7	62.1	80.5
Public	13.2	17.7	46.1	19.9	33.7	55.0	24.5	48.5	25.8	59.2	105.0
Exports	34.4	52.3	26.7	56.6	15.4	2.7	57.1	-6.0	64.4	67.9	152.5
Imports	47.1	62.4	29.6	28.5	69.5	29.7	29.2	20.6	7.8	72.8	210.0
GDP, market prices	16.7	28.8	23.9	27.3	38.6	26.7	27.9	30.0	47.7	69.1	100.8
GNP	18.2	30.5	25.4	28.3	37.7	25.5	26.0	29.3	47.9	70.4	101.6
Population	2.6	2.6	2.6	2.5	2.5	2.4	1.4	2.2	2.2	2.3	2.3
GNP/capita	15.2	27.2	22.2	25.1	34.4	22.5	24.2	26.5	44.6	66.6	97.1
Share of GNP:											
Consumption	81.6	83.6	77.8	77.2	80.1	80.3	78.5	79.0	78.9	79.	79.7
Private	68.9	70.6	66.2	65.3	69.1	68.4	66.0	65.7	65.6	65.1	67.5
Public	12.7	13.0	11.6	11.9	11.0	11.9	12.5	13.3	13.4	13.4	12.3
Investment	18.3	16.4	19.4	19.2	18.2	20.7	22.9	24.1	21.7	20.4	19.5
Private	9.1	8.2	9.7	10.2	9.5	9.9	12.2	11.9	11.2	10.7	9.6
Public	9.2	8.3	9.6	9.0	8.7	10.8	10.7	12.3	10.4	9.7	9.9
Exports	5.8	6.8	6.9	8.4	7.0	5.7	7.2	5.2	5.8	5.7	7.1
Imports	8.5	10.5	10.9	10.9	13.4	13.9	14.2	13.3	9.7	9.3	15.1
Trade deficit	2.6	3.7	4.0	2.5	6.4	8.1	7.1	8.1	3.9	4.1	7.9

Source: OECD, National Accounts: Main Aggregates 1960–87, and earlier issues. Division between private and public investment from World Bank, Turkey: Prospects and Problems (1975); and World Bank, Industrialization and Trade Strategy, 1982, and SPO data. Like estimates are not available.

Table 4

GNP and Its Components, Constant Prices, 1950–1980 (1968 prices)

	1950	1955	1960	1961	1962	1963	1964	1965	1966	1967	1968	1969
Level (billions of Turkish liras)												
Consumption	34.6	51.5	61.8	63.0	67.6	74.1	75.5	77.7	84.6	87.9	94.2	99.4
Private	30.3	45.0	53.6	54.1	58.3	64.1	64.7	66.4	72.4	74.7	80.1	84.4
Public	4.3	6.5	8.3	8.9	9.2	10.0	10.8	11.3	12.1	13.2	14.1	15.0
Investment	7.2	11.0	10.8	11.2	11.9	12.5	12.9	13.2	16.1	17.1	19.4	20.7
Private	4.3	5.8	5.6	5.9	6.1	6.4	6.0	6.3	7.5	7.7	8.5	9.3
Public	2.9	5.2	5.3	5.3	5.8	6.1	6.9	6.9	8.6	9.4	11.0	11.4
Stocks	—	—	—	—	—	0.8	0.7	0.3	2.0	1.1	0.8	0.1
Exports	2.2	3.2	3.9	4.0	4.2	4.6	4.8	4.9	5.5	6.0	6.0	6.4
Imports	3.2	6.8	5.2	5.5	6.7	7.7	6.1	6.042	7.5	7.0	8.2	8.3
Trade deficit	1.1	3.6	1.3	1.5	2.5	3.1	1.3	1.1	2.0	1.0	2.2	2.0
GDP, market prices	40.7	58.9	71.4	72.6	77.0	84.3	87.8	90.1	100.6	105.2	112.2	118.2
Net factor income from abroad	−0.1	−0.2	−0.3	−0.3	−0.3	−0.1	−0.2	0.3	0.6	0.3	0.3	0.4
GNP	40.6	58.7	71.1	72.3	76.8	84.2	87.6	90.4	101.2	105.5	112.5	118.6
Population (millions)	20.81	23.86	27.8	28.5	28.2	29.9	30.6	31.4	32.2	33.0	33.9	34.7
GNP/capita (TL)	1,951.7	2,459.2	2,559.9	2,541.6	2,725.7	2,817.6	2,860.6	2,878.9	3,143.9	3,194.8	3,322.0	3,415.7
Percentage change (average 50–55, 55–60, then annual)												
Consumption		8.3	3.7	1.8	7.3	9.7	1.9	2.9	8.9	3.9	7.2	5.5
Private		8.2	3.6	1.0	7.8	9.9	1.0	2.6	9.1	3.1	7.3	5.3
Public		8.7	4.9	7.3	4.2	8.5	7.6	4.8	7.4	8.7	6.8	6.5

(continued on next page)

12

Percentage change (average 50–55, 55–60, then annual) *(continued)*

Investment	8.9	-0.3	3.4	6.7	4.7	2.9	2.5	22.2	6.4	1⁻.4	6.4
Private	6.3	-1.0	5.9	4.0	5.2	-7.0	5.4	19.0	2.6	⊂.7	9.7
Public	12.4	0.4	0.8	9.0	5.0	13.5	-0.1	25.1	9.7	1⊂.5	3.8
Exports	8.1	4.2	1.7	6.1	9.4	4.1	2.6	11.7	8.4	⊂.1	6.9
Imports	16.1	-5.3	6.6	21.2	15.6	-21.5	-0.5	24.9	-7.8	1⁻.8	1.8
GDP, market prices	7.7	3.9	1.7	6.1	9.4	4.1	2.6	11.7	4.5	⊂.7	5.3
GNP	7.6	3.9	1.8	6.2	9.7	4.1	3.1	12.0	4.2	⊂.7	5.4
Population	2.8	3.1	2.5	-1.0	6.1	2.5	2.5	2.5	2.5	2.6	2.5
GNP/capita	4.7	0.8	-0.7	7.2	3.4	1.5	0.6	9.2	1.6	⊂.0	2.8
Share of GNP:											
Consumption	85.0	86.6	86.7	87.7	87.9	86.0	86.2	84.0	83.6	8⁻.0	84.1
Private	74.4	75.0	74.5	75.7	76.1	73.7	73.7	72.0	71.0	7.4	71.4
Public	10.6	11.6	12.2	12.0	11.9	12.3	12.5	12.1	12.5	1⁻.6	12.7
Investment	17.7	15.2	15.4	15.5	14.8	14.7	14.6	16.0	16.3	1⁻.3	17.5
Private	10.6	7.8	8.1	8.0	7.6	6.8	7.0	7.5	7.3	⁻.5	7.8
Public	7.1	7.4	7.3	7.5	7.2	7.8	7.6	8.5	9.0	.8	9.7
Exports	5.3	5.5	5.5	5.5	5.5	5.5	5.5	5.5	5.7	⁻.3	5.4
Imports	7.9	7.3	7.6	8.7	9.2	6.9	6.7	7.5	6.6	⁻.3	7.1
Trade deficit	2.6	1.8	2.1	3.2	3.7	1.4	1.2	2.0	0.9	⁻.0	1.7

(continued on next page)

13

(continued)

Table 4

	1970	1971	1972	1973	1974	1975	1976	1977	1978	1979	1980
Level (billions of Turkish liras)											
Consumption	101.8	114.4	121.9	124.6	134.2	147.3	160.9	165.3	167.6	163.8	166.0
Private	86.2	97.9	104.2	105.3	113.4	121.9	131.4	134.7	137.9	133.2	132.6
Public	15.5	16.5	17.7	19.2	20.8	25.4	29.5	30.6	29.7	30.6	33.4
Investment	23.5	22.3	25.6	28.5	29.1	34.0	39.3	42.2	37.6	36.9	33.5
Private	11.7	11.1	12.8	15.1	15.2	17.3	18.8	18.9	19.7	17.9	14.7
Public	11.8	11.2	12.8	13.4	13.9	16.7	20.5	23.3	17.9	19.0	18.8
Stocks	1.6	1.2	0.2	2.0	6.3	4.1	0.7	5.4	5.2	7.2	9.3
Exports	7.3	8.4	9.7	11.3	10.3	11.0	13.5	9.2	11.7	10.9	11.5
Imports	10.2	11.2	13.3	15.9	16.6	18.6	21.3	20.6	14.9	13.4	16.4
Trade deficit	2.9	2.7	3.6	4.6	6.4	7.7	7.7	11.4	3.2	2.4	4.9
GDP, market prices	123.9	135.2	144.1	150.4	163.2	177.8	193.2	201.6	207.3	205.5	203.9
Net factor income from abroad	1.5	3.0	4.4	6.0	4.8	3.6	2.5	1.8	1.9	2.9	2.2
GNP	125.4	138.2	148.5	156.5	168.0	181.4	195.8	203.4	209.2	208.4	206.1
Population (millions)	35.6	36.6	37.5	38.5	39.4	40.4	40.9	41.8	42.8	43.7	44.7
GNP/capita (TL)	3,522.2	3,780.7	3,959.4	4,069.1	4,264.3	4,495.3	4,782.6	4,860.9	4,890.6	4,763.5	4,605.8
Percentage change (annual)											
Consumption	2.4	12.4	6.6	2.2	7.7	9.8	9.2	2.7	1.4	-2.3	1.3
Private	2.2	13.5	6.4	1.1	7.6	7.5	7.8	2.5	2.4	-3.4	-0.5
Public	3.6	6.1	7.3	8.6	8.3	22.3	16.0	3.8	-2.8	2.9	9.2

(continued on next page)

14

Investment	13.5	-4.9	14.8	11.2	2.1	16.8	15.6	7.4	-10.9	-1.9	-.2
Private	26.2	-5.2	15.6	17.8	0.8	13.6	8.6	0.7	4.0	-9.3	-1.1
Public	3.2	-4.7	13.9	4.6	3.6	20.4	22.8	13.5	-23.1	6.4	-.9
Exports	14.3	15.5	14.6	17.5	-9.5	6.8	23.6	-31.9	27.2	-6.8	.1
Imports	22.0	9.7	19.0	19.8	4.4	12.2	14.0	-3.2	-27.5	-10.4	2.5
GDP, market prices	4.9	9.1	6.6	4.4	8.5	8.9	8.7	4.3	2.8	-0.9	-.8
GNP	5.8	10.2	7.4	5.4	7.4	8.0	7.9	3.9	2.8	-0.4	-.1
Population	2.6	2.6	2.6	2.5	2.5	2.4	1.4	2.2	2.2	2.3	.3
GNP/capita	3.1	7.3	4.7	2.8	4.8	5.4	6.4	1.6	0.6	-2.6	-.3
Share of GNP:											
Consumption	82.1	84.6	84.6	82.8	82.2	82.9	83.3	82.0	80.9	79.7	8.4
Private	69.6	72.4	72.3	70.0	69.5	68.6	68.0	66.8	66.5	64.8	6.0
Public	12.5	12.2	12.3	12.8	12.7	14.3	15.3	15.2	14.3	14.9	1.4
Investment	18.9	16.5	17.8	18.9	17.8	19.1	20.3	20.9	18.1	18.0	1.4
Private	9.4	8.2	8.9	10.0	9.3	9.7	9.7	9.4	9.5	8.7	.2
Public	9.5	8.3	8.9	8.9	8.5	9.4	10.6	11.5	8.6	9.3	.2
Exports	5.9	6.2	6.1	7.5	6.3	6.2	7.0	4.6	5.7	5.3	.6
Imports	8.2	8.3	9.2	10.6	10.2	10.5	11.0	10.2	7.2	6.5	.0
Trade deficit	2.3	2.0	2.5	3.0	3.9	4.3	4.0	5.6	1.5	1.2	.4

Note: Note slight differences in growth of GNP from Table 3 because of different revision periods.

Source: OECD, *National Accounts: Main Aggregates 1960–87*, and earlier issues. Division between private and public investment from World Bank, *Turkey: Prospects and Problems* (1975); and World Bank, *Industrialization and Trade Strategy*, 1982. Like estimates are not available. Net factor income from same World Bank sources.

15

less favorable terms and finally refused additional financing. By 1958
the annual rate of inflation was almost 20 percent—very high by world
standards at that time.[3]

By 1958 the economic situation had deteriorated sharply. Imports
had been drastically reduced, and many economic activities were
hamstrung by shortages of parts or raw materials. With a harvest
approaching, the absence of petroleum imports threatened to prevent
agricultural commodities from being harvested and shipped to port.
Under those circumstances and after several years of resistance, government officials signed an agreement with the International Monetary
Fund (IMF) to undertake a stabilization program.

Thereafter inflation diminished rapidly, while imports financed
by foreign credits received on agreement to the IMF program permitted
a fairly rapid expansion in economic activity.[4] By the early 1960s
growth had again resumed, and it was sustained at reasonably high
rates for most of the decade. As further discussed below, the foreign
exchange shortage of the 1950s led to import restrictions and licensing,
which provided a great deal of protection to domestic industry. This
encouraged import substitution (and discouraged exports) to a considerable degree, although inability to import capital goods and other
items used to install or increase capacity limited the extent of the effort.
In the early 1960s a newly formed State Planning Organization (SPO)
was given responsibility for designing development policy. The SPO
articulated the policy of encouraging industrialization through import
substitution and in the First Five Year Plan articulated the foreign
trade policies under which, after domestic production had begun,
imports would not be permitted except insofar as domestic capacity
could not meet domestic demand.[5]

Under these policies industrial output expanded rapidly during
the early and middle 1960s. Toward the end of the decade, however,
foreign exchange difficulties intensified. By 1970 the government once
again entered a stabilization program with the IMF, devaluing the
currency from 9 Turkish liras per U.S. dollar to TL15 per dollar and
attempting to stabilize the economy. As in the 1958–1960 devaluation episode, the intention was to rationalize the trade and payments
regime, but the fundamental philosophy of import substitution underlying the regime was not questioned.

In some regards the aftermath of the 1970 devaluation was similar
to that of 1960, but in others it was very different. Even more

than after the 1958–1960 devaluation, foreign exchange receipts increased sharply.[6]

Thus after the 1970 devaluation the large inflow of workers' remittances resulted in a rapid increase in the money supply, as the Central Bank did not have instruments with which to offset the inflow. Inflation accelerated over the 1971–1973 period. Economic growth was rapid, however, as there was little "foreign exchange constraint," and exports grew rapidly. This growth was in response to the incentives provided both by the devaluation and by special "incentives" for nontraditional exports that significantly raised the effective exchange rate received by exporters of nontraditional commodities.[7]

Table 5 provides data on major monetary and fiscal aggregates over the three decades under review. The inflation rate dropped from an estimated 20 percent in the 1955–1958 period to about 2.5 percent in the early 1960s. Although it rose somewhat in the later 1960s, it

Table 5

Money Supply, Public Finances, and Prices, 1950–1980

	1950	1955	1960	1965	1970	1975	1980
Money supply (M3) (bil.TL)	1.6	4.2	9.2	16.4	35.6	118.9	719.8
Consumer prices (1980 = 100)	—	2.2	4.5	5.2	6.7	13.8	100.0
Wholesale prices (1980 = 100)	1.8	1.8	3.6	4.0	5.6	13.0	100.0
Government (bil. TL)							
Expenditure	2.2	4.3	9.5	15.0	31.6	112.9	1,116.5
Revenue	2.3	4.1	9.3	13.4	28.8	109.0	956.7
Deficit (+)	−0.1	0.2	0.2	1.6	3.6	7.0	160.8
Share of nominal GNP:							
Government expenditure	23.3	22.6	20.4	19.6	22.0	21.6	25.2
Government revenue	23.6	21.7	19.9	17.5	19.5	20.3	21.6
Government deficit	−0.3	0.8	0.4	2.0	2.5	1.3	3.6
Average annual percentage change							
Money supply		21.3	17.0	12.3	16.8	27.3	43.4
Wholesale prices		0.0	15.5	2.3	6.8	18.2	50.5

Sources: International Monetary Fund, *International Financial Statistics Yearbook*, 1986 and 1989, for money supply, prices, and for government finances 1970 to 1980. Earlier government finance figures are from World Bank, *Turkey: Prospects and Problems* (1975).

never exceeded 10 percent. After the 1970 devaluation and the influx of workers' remittances, however, inflation accelerated rapidly.

For the international economy, the worldwide commodity boom (which had benefited Turkey's export earnings in 1972 and 1973) culminated in the threefold oil price increase that took place late in 1973. The government failed to take significant action in response to the oil price increase, instead permitting the current account to worsen rapidly, paying for the excess of expenditures over receipts by running down foreign exchange reserves and borrowing from abroad. Moreover, since most petroleum imports were on government account and the government failed significantly to increase domestic oil prices, the government's fiscal deficit also rose sharply up to 1980 (see Table 5).

This sequence of events gave further impetus to inflation. Simultaneously, the failure of the government to adjust the exchange rate or the domestic price of fuel resulted in sharply reduced rates of increase of export earnings and sharply increased rates of increase in demand for imports. In order to attract workers' remittances and other foreign currency held by Turks in deposits abroad, the government also embarked on a convertible Turkish lira deposit scheme, under which it provided guarantees in foreign exchange to those who deposited their funds with Turkish banks.

Over the next several years the situation worsened sharply. Despite occasional exchange rate adjustments, the failure of the exchange rate to be maintained in real terms further discouraged exports; the domestic inflation continued to accelerate; Turkish government debt mounted as the government attempted to finance imports; and convertible deposit accounts grew. By 1977 delays in obtaining import licenses were increasing sharply, real exports through official channels were falling, and real GNP was recorded to be growing at half the rate of the preceding three years.

The years 1978 and 1979 were ones of continuing and unresolved crisis. Despite several efforts at debt rescheduling and announced intentions to undertake fiscal reforms, inflation reached 100 percent by the end of 1979, while real output was declining. The five-year interval ending in 1980 recorded the slowest rate of economic growth of any such period since 1950 (Table 2). Given the relatively rapid rate of growth of the Turkish population, Turkish living standards increased little between 1975 and 1978, and real per capita incomes are estimated to have dropped by 5.8 percent from 1978 to 1980. By the end of 1979 Turkey's gross foreign exchange reserves were exhausted; imports of petroleum and other intermediate goods and raw materials had diminished sharply because of an inability to finance them, and economic activity was declining sharply, with shortages reminiscent of the 1958 predevaluation period.[8]

Thus, although Turkey had averaged a little over 6 percent annual growth between 1950 and 1975, its growth performance diminished sharply in the latter part of the 1970s, culminating in a balance-of-payments crisis and an inflationary spiral similar to those to be experienced by many other developing countries in the early 1980s.

Before turning to the evolution of the Turkish trade and payments regime before 1980, two other aspects of the Turkish economy require brief attention. First, it is desirable to examine the behavior of Turkish investment and savings over the thirty years before 1980. The basic data are given in Tables 3 and 4.

Turkish savings and investment rose significantly over the three decades after 1950. Starting from 6.6 percent of GNP in 1950, private investment stayed steady, measuring 6.9 percent by 1965, rose to an estimated 12.2 percent of GNP in 1976, and then declined to 9.6 percent in 1980. Public investment, however, rose rapidly from 4.4 percent of GNP in 1950 to reach 12.3 percent of GNP in 1977. The excess of investment over savings was financed primarily by official capital inflows, which constituted as much as 4 percent of GNP in the early 1960s and averaged 2.4 percent of GNP annually during that decade. After 1970 capital inflows were less important as a source of investment finance but still averaged about 1.5 percent of GNP during the 1970s.

The final aspect of Turkey's economic structure that deserves attention is the role of the public sector. The shares of government expenditures in GNP and public savings and investment have already been examined. It remains to note the role of the state economic enterprises (SEEs).

Like most developing countries, Turkey had established a number of government-owned enterprises devoted to production and other economic activities. This had begun in the 1930s, when the impact of the Great Depression led to a decision to adopt *étatist* policies with respect to economic activity. Some SEEs were established to undertake the mining and sale of Turkish minerals, especially copper and chrome. Some others were established to undertake production of items such as textiles, clothing, and footwear alongside private enterprises engaging in the same lines of activity. Still others were engaged in banking, agricultural financing, transport, and other commercial services.

By the late 1950s approximately half of value added in manufacturing in Turkey was produced by SEEs. Similarly, SEEs accounted for more than half of investment in manufacturing. Although their relative rate of expansion varied somewhat depending on which government was in power and other factors, the SEEs were and remain an important part of Turkish economic life.

SEEs had been engaged in many lines of economic activity, especially import substitution. Their output is important in almost all manufacturing sectors, but even in those that export, SEEs tend to produce almost entirely for the domestic market. For example, although the SEE Sumerbank was a major producer of textiles, which are an exportable, almost all exports originated in private sector firms. Sumerbank produced much more for the domestic market, developing nylon, polyester, and other import-substitution production lines. SEEs were generally given preference in receiving import licenses and also credit. When they incurred losses, these were generally financed by Central Bank credits. Losses originated in part because SEEs were inefficient producers but also because the government tended to impose price ceilings on SEE outputs during periods of inflation.[9]

The Evolution of the Turkish Trade and Payments Regime

Two driving forces have influenced the Turkish trade and payments regime. On one hand, the Turkish government was strongly committed to a policy of industrialization through import substitution throughout the 1960s and 1970s. On the other hand, the government was equally committed to maintaining a fixed nominal exchange rate despite domestic inflation, with the result that there was almost always excess demand for foreign exchange. Foreign exchange shortage therefore impelled many policy actions and interacted with the policy of encouraging domestic industry through import substitution.

Like the governments of most other developing countries in the 1950s and 1960s, the government of Turkey was committed to accelerating development by encouraging industrialization. While a number of incentives were given to new industries, including access to preferential credit, tax credits, and investment incentives, in practice the most powerful inducement was the principle, enunciated in the First Five Year Plan, that imports would be restricted when domestic production started and prohibited when domestic production was adequate to serve the internal market.

The result was that domestic prices of import-substitution commodities could be well above international prices. Because of quantitative restrictions, imports could not in any event enter legally; so the tariff equivalent of import prohibitions or quotas could be greatly above the legal tariff rate. Baysan and Blitzer provide estimates of the effective protective rate (EPR) equivalents of quotas and tariffs for manufacturing industries in 1973—a year when foreign exchange was relatively easy. According to their estimates, paper and paper products were accorded an EPR of 154 percent, plastic products 358 percent, iron and steel basic industries 203 percent, nonelectric machinery 108 percent, and so on. By contrast, EPRs for agricultural commodities and many minerals products—all exportables—were negative. Even textiles and wearing apparel—exports to some degree during the 1960s and 1970s—received less than 20 percent protection.[10]

As in most developing countries, import-substitution policies in Turkey were increasingly economically costly as they continued. The EPR estimates already cited provide one indication. But the rising cost was also reflected in a rapidly rising incremental capital-output ratio (ICOR): according to Balassa's estimates, the ICOR rose from 1.6 in 1963–1967 to 2.4 in 1968–1972 to 4.7 in 1973–1977. In constant 1976 prices, the average investment per job created rose from TL267,000 in the 1963–1967 period to TL572,000 a decade later.[11]

Import-substitution policies were defended on infant industry grounds, although high levels of implicit protection lasted considerably longer than infant industry considerations would suggest were warranted. In addition, during most of the 1960s and 1970s, foreign exchange shortage bedeviled Turkish policy makers. Indeed, most of the features of the trade and payments regime and most of its effects on incentives were the result of responses of policy makers to the exigencies of their balance-of-payments position. It is therefore important to review the various twists and turns taken by foreign exchange shortage in the period before 1980.

For purposes of understanding the means used to contain excess demand for foreign exchange, it suffices to start with the stabilization program of 1958. Before that program the Turkish trade regime had become increasingly chaotic, with efforts to contain excess demand for foreign exchange through both price and quantitative measures. There were a variety of surcharges upon imports, some of them exceeding 100 percent of the value of the import at the official exchange rate, in addition to tariffs. There were numerous effective exchange rates for exports, again with some export premiums exceeding the official exchange rate by more than 100 percent. There was import licensing, and once licenses were received, importers queued at the Central Bank until foreign exchange became available. As the exchange rate had become increasingly overvalued in the mid-1950s, delays in receiving foreign exchange mounted rapidly and, in fact, became the principal instrument through which imports were restricted.

By 1958 the flow of imports through legal channels had virtually halted. A large number of these imports—including petroleum and refined petroleum products, most inputs to domestic manufacturing, spare parts for capital equipment, medicines, fertilizers, pesticides, and even coffee—had no import-competing production. The absence of imports thus led to sharp dislocations. Factories were operating at low levels of capacity utilization or else shut down completely. As a consequence, the level of industrial production was falling sharply. Only after a prolonged period of economic dislocation did the prime minister consent to an IMF program.

The program had three major parts: it aimed at monetary and fiscal restraint to reduce domestic inflation and inflationary pressures; it sought to rationalize the trade and payments regime in the context of a more realistically valued exchange rate; and it made an effort to restructure and rationalize Turkish debt while simultaneously providing enough new money so that Turkish import flow could resume.[12]

For present purposes the significant components of the 1958 program relate to the second part. Two features require attention: First, the pattern of reforms set in that year and broadly repeated in 1970 clearly influenced the responses of private decision makers to the initial phase of the 1980 reforms. Second, as part of the reform the "import programs" were established that became the basis for regulating imports and protecting domestic manufacturers until after 1980.

Turning first to the pattern, the nominal devaluation of 1958 was massive: from TL2.80 per U.S. dollar to TL9.00. The effective devaluation was far smaller, however. In part it was smaller because, until 1960, the devaluation was effected with surcharges over the official exchange rate that applied to all transactions except some traditional exports.[13] It was also smaller because some import surcharges and export subsidies had existed before devaluation and thus reduced the magnitude of the change.

The 1958 devaluation was followed by a several-year period of relative balance-of-payments ease. This meant that, during the initial period after the stabilization program was inaugurated, the black market rate was very little greater than the official rate and that importers were able to obtain foreign exchange relatively rapidly once they received an import license.

The devaluation, however, was to a new, fixed nominal exchange rate. While the rate of inflation fell sharply, the Turkish inflation of the 1960s was still between 5 and 10 percent—significantly greater than the rate of increase of dollar prices in world markets, which was less than 1 percent annually during that decade.[14]

Moreover, Turkish government developmental expenditures rose sharply after 1962, thereby significantly increasing the demand for foreign exchange. Because of these two factors, foreign exchange shortage mounted again during the 1960s. By 1965 delays of several months were occasionally experienced before importers were able to obtain foreign exchange after they had their import licenses; by 1969 the delays were often eight months and longer. Thus the liberalization in the early 1960s of the import regime was short-lived, and simultaneously the attractiveness of exporting at the new rate of TL9 per U.S. dollar diminished throughout the decade.

The establishment of import programs in 1958 was the second enduring feature, from the viewpoint of understanding the background to the 1980 reform program. In reaction both to the lengthy delays for import licenses that prevailed before 1958 and to an apparent randomness in their allocation among importers of medicines, spare parts, intermediate inputs, and luxury consumer goods, the practice of establishing "import lists" began. Three lists were established.

An important feature of the import regime was that any commodity that did not appear on a list could not legally be imported. Thus, once an item was domestically produced, it was accorded virtually unlimited protection through the simple device of removing it from any import list. Those commodities that were legally importable were divided among the three lists. One list indicated items that could be imported only under bilateral trading arrangements Turkey had with a number of countries, primarily in Eastern Europe and the Middle East. The bilateral list was rather marginal, although if the authorities deemed that a commodity was available from those sources, they attempted to encourage purchases from bilateral sources by restricting the quantities that could be imported under the other lists. The two remaining lists were the significant ones. They were the liberalized list and the quota list.

It was intended, and usually accomplished, that imports on the liberalized list be freely importable during the period of the import program (six months) subject only to the individual's obtaining the requisite foreign exchange from the Central Bank. In contrast, the quota list indicated the quantitites of individual items that could be imported.

In the early 1960s and early to middle 1970s, the two lists functioned reasonably in accord with intentions: items on the liberalized list—primarily raw materials, intermediate goods, capital goods, and spare parts—were fairly freely importable, and items on the quota list were in restricted supply. For this latter group of items, complex procedures were established to allocate available quotas to various producers or importers who had claims to them.

Although the quota list was intended to be more restrictive than the liberalized list, the system was reversed during periods of balance-of-payments difficulty. In the late 1960s and again after the mid-1970s those with quota rights under the quota list generally received their import licenses early in the import program period and then applied immediately to the Central Bank for foreign exchange. Ironically, those who wished to import items on the liberalized list later in the import program period were subject to delays of increasing length as balance-of-payments difficulties mounted, and in that sense the liberalized list was increasingly illiberal in periods before devaluation and stabilization programs.

Thus the 1958 stabilization program laid the foundations for the import regime that was to prevail in Turkey until the 1980s. In its aftermath export earnings grew fairly rapidly, and there were several years during which foreign exchange difficulties were not perceived as a major restraining factor on Turkish development policy.

When foreign exchange stringency began once again to appear in the mid-1960s, another feature that was to prevail until the 1980s was added to the trade regime. That was the practice of setting export subsidy rates for individual categories of nontraditional exports. The intention at first was to provide additional incentives for certain categories of nontraditional exports. As domestic inflation proceeded at a fixed exchange rate, the magnitude of these incentives increased. Thus by 1970, when the exchange rate was still officially TL9 per U.S. dollar,[15] a variety of nontraditional exports were subject to effective exchange rates ranging up to TL25 per dollar.

The practice of setting commodity-specific export rebate rates was abandoned in 1975, when export lists were established.[16] For present purposes the important point to note is that export subsidies of a variety of kinds were employed in conjunction with the trade and payments regime by the mid-1960s. Although at that time they probably served more as a partial offset to the disincentives to export created by the import regime, the export lists were readily at hand as a policy instrument through which exports could be encouraged in the 1980s.

Thus by the late 1960s the policy instruments that would be used throughout the 1970s were already established. The 1970 devaluation was followed by accelerating inflation in Turkey. During the 1970s the nominal exchange rate was altered, though generally by less than the percentage inflation differential between Turkey and the rest of the world and generally only after a time lag (see Chapter 4, Table 9). As Turkey's inflation rate approached 100 percent in the late 1970s, these time lags were themselves highly significant. They certainly must have reinforced the expectations, already generated by the two major stabilization episodes, that exchange rate changes would not for long be reflected in increased attractiveness of the export alternative. We turn, then, to a closer look at the situation as it evolved in the late 1970s.

The 1975–1980 Period: Recurring Crisis and Stagnation

The 1970 devaluation was followed by a massive increase in foreign exchange receipts. These originated in increased export earnings but also in workers' remittances. The current account, which had been in deficit by $108 million in 1969, showed a $44 million deficit in 1970 and then turned to a surplus of $43 million in 1971. By 1973 the current account surplus had reached $660 million. This was the first time since the early 1960s that foreign exchange shortage was not a dominant factor in policy formulation. Foreign exchange reserves rose from $26 million in 1968—less than three days' imports—to $2.0 billion by 1973, an amazing turnaround from the situation in the 1960s.[17]

Although part of the improved foreign exchange situation was a consequence of reversed speculative flows, it nonetheless permitted an economic boom. Real GNP grew at annual rates of 10.2, 7.4, 5.4, 7.4, and 8.0 percent in the five years from 1970 to 1975. It appeared that economic growth was, if anything, accelerating somewhat from its already rapid pace of the 1960s. As late as 1975 the only sign of difficulty that might have been perceived from the behavior of the domestic economy was the acceleration in the rate of inflation. Internationally, however, the current account had swung sharply into deficit after the oil price increase of 1973, reaching a negative $1.6 billion by 1975 and a negative peak of $3.1 billion by 1977 (almost twice export earnings in that year). At that point the authorities were unable to continue financing imports, and the situation deteriorated sharply. Real GNP was actually lower in 1980 than it had been in 1978.

From that period onward the Turkish economy (and body politic) was in increasing distress. In 1977 and again in 1978 the authorities entered into agreements with the IMF and the international creditors, but both agreements were rapidly outdated by the continuing acceleration of inflation and deterioration in the general situation. In this section we attempt to diagnose the phenomena that led to the crisis of the late 1970s. An understanding of the two aborted stabilization programs is important in the context of the 1980 program. Discussion of those episodes is therefore deferred to Chapter 3.

Real GNP grew only slowly after 1976, especially compared with the average annual rate of growth of almost 6.5 percent from 1960 through 1975. Per capita income in fact was falling after 1977. Several factors contributed to the slowdown in growth. These included the inflation and the consequent distortion of relative prices, the overvaluation of the exchange rate, and labor difficulties. The inflation can be traced to a combination of factors, including the failure of economic policy to adjust to the oil price increase of 1973, sizable fiscal deficits, and a convertible lira deposit scheme that left the economy extremely vulnerable to acceleration in the rate of inflation.

There is no dispute about the fact that the rate of inflation rose sharply after 1975 and was accelerating dangerously by late 1979. The annual inflation rate was 17.5 percent between 1975 and 1976, 26.8 percent in 1977, 45.5 percent in 1978, and 58.7 percent in 1979. It reached 110.2 percent in 1980.

There is also no disagreement about the extreme overvaluation of the Turkish lira in the late 1970s. Although the price level in 1975 was 134 percent above the 1970 level (see Table 5), the official exchange rate still stood at TL15 per dollar, virtually unchanged from 1970. Thereafter it was 16.50 at the end of 1976, 19.25 in 1977, 25.00 in 1978, and 47.10 at the end of 1979. By any measure the degree of overvaluation of the official exchange rate increased greatly during the 1970s. If one takes a purchasing power parity measure of the official exchange rate, the GNP deflator had increased by 150 percent between 1970 and 1975 with almost no change in the exchange rate. From 1975 to 1979 the GNP deflator rose 258 percent while the official exchange rate was adjusted by 165 percent. Thus, even without making any allowance for Turkey's deteriorated terms of trade resulting from the oil price increase, the exchange rate had been permitted to become overvalued by a massive amount.

The consequences of exchange rate overvaluation were several. First, the disparity between the official and the free market rate rose sharply. Early in 1975 this differential was relatively small—averaging under 10 percent over the first part of the year. Even at the end of 1976 it stood at just 9.7 percent above the official exchange rate. During 1977 the lira was devalued vis-à-vis the U.S. dollar from 16.50 at the end of 1976 to 19.25. By the end of 1977, however, the free market exchange rate stood at TL26.25, leaving a differential of 36 percent. The official rate was changed to TL25 per dollar in 1978, but by the end of that year the free market exchange rate was 51.6 percent above the official rate. It rose even further early in 1979, reaching a 91.4 percent differential in March of that year, when the official rate was still TL25 per dollar while the free market rate was 47.85. That differential was eliminated with a devaluation, to TL47.1 = US$1 in June 1979. It nonetheless started rising again, reaching 15 percent by the end of 1979; in January 1980 the official rate was changed again to TL70 = US$1. Thereafter the official rate was altered at increasingly frequent intervals, and disparities between the free market and the official rate of the order of magnitude that had been seen in the 1970s were not repeated.

A second and related consequence was that the evidence of exchange rate overvaluation provided incentives for underinvoicing of exports and overinvoicing of imports, for smuggling, and for Turkish workers to refrain from repatriating their savings without special inducements. This was a major motive for the establishment of convertible lira deposit accounts.

The overvaluation of the lira also resulted in a sharp deterioration in the official trade and balance-of-payments figures. Officially recorded exports were rising through 1976 but were fairly stagnant thereafter until 1980 and the devaluation and stabilization program of that year. Even by 1975 the current account deficit had been massive, in large part because of the higher price of oil but also because the inflation-driven real exchange rate appreciation increased the demand for imports. After 1975 Turkish importers were simply unable to obtain additional foreign exchange or foreign credits, and the restrictiveness of the trade regime increased in response to increases in demand for imports.[18] The magnitude of the recorded current account deficits in the late 1970s therefore fails to reflect the pressure of excess demand.

A natural corollary of these events was a sharp buildup in Turkish foreign debt. Table 6 gives particulars, based on World Bank data, from which evidence regarding short-term debt is not available before

Table 6

Turkish Foreign Debt and Debt Ratios, 1970–1980 (millions of U.S. dollars)

	1970	1975	1976	1977	1978	1979	1980
Total debt	1,960	3,585	4,258	11,419	14,829	15,889	19,040
Long-term debt (LTD)	1,886	3,342	3,867	4,917	7,021	11,660	15,496
Public	1,844	3,182	3,619	4,438	6,464	11,030	14,961
Private	42	160	248	479	557	630	535
IMF	74	243	391	409	622	633	1,054
Short-term debt[a]	—	—	—	6,093	7,186	3,596	2,490
Debt ratios							
Debt/exports	3.33	2.56	2.17	6.51	6.48	7.03	6.54
LTD/exports	3.21	2.39	1.97	2.80	3.07	5.16	5.33
Service/exports[b]	0.30	0.21	0.19	0.24	0.25	0.34	0.38

a. Short-term debt figures before 1977 included within long-term figures.
b. Debt service is the ratio of payments of interest and of public and privately guaranteed principal to exports.
Source: Debt figures from World Bank, *World Debt Tables and Supplements*, 1988–1989. Exports from IMF, *International Financial Statistics Yearbook*, 1988.

1977. By 1979 Turkish short- and long-term debt, almost all of which was public or publicly guaranteed, stood at US$15.89 billion; this was more than seven times exports of goods and nonfactor services. Even counting workers' remittances, the debt was more than three times exports of goods and all services.

By the end of 1979 the foreign exchange situation was truly desperate: not only were all lines of credit fully utilized, but suppliers were refusing to ship without advance payment. It was reported that Turkish embassy employees in some foreign countries had not been paid for several months. In Turkey oil imports were drastically reduced, and many houses, offices, and factories were unheated in the exceptionally cold winter of 1979–80.

Foreign exchange difficulties in themselves would have been sufficient to lead to underutilization of capacity in import-substitution industries dependent on imports of needed intermediate goods and raw materials and to curtail economic activity in transport and communications and other oil-dependent activities. They also contributed to accelerating inflation, which in itself was further contributing to economic distress. Inflation had its roots in the financing of oil imports, in a sizable fiscal deficit, which reached 10 percent of GNP by 1980,[19] and in convertible lira deposits.

To compound matters still further, however, the late 1970s were a period of political instability and general economic upheaval in Turkey. One symptom (and perhaps cause) of this was the occurrence of exceptionally disruptive strikes by a variety of unions. In private sector manufacturing, an average of less than 200,000 man-hours were lost annually to strikes in the years 1970 to 1975; by contrast, 1.2 million man-hours were lost in 1976 and 3.9 million man-hours in 1980.[20]

At a more fundamental level, the Turkish elections of 1977 had failed to return either major party to power with a majority sufficient to govern. Each major party had to gain the support of one or both of two smaller parties, which contributed significantly to political instability. A minority government was therefore ruling from 1977 until a military takeover eight months after the January 1980 reform program was introduced.[21]

All observers would agree that the Turkish economic situation deteriorated drastically in the late 1970s and that the factors already mentioned were hallmarks of that deterioration. The questions that remain are twofold: why was the domestic inflation rate permitted to accelerate so rapidly, and why was the lira permitted to become so overvalued? Here different analysts have different answers to the questions. Baysan and Blitzer (1988), for example, characterize economic policy making as being "neither consistent, stable, nor very rational." In their analysis,

> Despite unfavorable external circumstances, successive Turkish governments attempted to maintain or even accelerate the aggregate economic growth rates achieved during the first two five-year plans. . . . Because it was based on inflationary policies, heavy borrowing, and postponement of adjustments called for by changing world factor prices, the growth process soon proved to be temporary.[22]

Dervis, de Melo, and Robinson attempted to decompose the overvaluation of the lira into three parts: that attributable to the 1973–74 oil price increase, that resulting from excess demand following from the government's large investment program, and that resulting from increases in the prices of commodities imported by Turkey. In their analysis the total change in the equilibrium exchange rate could be decomposed into that resulting from differential inflation as a consequence of the government's investment program and other domestic inflationary pressures, 37 percent; the oil price increase, 21 percent; lower workers' remittances as a consequence of Europe's slower growth, 18 percent; the increase in Organization for Economic Cooperation and Development (OECD) export prices, 11 percent; and other factors, 13 percent. They therefore rejected any unicausal interpretation of the Turkish difficulties, though pinpointing the failure to alter policies in response to external events as having generated the crisis.[23]

The OECD diagnosis focused on the absence of policy change in response to changing circumstances:

> The current economic crisis has its roots both in the oil crisis of 1973–4 and the slowdown in world economic activity, that made the called-for adjustment to the changed external economic environment difficult. . . . Whilst oil price developments were an aggravating factor in respect of the balance-of-payments deficit and rising domestic inflation, the situation need not have become so serious if domestic policies had been adjusted in time to cope with the balance-of-payments problem. However, investment demand was allowed to remain high. . . . Similarly, the balance-of-payments policy

remained traditionally inward-looking, favouring import replacement rather than export growth.[24]

Amelung, by contrast, refers to a paralysis in policy making:

Following Demirel's failure, Ecevit formed a minority government backed by recently defected independents from the JP [Justice party]. Virtually, economic policy-making was reduced to restricting imports and taking up foreign loans in order to cover the foreign exchange gap. The embarrassment of economic decision-makers and their lack of conception were reflected in the Fourth Five Year Development Plan for 1979–83, which was delayed one year due to lacking majorities. The political crisis which accompanied the economic exhaustion of ISI [import-substitution industrialization] was not only reflected in a splintering of the party system; widespread civil and political unrest throughout 1978 prompted a declaration of martial law.[25]

Amelung attributes the political crisis to difficulties associated with the earlier import substitution strategy.

Celasun and Rodrik take an entirely different line. In their view the Turkish policy response was little different from and no worse than that of many other oil-importing developing countries in the 1970s. They summarize their argument as follows:

The proximate cause for Turkey's debt crisis can be observed in the rapid deterioration of her current account during the period. . . . While the initial deterioration can be accounted for by the oil shock, the trend after 1975 requires additional explanations.

What lay behind these deficits and were they large enough to have brought about the crisis? . . . The counterpart to these deficits was an increased investment effort, mainly by the public sector. Hence, external borrowing was used primarily for investment purposes, and not for consumption. Secondly, while consumption and investment decisions in the economy were considerably distorted by inappropriate pricing policies, mainly an overvalued exchange rate, these alone would not have brought about the crisis. What probably tipped the balance was the dynamics of the debt process itself. To prevent private-sector crowding-out and to ensure foreign exchange availability for its own needs, the government subsidized private-sector foreign borrowing by providing blanket protection against foreign-exchange risk. . . . The implicit subsidy on foreign borrowing was larger the greater the likelihood of a crisis; in turn, the crisis became more likely as borrowing skyrocketed.[26]

The "blanket protection" was in the form of convertible Turkish lira deposits (CTLDs). Starting in 1975 the government permitted nonresidents to open deposit accounts in Turkish commercial banks; the government then guaranteed principal and interest against all foreign exchange risk arising out of devaluations. The lender would deposit foreign exchange in a Turkish commercial bank; the commercial bank would then surrender foreign exchange to the Central Bank in return for Turkish liras; when payments became due, the commercial bank presented Turkish liras to the Central Bank in return for foreign currency. If there had been any devaluation in between, the Central Bank had to absorb the losses.

Celasun and Rodrik estimate the subsidy component of the CTLD scheme as being US$203 million in 1975 and rising to $1.2 billion in 1977, equal to 1.7 percent of GNP at that time.[27] They estimate that CTLDs constituted $1.2 billion at the end of 1975 and had risen to $6.1 billion by the end of 1977.[28] In their view it was this explosive financing, which became more costly as the lira was devalued, that led to an earlier crisis than occurred in other developing countries.

For purposes of analyzing the 1980 reform program and its aftermath, it is unnecessary to attempt to infer causation among the alternative views set forth above. All agree that there was a failure to adjust domestic spending or relative prices to the 1973 oil price increase and that continuing growth in the three years following 1973 was financed by running down foreign reserves and borrowing from abroad. All agree also that there were inefficiencies associated with import-substitution policies and that export earnings failed to grow both because of those policies and because of the overvaluation of the exchange rate. The CTLDs certainly increased the losses of the Central Bank and contributed to accelerating inflation, as did continuing fiscal deficits. Without the ability to borrow from abroad to the extent that the CTLDs permitted, the Turkish authorities might have been forced to take action sooner. Whether they could have done so, however, is an open question. Given the paralysis of 1978 and 1979, the absence of CTLDs might simply have implied an earlier slowdown in growth and a longer period of crisis, rather than an earlier successful change in policy regimes.

What is clear is that, by January 1980, the Turkish economy had been in a state of crisis for almost three years. The rate of inflation was accelerating; factory shutdowns and excess capacity were increasing as imports were increasingly unavailable; foreign exchange reserves were nonexistent, and the government was heavily in arrears on foreign debt; and real output was falling. It was in that crisis atmosphere that the policy reforms of January 1980 were undertaken. They are the subject of Chapter 3.

3

The Overall Reforms of the 1980s

By the end of 1979 the body politic and the economy of Turkey were in chaos. Politically, the coalition government of Prime Minister Bülent Ecevit's Republican People's party (RPP) had fallen in 1979. It was replaced by a coalition government led by Prime Minister Süleyman Demirel of the Justice party. Throughout the latter half of the 1970s, however, civil unrest had been increasing; by 1979 there were three political killings a day, and parts of Turkey were placed under martial law by the Ecevit government. Political violence continued to mount throughout the year. On the economic front inflation had reached an annual rate of 100 percent and was still accelerating; shortages and dislocations associated with dwindling imports were intensifying; debt service payments had fallen into arrears; there were long waits for foreign exchange allocations at the Central Bank even when importers had received import licenses; and strikes and other work stoppages were increasing in intensity. To add to the Turks' misery, the winter of 1980 was the coldest in the Anatolian plateau in many years, and heating fuels were in greatly limited supply. Parliament itself was without heat.

In many regards, however, the situation was not fundamentally different from what it had been since 1977, except in the sense that economic and political deterioration had been in process longer. The major difference from the years 1977–1979 was that the Demirel government chose to adopt a major program of economic reforms, with the support of the International Monetary Fund (IMF) and the donor community; under Ecevit these reforms had been strongly

34

resisted, although two programs had been inaugurated in the 1978–1979 period.

The focus in this chapter is on the overall outlines of the reform program that began with Prime Minister Demirel's announcement on January 26, 1980, and the reform program as a whole is described. In Chapter 4 the focus is on the trade and payments regime and the shift in incentives among nontradable, exportable, and import-competing activities.

The reform program gained and lost momentum from time to time, and the emphasis also shifted. Overall it is useful to think of policy formulation as having been in two distinct phases. A first phase, lasting from the September 1980 announcement until 1983, focused primarily on economic stabilization, although changes in the real exchange rate and announced intentions to rely more on private sector activity were also very important. The first phase of reforms can be said to have ended with the events leading up to the elections of 1983. These included the "Banker Kasteli affair"[1] and the abandonment of a tight credit program with expansionary monetary and fiscal policies before the 1983 elections. The second phase began after the 1983 elections and has lasted to the time of writing. The emphasis has been on increased support for private sector economic activity (including the construction and upgrading of infrastructure), liberalizing the trade and payments regime and shifting the orientation of the economy away from its earlier inner-oriented structure, and improving the functioning of finanacial markets.

Each of these main periods and the major reforms undertaken within them are considered in this chapter. To understand the reform program of 1980, however, it is necessary to begin by considering the two earlier programs that had been announced. That is the subject of the first section. The next section covers the basic features of the January program as it was initially announced and perceived. The following section examines the follow-up policies that were instituted in support of the program from January 1980 to the end of 1983. The next sections cover the role of debt and debt restructuring in the 1980–1983 period and trace the evolution of macroeconomic aggregates in that period. The following section focuses on the overall characteristics of the reforms taking place in the trade and payments regime in the 1984–1989 period. The final section outlines the major policy reforms in other markets that were effected during the

1984–1989 period and provides a brief overview of macroeconomic performance in the 1980s. An evaluation of the entire reform package is left to Chapter 5, after changes in the trade and payments regime and the response to them have been considered. The reader may find it useful to consult the Chronological Appendix, which provides a summary of the major policy changes.

The IMF Standbys of 1978 and 1979

The economic situation was already very difficult when Ecevit became prime minister early in 1978.[2] Short-term indebtedness was high, in part because of the buildup of short-term convertible Turkish lira deposits (CTLDs) during the Demirel government's tenure in office and in part because of the shortfall of exports and the dropoff in workers' remittances.

The Ecevit government had inherited an economically difficult situation. Its diagnosis of the situation appears to have been that unavailability of foreign exchange was restricting imports, which in turn were constraining domestic production levels. The solution, therefore, should be to seek foreign aid and foreign loans to permit an increased import flow, which would increase production and generate more exports. While it was recognized that the fiscal deficit should be reduced somewhat to curb inflation, a larger role for government in the economy in the future was anticipated. As aptly put by Okyar:

> It appears that the political views and ideological complexion of the left-of-center Ecevit government created almost insurmountable barriers in the way of arriving at a correct diagnosis of the situation, let alone taking decisive measures to counter it. The Ecevit government appeared convinced of the paramount virtues of government intervention in the economy, in the form of creating state economic enterprises or of intervening in the market mechanism, either directly or through subsidies. In addition, it was emotionally inclined towards a self-sufficient, even autarkic view of economic development, which restricted to a minimum the foreign role in the economy. The People's Republican Party had, in recent years, espoused undefined causes and slogans, such as total economic independence and anti-imperialism. The necessity of resorting to IMF cooperation and advice when the Party assumed power early in 1978 made the Ecevit

government extremely uneasy and unhappy. . . . In the Turkish government's view, there was nothing structurally wrong with the Turkish economy or with the economic development policies followed in Turkey between 1960 and 1978. The causes of the crisis in foreign payments and the quickening trend in inflation that arose in the middle of 1977 were ascribed to the faulty—but quickly repairable—policies, and the events mentioned above. Correspondingly, all that was needed to restore the situation was additional foreign financing and the rescheduling of short-term debts to help the balance of payments, and a period of restraint in public sector finances to control internal inflation.[3]

After discussions with IMF staff, the IMF and the Turkish government reached a standby agreement covering a two-year period, with 300 million special drawing rights (SDR) to be released over two years in three tranches. The Turkish lira was devalued from TL19 to TL25 per U.S. dollar. Turkey was to be entitled to make purchases under the standby subject to observing the following conditions:

- Ceilings were set for successive periods on net domestic assets.

- Limits were established on the amount of additional foreign borrowing the government might undertake.

- Turkey was not to incur any additional arrears in foreign payments.

- Debt rescheduling was to be carried out and completed by November 1978, with provision for eliminating all past arrears.

- Commercial banks would continue to be required to maintain a liquidity ratio of at least 15 percent.

- No new restrictions on international payments, multiple currency practices, bilateral payments agreements with IMF members, or limitations on imports would be introduced.[4]

By September, however, the Turkish minister of finance wrote to the IMF, noting that the IMF conditions had not been met and requesting higher ceilings than had been negotiated. In particular, Central Bank net domestic assets had risen to TL229.1 billion, more than 2 percent above the negotiated ceiling of TL224 billion. New arrears in foreign payments had been incurred, and new restrictions on imports were to be imposed. The Turkish government stated that the need for revision was attributable to the effect of extreme shortages of imports on domestic production and on tax receipts. There were also difficulties in debt rescheduling.

Although the IMF board approved modifications to the standby, it apparently did so reluctantly. The IMF staff made clear their difference in viewpoint from the Turkish government, attributing the failure to meet the conditions of the standby to the insufficient profitability of Turkish exports (because of exchange rate policy under continuing inflation) rather than to import scarcity.[5] Meanwhile, inflation in Turkey continued to accelerate, rising from an estimated annual rate of 21 percent in January to 57 percent in July 1978. IMF staff also expressed discomfort with the wage increases of 40–80 percent that had been negotiated by Turkish trade unions.

Economic conditions continued to deteriorate. Inflation accelerated, wage settlements were growing ever larger, import shortages intensified, and double pricing of government-controlled commodities such as sugar, cigarettes, and cooking oil became almost standard. The black-market exchange rate was over 40 percent above the official exchange rate when the third tranche of the standby was due to be released in November 1978. As reported by the *Economist,* by that time the IMF was insisting on a further 30 percent devaluation and sharp cutbacks in the government's fiscal deficit (including large increases in prices of commodities sold by state economic enterprises; these SEEs were incurring large losses at the prices at which they were selling, which were then financed by Central Bank credits). The Ecevit government, however, was resisting, insisting that social unrest could assume unacceptable proportions if the prices of SEEs were increased and that devaluation would increase import prices. It proposed instead to increase the size of export subsidies.[6] In consequence, the third tranche was not released.

In March 1979 the government introduced a somewhat restrictive budget in Parliament, and in April a first meeting took place between the Turks and the IMF regarding the possibility of a second standby. Another devaluation was announced on June 11, 1979, with the exchange rate moving from TL26.5 to TL47.1 per dollar for most commodities. For agricultural goods subject to domestic price supports and imports of petroleum and inputs into fertilizers, the exchange rate was to be TL35 per dollar. A letter of intent was finally signed dated June 30, 1979, in which it was requested that the two-year standby of 1978 be canceled and a new one-year standby be entered into for

SDR 250 million. This time the government stated its intention of slowing down the rate of inflation, raised the deposit and lending interest rates by 5.5 percentage points (still well below the rate of inflation), and put new ceilings on net domestic assets of the Central Bank and net Central Bank credit to the public sector. The standby was approved by the IMF in July 1979, which paved the way for an Organization for Economic Cooperation and Development (OECD) consortium package of aid of about $1 billion and another round of debt rescheduling.

Despite the new aid, inflation continued to accelerate, and the government failed to curb its expenditures or to reduce its drawing on the Central Bank. Domestic levels of production were falling, and the foreign exchange crisis intensified. In October 1979 partial elections led to a severe defeat for Prime Minister Ecevit's RPP. Ecevit was succeeded once again by Demirel, who formed a minority government in November 1979.

Thus, twice in the two-year period preceding January 1980, the Turkish government had announced a stabilization program supported by the IMF and the OECD consortium. Twice the government's announcement of its intention to adhere to net domestic credit ceilings and other measures had not been realized. Indeed, each announcement was followed by a subsequent worsening of the economic environment. The electoral defeat of the RPP in October 1979 certainly signaled popular discontent with the economic and political situation. In that sense it provided something of a mandate for action. In other regards, however, the situation was much the same as it had been earlier: a minority government, without a consensus or popular backing for a course of action, was once again in power.[7] It was in this context that the reform program of January 24, 1980, was announced.

The January 1980 Reforms

When Prime Minister Demirel assumed office in November 1979, he appointed Turgut Özal as planning undersecretary—a top economic post in the Turkish government. Regardless of political viewpoint, any diagnosis of the problems of the Turkish economy at that time would have concluded that, if the downward spiral in output was to be halted, it was essential to find means of financing an increased flow of imports. That meant arranging additional financing with the IMF and the OECD consortium of donors. Likewise, it was straightforward to conclude that the ceilings negotiated under the July 1979 letter of intent would soon be greatly exceeded and that the targets established in the second standby, like those in the first, would not be realized.

In these circumstances there were two choices. One was to approach the IMF in an effort to renegotiate ceilings and conditions for release of the second tranche of the existing standby. The other was to develop an economic program, implement it, and then approach the international community for financial support. The new government chose the latter policy, developing and announcing its program and only then seeking rapprochement with the IMF and the OECD consortium.

There was little public discussion of a reform program. Even within the bureaucracy, very few individuals were involved in its preparation. It is estimated that not more than ten bureaucrats were involved in preparation of the January 24, 1980, stabilization plan. It was the work of a very small group of technocrats, led by Özal.[8]

The plan was announced by Prime Minister Demirel on January 24, 1980, and further elaborated in a series of meetings with journalists over the next few days. The plan had two key, interrelated objectives: to reverse the downward spiral in economic activity and to stem the inflationary spiral. Unlike earlier policy packages, however, the plan immediately stated that there would be a fundamental change in underlying economic policies. It was intended to strengthen market forces and competition by opening up the Turkish economy to the rest of the world; simultaneously state controls over economic activity were to be reduced. Moreover, in his initial unveiling of the program, the prime minister made clear that the measures he then described would be followed by other policy changes (some of which would require legislation).

The initial program had three major components: (1) exchange rate policy; (2) internal price policy; and (3) institutional reforms.[9]

Trade and Exchange Rate Policy

The Turkish lira was immediately devalued, and it was announced that henceforth exchange rate policy would be more flexible, with more frequent devaluations in the future as warranted to maintain the attractiveness of exports. Simultaneously several other measures were taken to encourage exports and to reduce the restrictiveness of the import regime. The official exchange rate was changed from TL47 to TL70 per U.S. dollar. Although some exceptions were continued, the earlier multiple exchange rate system was considerably unified.[10]

For agricultural exports subject to domestic price supports, a special fund was established with the Central Bank, and levies were established on various export commodities, which were intended to capture the difference between the export price and the domestic price. The proceeds of the fund were to be used to subsidize farmers' inputs and to provide other support to them.[11]

A variety of other measures were also taken that had the effect of liberalizing the regime. Banks authorized to hold foreign exchange were permitted to retain up to 80 percent of their receipts, using them to cover acceptance credit obligations and to finance imports of oil, petroleum products, fertilizers, and pharmaceutical raw materials. The allowance for Turks traveling abroad was raised, and trade in gold was substantially liberalized.

In addition, a number of incentives for exporters were introduced or enhanced. Exporters were permitted to retain 5 percent or $10,000 of their receipts (whichever was larger). Moreover, all duties on imports used in export production were eliminated, and administrative procedures relating to exports were to be greatly simplified. Provisions were made for subsidized export credits, and export subsidies were retained.

Finally, the import regime was liberalized in several ways. The coverage of the liberalized list was enlarged, and advance deposit requirements on imports were generally reduced.[12] In addition, the quota list, which had previously been issued once a year, became semiannual.

It was made clear that all these moves were intended as first steps. Further liberalization of the import regime, continuing greater flexibility in exchange rates, and other changes were to follow. Except for these statements of intent, however, the actual changes in the trade and exchange rate regime were not dissimilar from those made in the 1958 and 1970 devaluation-stabilization programs. Even when compared with the 1978 and 1979 standby announcements, the January 1980 changes in the trade and payments regime were not qualitatively or quantitatively dissimilar.[13] The differences lay in the statement of intent and possibly, to a smaller extent, in the fact that there was a tendency toward simplification of regulations, rather than a move toward greater complexity of controls.[14]

Controls over Prices

If the international community perceived the devaluation and liberalization steps as the start of a reform program, it was the increase in prices of SEEs and the removal of price controls more generally that was immediately felt by more Turkish households.

SEEs have been important in Turkish economic life since the 1930s, providing power, transportation, communications, and about 40 percent of manufacturing value added. During the late 1970s their real expenditures and deficits grew rapidly. Transfers to SEEs from the consolidated Turkish government budget to cover their operating losses and investments rose from TL31.7 billion in 1977 to TL79.7 billion in 1979. This contrasted with a total consolidated budget deficit of TL52.2 billion in the former year and TL84.0 billion in the latter. The OECD attributed the government's overshooting of its expenditure targets largely to rising transfer payments, of which transfers to the SEEs were the largest component.[15] There was little question that ceilings on Central Bank credits were broken as government fiscal requirements driven by SEE deficits dictated Central Bank financing.

Once inflation had begun to accelerate, successive governments had prevented SEE prices from rising in an attempt to keep the recorded rate of inflation down. They had then belatedly raised SEE prices, usually by less than would have permitted them to cover costs at existing cost and output levels. By this time the monetary creation associated with the SEE deficits incurred during the earlier period of price suppression had unleashed additional inflationary pressures and price increases, with the result that SEE deficits would again widen, with further inflationary impetus.

In the January 1980 program it was announced that henceforth prices of SEE outputs (except coal, fertilizers, and electricity) would be freely determined and government subsidies would no longer be given (with a few exceptions). The average percentage increases associated with the January 1980 announcement were as follows: 100 percent for fuel oil, coal, lignite, railways, maritime transport, and textiles; 45 percent for gasoline; 120 percent for diesel oil and electricity; 75 percent for steel and post, telegraph, and telephone (PTT) services; 300 percent for paper; 400 percent for fertilizer; 55 percent for cement, cigarettes, and beverages; and 80 percent for sugar.[16]

In one of his press conferences explaining the program, Prime Minister Demirel pointed out that the price increases already undertaken were expected to reduce the losses of the SEEs by TL290 billion in 1980 and the remaining deficit was expected to be TL62 billion.[17]

In addition to the measures providing for the SEEs to establish their own prices and to refrain from financing deficits from the government budget, the prime minister also announced the abolition of the Committee for Price Control within the Ministry of Industry. This committee had been responsible for controlling prices of private sector outputs. This measure was aimed at returning private sector pricing to market forces and at eliminating black markets and double pricing, which had been frequent occurrences in the late 1970s.

There can be little question but that the part of the program raising prices was both necessary and extremely painful. The immediate impact of SEE price increases, which went into effect immediately and whose magnitude was known, was very great on large groups in society. The sharp increases in prices of transport meant, in some cases, a high decrease in income once transport to and from work had been paid for. The elderly, living on fixed pensions, felt alarm about how expenses would be covered at all. Thus political attention initially focused on the SEE price increases rather than the trade and exchange rate aspects of the policy changes.

Institutional Changes

For purposes of this study, the changes in the trade and exchange rate regime and the price increases are of central importance. The SEE price increases were certainly a key element in reducing the rate of inflation, which was both politically essential and a prerequisite for the maintenance of the new, more outer-oriented trade policies.

The announced change in trade policies, however, was only part of a broader change that was intended to increase reliance on the private sector and reduce government controls over economic activity. In announcing the program, therefore, Prime Minister Demirel indicated several organizational changes that were designed to bring about the first steps in this shift. First, two new coordinating committes were established, one to coordinate economic policy (Coordination Committee) and the other a Money and Credit Committee. The Coordination Committee was to be chaired by the undersecretary of the State Planning Organization (Özal at that time), with membership of senior officials from the Ministries of Finance, Industry and Technology, Energy, Foreign Affairs, and the Central Bank. As its name implies, the Coordination Committee was to give the undersecretary of the State Planning Organization an instrument through which he could influence the actions of the other economic ministries. It was charged with coordinating policies related to development plans and annual programs, preparing import and export regimes, and coordinating all economic relations with other countries and international organizations. The Money and Credit Committee was to be chaired by the undersecretary of the Prime Ministry, with the undersecretaries of the Ministries of Finance and Commerce and the governor of the Central Bank as members. It was to coordinate money and credit policies and to ensure that credit allocations were consistent with general policies.

The second organizational change was the creation of two new departments, a Department of Foreign Investment and an Investment and Export Promotion and Implementation Department. The former was designed to provide one bureaucratic location for the approval of foreign investment applications, which had previously been dealt with by a variety of ministries. The latter was charged with simplifying government regulations on investment incentives and exports. It replaced a number of scattered agencies that had previously been involved in these activities.[18]

The Follow-up to the Initial Announcement

Once the initial program was announced, the Turkish authorities approached the IMF and the consortium of OECD countries in an effort to obtain new money and short-term relief from debt-servicing obligations.[19]

Discussions proceeded during February and March 1980. The IMF staff highlighted two policy issues in addition to those addressed in the January program. On one hand, nominal interest rates were so low that real interest rates were negative, forcing credit rationing and discouraging savings. On the other hand, IMF staff were still concerned over the magnitude of wage settlements continuing to take place. The Turkish authorities were not highly receptive to discussion of either of these issues, arguing that financial deregulation should await the reduction in the rate of inflation that was expected to follow from the January measures and that incomes policy should not be necessary in a democratic society once monetary-fiscal policy had brought inflation under control.[20]

After several months of discussion, the government of Turkey and the IMF signed a three-year standby for SDR 1.25 billion six times Turkey's quota and the largest credit extended by the IMF to that date—on June 18, 1980. The terms of the letter of intent are not public but are known to have included the usual ceilings on net domestic assets of the Central Bank and on net borrowing by the public sector, along with provisions to liberalize the import regime as circumstances permitted, to refrain from adopting multiple exchange rate practices, and to prevent the accumulation of any new payments arrears.

In the standby agreement the Turkish government agreed to undertake some degree of financial liberalization within two years. In fact, on July 1 the borrowing and lending rates of the commercial banks were entirely liberalized, to be determined by market forces (apparently this was totally unexpected by the IMF). Representatives of the main commercial banks, however, apparently met quickly and agreed on rates to be charged among themselves. The result was that lending rates for commercial credit rose from 25 percent to over 60 percent a year while sight deposit rates rose only slightly from 3 to 5 percent a year.[21]

Despite the resumption of import flows and therefore a pickup in domestic production, political violence in Turkey continued throughout the summer of 1980. On September 12 of that year, the military dissolved Parliament and suspended all civilian institutions. A Military Council named a general, Kenan Evren, as president, appointed a new cabinet, and included Özal as deputy prime minister, thus signaling that the economic program would be continued.

Among its early actions, the Military Council banned strikes; outlawed the radical trade union, Devrimci İşçi Sendikaları Konfederasyonu (DİSK, in English, Confederation of Revolutionary Labor Unions); and suspended collective bargaining wage negotiations. Instead, a High Arbitration Council was established to decide on wage increases, to be based on such criteria as prevailing economic conditions and cost of living. It is estimated that wage increases in 1981 averaged about 25 percent, down from a 60–70 percent increase in 1980.[22] Simultaneously, in a move intended to guard against unemployment, the Military Council issued a decree preventing the discharge of workers.

Over the following year and a half the government adhered fairly strictly to the ceilings agreed on with the IMF and simultaneously further liberalized the import regime. After the maxidevaluation of January 1980, there were ten further devaluations of the lira over the subsequent fifteen months. Then, starting in May 1981, the Central Bank was given the authority to set exchange rates daily; this inaugurated a period that still continues in which exchange rates are changed almost daily. Although there have been changes in the real exchange rate (see Chapter 4, Table 9), the system can most aptly be described as a crawling peg.

By early 1983 nominal interest rates were high, and inflation was decelerating. Whether as a consequence of the credit squeeze or for other reasons, a prominent Turkish financier was unable to meet his obligations, and the ensuing panic resulted in sharp increases in interest rates and a scramble for liquidity. The military government reacted by firing Özal and replacing him with an economic team much less strongly committed to carrying out the reform program.[23] The new team relaxed the monetary and fiscal restraints on economic activity, and inflation began to accelerate.

Shortly thereafter the military government announced that elections would be held in the fall of 1983 under a new constitution that retained considerable power for the president. The government also announced the candidate whom it supported. Özal thereupon announced that he would be a candidate for prime minister and organized the Motherland ANAP party. During the election campaign government spending increased substantially, which resulted in further acceleration of inflation. Altogether the military government permitted three candidates, including Özal, to contest the election. The Motherland party and Özal won by a substantial plurality and returned with a majority in Parliament.

Thus by late 1983 a new, democratically elected government was in power.[24] It had a considerable mandate to carry out further reforms, and it had the parliamentary majority to carry them through. Thus the end of 1983 and 1984 witnessed the announcement of a number of significant measures, which further liberalized the economy.

Turkish Debt

An understanding of Turkey's experience with debt is important for analyzing subsequent developments in Turkey and also contains lessons for the rest of the world. For Turkey was unable to service debt voluntarily during the late 1970s and rescheduled debt as early as 1979. This was long before the debt crisis erupted for most other developing countries. Moreover, when other countries were experiencing major difficulties—during the worldwide recession of 1980–1983—in servicing their debt, Turkey had resumed voluntary credit-worthiness status.

Some observers, including especially Sachs, believe that Turkey's impressive growth performance in relation to other heavily indebted countries in the 1980s was in significant part a result of differences in net capital flows.[25] Not only did Turkey reschedule, but it also received significant new credits during the early 1980s. For these reasons a careful examination of borrowing and debt is called for.

With the formal approach by the Turkish authorities to the IMF in early 1980 after the program was announced, the way was cleared for the Turkish authorities to seek debt rescheduling. There had already been a massive rescheduling in 1979.[26] That had included a three-year grace period and then a five-year repayment period. In July 1980 the OECD consortium reached agreement with Turkey covering obligations to official creditors due through June 1983 as well as a restructuring of other maturities and arrears that had accumulated since 1979. The agreement involved about $3 billion in principal and interest and extended the grace period on the debt that had earlier been rescheduled for another two years.[27]

Almost all the rescheduled commercial debt was to be paid at an interest rate 1.75 percent above the London interbank offer rate (LIBOR). It is estimated that the total debt rescheduled amounted to about $6.5 billion. Some of this was outright relief, but most of it was rescheduling. This left a bunching problem for Turkish debt-servicing obligations that would emerge in 1985–86.

In addition, Turkey received new credits from the IMF, the World Bank, and the OECD consortium. Net transfers to Turkey are estimated to have been $1,274 million in 1980, $566 million in 1981, $274 million in 1983, and a negative $586 million in 1983.[28] After 1983 net transfers from private creditors were consistently negative, averaging a negative $320 million per year.

Table 7 provides estimates of Turkish external debt from 1975 to 1988. Turkey continued borrowing from 1980 to 1987. Although debt increments were very modest in the 1980–1983 period, borrowing rose sharply in the 1985–1987 period. Indeed, at the end of 1987

Table 7

Turkish Foreign Debt and Debt Ratios, 1975 and 1980–1988 (millions of U.S. dollars)

	1975	1980	1981	1982	1983	1984	1985	1986	1987	1988
Total debt	3,585	19,040	19,181	19,677	20,289	21,567	25,977	32,784	40,818	38,700
Long-term debt (LTD)	3,342	15,496	15,665	16,458	16,441	16,961	19,892	24,788	31,356	30,697
Public	3,182	14,961	15,225	16,064	16,042	16,536	19,533	24,285	30,490	30,162
Private	160	535	440	394	399	425	359	503	866	535
IMF	243	1,054	1,322	1,455	1,567	1,426	1,326	1,085	770	299
Short-term debt[a]	—	2,490	2,194	1,764	2,281	3,180	4,759	6,911	8,692	7,704
Debt ratios										
Debt/exports	2.56	6.54	4.08	3.34	3.44	2.92	3.15	4.32	3.95	3.27
LTD/exports	2.39	5.33	3.33	2.79	2.78	2.30	2.41	3.27	3.04	2.59
Service/exports[b]	0.21	0.38	0.38	0.40	0.40	0.32	0.45	0.46	0.48	0.56

a. Short-term debt figures before 1980 included within long-term figures.
b. Debt service is the ratio of payments of interest and of public and publicly guaranteed principal to exports.
Source: Debt figures from World Bank, *World Debt Tables and Supplements*, 1988–89. Exports from IMF, *International Financial Statistics*, 1988 *Yearbook* and February 1990 issue.

Turkish debt was double what it had been in 1980. The debt-export ratio fell from its high of 6.54 in 1980 to a low of 2.92 in 1984 but thereafter began rising again. Similarly, except for 1984, debt service obligations absorbed more than 40 percent of export earnings in each year after 1982.

Turkish debt and debt-servicing obligations have remained relatively large in the period since 1980. Certainly the debt reschedulings of 1979, 1980, and 1981 brought the Turkish economy a period of relief from heavy debt-servicing obligations. It remains for Chapter 5 to assess how important debt postponement and relief and new money were in permitting the relatively successful performance of the Turkish economy.

Turkish Economic Activity Levels, 1980–1983

The initial results of the January 1980 program were highly visible to all in Turkey. Shortages disappeared as import flow resumed and as power outages, petroleum shortages, and other bottlenecks disappeared while destocking of inventories also took place.[29]

In its initial phase the major success of the program was to bring about a reduction in the rate of inflation. By early 1981 it was estimated that the rate of inflation had dropped to 35 percent from its high of 133 percent in February 1980.[30] For the entire year of 1981 the rate of inflation was 36.6 percent. It fell to 30.8 percent in 1982. It accelerated slightly in 1983, to 31.4 percent, as the increase in government expenditures accompanying the election was felt. The first two years of the program, however, must be deemed to have been successful in achieving their objective of reducing the rate of inflation.[31]

Likewise, the balance-of-payments situation rapidly improved. Exports rose sharply and were more than 50 percent over their corresponding 1980 level for the first half of 1981.[32] Industrial exports rose even more rapidly and were more than double their 1979 level by 1981. By 1983 Turkish export earnings were $5.7 billion, up from $2.9 billion in 1980.

The increase in exports, combined with the new money that was received at the time of debt rescheduling, permitted a significant reduction in the current account deficit (from $3.4 billion in 1980 to under $1 billion in 1982) and a major increase in imports.[33]

Imports rose from $5.1 billion in 1979 to $7.9 billion in 1980 and $8.9 billion in 1981 and 1982.

Thus, in their immediate objectives, the 1980 reforms were quite successful. They resulted in sharply increased exports and in a major reduction in the rate of inflation. The impact on overall economic activity was more mixed, however. Real GNP grew at rates significantly above those of the late 1970s (see Table 1 in the Data Appendix) but still well below the rates of growth realized in the 1960s and early 1970s. Likewise, unemployment appeared to be rising, and the decline in real wages for industrial workers was quite steep.

By the end of 1983, therefore, it could have been asserted that the initial effect of the policy package was on balance strongly positive. Exports had increased sharply, against the background of worldwide recession and therefore difficult conditions for growth. Inflation had decelerated and appeared to be moderating still further. At a more fundamental level, however, there were still significant trade barriers and pervasive public controls over private economic activity. It was in this climate that the second phase of the reform program began in 1984.

The Second Phase of Policy Reform, 1983 to ?:
An Overview

The first phase of the policy reform program really ended when Özal was replaced. Mid-1983 was a time when elections were in prospect, and the focus was on the political issues associated with the resumption of civilian government under a new constitution. By the time elections had taken place, some of the reforms that had been instituted in 1980 had been at least partially reversed. Inflation had already accelerated from an annual rate of about 30 percent in 1982 to over 50 percent in the summer of 1983. The real exchange rate had appreciated somewhat, by about 8 percent between December 1982 and the first quarter of 1983.[34]

Export earnings, however, were continuing to increase rapidly, debt rescheduling and new credits had significantly eased the pressures of debt-servicing obligations, and real output was rising, albeit slowly. Moreover, real interest rates remained slightly positive, and the exchange rate was adjusted daily. The fiscal deficit had been reduced to less than 3 percent of GNP, much lower than in the late 1970s, though higher than in 1981 and 1982. While it could be said that the momentum of reform had been weakened, if not entirely lost, the major changes had not been undone. Unlike the situation early in 1980, therefore, there was no crisis nor even a significant detectable worsening in economic indicators.

Nonetheless, the new Özal government moved quickly to regain the momentum of policy reforms. Changes proceeded rapidly over the next three years. The reform package and objectives after 1983, however, differed in important ways from those in the 1980–1982 period. The earlier reforms had had two primary objectives: the retardation of inflation and the reduction in the current account deficit; and structural changes within the economy, especially with regard to the role of import-competing and export industries, on one hand, and the role of the private and public sectors, on the other. After 1983 the emphasis shifted squarely to the latter set of objectives. Almost all the changes introduced after Özal became prime minister focused on the structure of the economy and its outward orientation: government expenditures began rising again, and inflationary pressures were again felt in the economy.

Thus, if the 1980–1982 period was successful in reducing inflation and stabilizing the economy but less so in resuming growth with a new, outer-oriented economic structure, the period after 1983 was more successful in continuing structural change and achieving more rapid economic growth and less successful in maintaining underlying macroeconomic balance. Indeed, starting in about 1986 macroeconomic instability, reflected in accelerating inflationary pressures, has been the Achilles heel of the reform program.

In this section we do three things. First we discuss the reforms in the trade and payments regime that were introduced starting in late 1983. Next we review other policy reforms that were undertaken after the new government came to power. Finally we assess overall government sector performance and the overall growth performance since 1983.

Further Reforms in the Trade and Payments Regime, 1984–1989

There is no question that considerable progress had been made in altering the trade and payments regime after 1980. The daily adjustment of the lira after 1981 resulted in much greater stability of the real exchange rate than had prevailed in the 1970s. Nonetheless, many restrictive aspects of the Turkish trade regime of the 1960s and 1970s were still intact in mid-1983. Much of the increased incentive for exporting that had been accomplished in the first phase of the reform program had been effected by special export incentives, rather than by dismantling the protection accorded to import-competing goods.[35]

One of the first policy pronouncements of the new Özal government after the November elections was an affirmation of its determination to continue integrating Turkey into the world economy. The "second stage" of the reform program then began with an announcement in December 1983 that henceforth the authorities intended to provide incentives more through the exchange rate, and less through special export incentives, than they had earlier done. They further indicated that they intended to move toward a unified exchange rate for all transactions.

Several steps were immediately taken in this direction. When the 1984 import program was announced, it was fundamentally altered from that of earlier years. Before 1984 the import lists were positive lists. That is, they enumerated those commodities eligible for importation. Those commodities not listed were deemed ineligible for import licensing. The January 1984 program, by contrast, was a negative list— all items not specifically mentioned were eligible for importation. In itself, the shift from a positive to a negative list is a liberalizing move. In fact, about 200 items were listed as ineligible for importation, and a number of other import-competing items were listed as eligible for importation only with permission. Since many more than 200 items had previously been omitted from the lists, the net effect was to free many commodities from quantitative restrictions. Simultaneously with the announcement of the new lists, tariff reclassifications were announced, with an average reduction in tariff rates of about 20 percent. Further liberalization was undertaken in later years, as the number of items requiring import licenses was further reduced.[36] The maximum rate of import duty was lowered to 50 percent, additional items were removed from the import lists, and import procedures were simplified.

There were some conflicting currents, however. As import duties were reduced and items removed from the negative lists, several special funds were created. These funds, which were off-budget items, were for particular purposes, such as a Housing Fund and a Support and Price Stabilization Fund (SPSF). While the rates of levy for these funds were far below earlier tariff levels (reaching a maximum of 10 percent for the SPSF in 1989) and applied uniformly to a large number of imported commodities, they were increased several times, and their scope was generally extended.[37] It would be surprising if this did not lead to expectations of further increases.

Potentially more damaging was the establishment of a Foreign Exchange Risk Insurance Scheme (FERIS) in April 1984. It was intended to encourage domestic producers to be willing to undertake investment: the stated rationale was that with daily devaluations, potential investors were refraining from borrowing to finance imports of capital goods because of exchange risk; FERIS was introduced with the stated purpose of covering that risk. In practice FERIS increased the fiscal difficulties of the government in raising resources for debt service as the exchange rate was depreciated to keep pace with inflation: since the private sector earned and earns most foreign exchange, the government must raise revenue to purchase foreign exchange from the private sector. When it must raise revenue to purchase foreign exchange and simultaneously must compensate private producers for increased debt-servicing costs arising from the exchange rate change, there is a double burden on the government budget.

After early 1983 the continuing alteration of value of the lira in foreign currencies once again kept pace with or even exceeded the rate of inflation. Baysan and Blitzer estimate that, on average, the real exchange rate depreciated by about 3.6 percent annually from May 1981 to May 1986.[38]

By 1987, however, inflationary pressures were increasing sharply. In an effort to contain them, the authorities began depreciating the lira less rapidly than the rate of inflation. The consequence was a real appreciation of the lira, which lasted until February 1988. By that time speculation regarding future devaluations resulted in a sizable capital outflow, and the Central Bank reversed its policy and tightened credit significantly.[39] As inflationary momentum accelerated in 1988 and 1989, changes in the nominal exchange rate once again lagged behind changes in the rate of inflation. It is not entirely clear how much of this lag was the result of deliberate policy by the authorities and how much was the result of a change in the exchange rate regime whereby market transactions became a larger element in the determination of the exchange rate. Regardless of the cause, by the start of 1990 the real exchange rate had appreciated by an estimated 20 percent over its end-1988 level. Thus toward the end of the 1980s difficulties with excess demand and inflation resulted in some departures from the earlier commitment to maintenance of the value of the real exchange rate.[40]

In addition to measures that liberalized imports and increased the uniformity of incentives, the government reduced restrictions surrounding convertibility of the lira and announced that steps would be taken to make the lira convertible. Foreign banks were encouraged to open branches in Turkey. Other immediate moves included liberalizing restrictions on the amount tourists could take abroad and widening the band within which commercial banks could deal in the foreign exchange market in Turkey. Subsequently Turkish residents were permitted to open foreign bank accounts and make payments, withdrawals, and transfers abroad. After July 1988 foreign investors were permitted to enter the Turkish capital market, and by June 1989 foreign investment funds were allowed to operate in Turkey. Also in 1989 Turkish residents were given the right to purchase foreign securities freely and could purchase up to $3,000 in foreign currency without restriction.

Finally, steps were taken to increase the attractiveness of Turkey for private foreign investors. Measures included the easing of conditions governing the transfer of profits and repatriation of capital, as well as the general relaxation of capital and exchange market controls.

Reforms in Other Markets

Although the focus in this monograph is on reforms in the trade and payments regime, those reforms were part of an overall policy package. Given the importance of those other reforms, it would be misleading to analyze the effects of changes in the trade and payments regime without recognizing that the entire policy environment was changing for decision makers.

Financial sector reforms were far reaching. A financial crisis had developed in the summer of 1982, which led to the replacement of Özal at that time.[41] In the aftermath of that crisis, interest rates were once again regulated by the Central Bank, although they were generally set to realize positive real rates of interest. Instead of the sudden liberalization that was believed to have resulted in the earlier difficulties, a series of measures were undertaken over the next several years that strengthened the supervisory powers of the Central Bank over the banks.[42] Legal reserve requirements and required liquidity ratios were reduced, taxes on financial transactions were reduced, and an inter-bank money market was opened in 1986. In addition, the Istanbul Stock Exchange was reopened in 1986. In October 1988 banks were once again authorized to set the interest rates on deposits and credits, except for the rate on official deposits.[43] In 1988 and 1989 the removal of legal prohibitions on the entry of foreigners into the Turkish financial markets further liberalized the financial system.

These measures greatly reduced the degree of financial repression in the Turkish economy. New security issues rose from less than 2 percent of GNP in 1981 and 1982 to 5 percent of GNP by 1987, and the composition of financial assets held by Turkish residents shifted sharply toward time deposits and other interest-bearing assets. The ratio of the stock of financial assets to GNP rose from 0.293 in 1980 to 0.508 by 1987, the latest year for which data are available.

Simultaneously there were significant reforms in the tax structure. In the 1970s a tax structure had evolved in which personal income taxes, which were paid primarily by wage and salaried employees, were the major source of government revenue. In the early 1980s the marginal rate of taxation was significantly reduced from 40 to 25 percent, and brackets of income were rearranged to increase the elasticity of tax revenue with respect to income. Corporate taxes were set at a uniform rate, initially of 50 percent, but were later lowered to 40 percent in 1981 and raised to 46 percent in 1986. SEEs were gradually made subject to the same rates of taxation as private enter-prises. Finally, a 10 percent value-added tax was introduced in 1985, which moved reliance even further away from personal income taxes.[44]

Later years saw even further measures. In 1988 and 1989 penalties for tax evasion were strengthened, and the Ministry of Finance was empowered to compel the closure of enterprises that were found to have systematically evaded their tax obligations. In addition, a program for privatization of SEEs was begun, although progress was slow and few enterprises had been sold by late 1989.

The combined effect of these measures was to shift the structure of tax revenues. In 1980, 43.5 percent of all taxes had come from personal income taxes, 4.1 percent from corporate taxes, and 25.6 percent from indirect taxes. By 1987 personal income tax receipts accounted for 24.9 percent of revenue, corporate taxes for 10.7 percent, and indirect taxes for 32.0 percent.

In addition to tax reforms, a number of measures were taken to increase incentives for efficiency of SEEs and to reduce the degree to which they might borrow from the Central Bank to finance their deficits. Before 1985 these measures seemed to have improved the financial performance of those enterprises. Before the elections of 1987, however, prices of SEEs were controlled, and financial performance significantly deteriorated.[45]

Overall Economic Performance in the 1980s

The previous section contained a discussion of policies that were changed by the Turkish government during the 1980s. Before turning to results, we mention several policies that were unchanged or changed in ways not conducive to reform.

Significant structural reforms in the financial sector, in public finances on the revenue side, and with the trade regime were accomplished. Further, the government clearly signaled its intention to rely increasingly on private economic activity for the production of most goods and services.

Despite this, there was considerably less success in curtailing public expenditures. In part this was attributable to a perceived deficiency of transport, communications, and other facilities in support of an outer-oriented trade strategy. In part, however, there appear to have been political pressures to maintain public expenditures. In 1980 general government expenditures constituted 25.0 percent of GNP; by 1984 they had fallen to 20.6 percent of GNP. Thereafter, however, the growth of public spending outstripped that of GNP: by 1987 general government expenditures accounted for 21.9 percent of GNP.[46]

The inability to raise government revenues more rapidly or to curtail the growth of public sector expenditures resulted in sizable public sector borrowing requirements and fiscal deficits. The general government deficit stood at 4.0 percent of GNP in 1980. It fell to 2.3 percent of GNP in 1982 and rose to 3.0 and 5.3 percent of GNP in the subsequent two years. It then once again fell to 2.8 and rose to 3.6 percent of GNP in 1985 and 1986 respectively. In 1987, however, it rose sharply to 4.5 percent of GNP and fell back to 3.4 percent in 1988. For 1989 it was estimated that the general government deficit would stand at 2.6 percent of GNP.[47]

In addition to those deficits, the activities of the SEEs must be taken into account. Their deficits, which were 5.8 percent of GNP in 1980, fell to less than 3 percent in the years 1981–1984, rose somewhat (to a peak of 4.2 percent) to 1987, and fell thereafter to 2.4 percent in 1989. Consolidating SEE deficits and general government deficits, the public sector deficit fell from 10.5 percent of GNP in 1980 to 4.7 percent in 1986, rose to 7.8 percent in 1987, and fell thereafter to an estimated 5.6 percent of GNP in 1989.

These numbers, of course, are indicative of why inflation has continued to be a major problem in Turkey. Whereas reforms appear to have acquired momentum and been highly successful in the financial markets, in the trade and payments regime, and in the structure of taxation, they have not yet reconciled the sources of government revenue with the claims on government expenditures. It is evident that over the longer term further policy reforms will be needed.

With that background in mind, it is possible to turn to economic performance over the 1980–1989 period. Detailed data are available in the Data Appendix tables. Summary data are provided in Table 8.

The initial stabilization years were ones of slow growth. Even though real GNP had fallen in 1979 and 1980, growth was only 4.2 percent in 1981, 4.5 percent in 1982, and 3.3 percent in 1983. Starting in 1984, however, growth proceeded considerably more rapidly, averaging over 6 percent for the next four years. Growth slowed substantially in 1988—presumably in response to the 4th of February package— and again in 1989. The first preliminary estimate is that real GDP rose 1.7 percent.

Interestingly, agricultural output grew relatively rapidly during the 1980–1988 period. Turkish agricultural output is strongly influenced by weather conditions, and therefore there are sharp year-to-year fluctuations. Nonetheless, overall agricultural growth averaged about 4 percent annually.[48] Industrial growth has been even more rapid, averaging in excess of 7 percent annually, although the slowdown in 1988 and 1989 was fairly pronounced. As a consequence of these differential rates, the share of agriculture in GNP fell from 24 percent in 1980 to 19 percent in 1989 while that of industry rose from 22 percent to 26 percent.

Table 8

Indicators of Turkish Economic Performance, 1980–1989
(GNP in billions of Turkish liras; exports and imports in billions of U.S. dollars)

	1980	1981	1982	1983	1984	1985	1986	1987	1988	1989
Real GNP[a]	206.1	214.7	224.4	231.9	245.6	258.2	279.0	299.7	310.9	316.3
Agricultural GNP	45.3	45.3	48.2	48.1	49.8	51.0	55.1	56.2	60.8	54.0
Industrial GNP	40.8	43.9	46.0	49.7	54.7	58.1	63.2	69.2	71.4	73.6
GNP deflator (% change)	103.8	41.9	27.5	28.0	50.1	43.9	30.9	38.3	65.8	66.8
Exports	2.9	4.7	5.7	5.7	7.1	8.0	7.5	10.2	11.7	11.6
Imports	7.9	8.9	8.8	9.2	10.7	11.3	11.1	14.2	14.3	15.8

a. 1968 prices.

Source: Data Appendix, Tables 1, 11, 14, and 15.

Whatever the future may hold, it seems clear that the policy reforms of the 1980s have altered the Turkish economy irrevocably. The chronic balance-of-payments crises and foreign exchange shortages that had plagued Turkish policy makers in earlier decades had disappeared; no longer was it believed that Turkish producers were simply incapable of exporting. Regardless of whether problems still remaining (see Chapter 5) imperil the short-term continuation of reform efforts or whether further measures succeed in ameliorating them, the 1980s were certainly a decade of major economic progress for Turkey.

4

Reforms in the Trade and Payments Regime

As the narrative of Chapter 3 demonstrates, a number of changes were made in the trade and payments regime in the 1980s with the express purpose of making exports more attractive to domestic producers and import-substituting production somewhat less profitable than it had been in the preceding decades. The relative attractiveness of exporting depends on the return producers can obtain when they produce a dollar's worth of exportables for sale in the international market contrasted with their return when they produce a dollar's worth of import-competing goods (valued at international prices) for sale in the domestic market.

In this chapter we first examine the behavior of the real exchange rate during the 1980s. Thereafter we make an effort to quantify the changes in protection for import-competing industries, to estimate the real effective exchange rate for import-competing activities. Then we calculate the value of export subsidies and incentives and derive the real effective exchange rate for exports. On that basis the shift in relative profitability and therefore in the bias of the trade and payments regime resulting from the reforms instituted in the 1980s may be calculated.

Nominal and Real Official Exchange Rates

In May 1981 it was announced that the exchange rate would be adjusted frequently, if not daily, to maintain the real value of foreign exchange to exporters. Indeed, for much of the period the real exchange rate depreciated: there was a deliberate policy to devalue the currency by somewhat more than the inflation differential between Turkey and foreign countries.

Table 9 presents the official exchange rate, the Turkish wholesale price index, the U.S. dollar price index, and a weighted average (by share of Turkish exports) of Turkey's trading partners' price index for the period 1975 to 1990. The purchasing power parity (PPP) exchange rate can be calculated vis-à-vis the United States and Turkey's

Table 9

Nominal and PPP Exchange Rate for Turkey, 1975–1990

	Nominal exchange rate (liras per dollar)	Turkish wholesale price index	U.S. price index	PPP NER Turkey– United States	G-7 price index[a]	7-country PPP NER
1975	14.44	2.80	56.60	291.90	71.50	368.80
1976	16.05	3.30	59.30	288.40	71.80	349.20
1977	18.00	4.10	62.90	276.10	79.00	346.90
1978	24.28	6.10	67.80	269.90	96.20	382.80
1979	31.08	10.00	76.30	237.10	105.20	326.90
1980	76.04	21.00	87.10	315.40	119.50	432.60
1981	111.22	28.70	95.00	368.10	111.30	431.50
1982	162.55	35.90	96.90	438.70	107.90	488.40
1983	225.46	46.44	98.10	476.30	104.90	509.50
1984	366.68	69.82	100.50	527.80	100.30	526.80
1985	521.98	100.00	100.00	522.00	100.00	522.00
1986	674.51	129.57	97.10	505.50	121.40	631.90
1987	857.21	171.08	99.60	499.10	133.70	669.80
1988	1,422.35	287.92	103.70	512.30	147.20	727.10
1989	2,121.70	488.20	108.80	472.80	145.00	630.10
1990	2,608.60	769.00	112.70	382.30	166.20	563.70

Note: Exchange rates are yearly averages of selling rates. PPP exchange rates are calculated by taking the ratio of the partner country wholesale price index to the Turkish price index and multiplying the resulting number by the Turkish official nominal exchange rate.

a. The G-7 countries are Canada, France, the Federal Republic of Germany, Italy, Japan, the United Kingdom, and the United States. The G-7 index is a weighted average of each nation's wholesale price index converted by the price of national currency in U.S. dollars. Weights are calculated as the sum of exports and imports from Turkey to each country as a share of Turkey's total exports and imports to the G-7. The index falls between 1980 and 1985, since a U.S. consumer who purchased goods from the U.S. and other G-7 countries in the same ratio as a consumer in Turkey would pay progressively less, because of the appreciation of the dollar.

Sources: Official Turkish exchange rate and wholesale prices: *International Financial Statistics* (June 1, 1991) and *Yearbook* 1990.

partners. There was significant real appreciation of the Turkish lira in the late 1970s, especially against the U.S. dollar. Contrasted with the U.S. dollar, the official real lira appreciated by 23 percent between 1975 and 1979; compared with a weighted average of Turkey's G-7 trading partners, the appreciation was 13 percent.

After 1980 the real value of foreign currency rose continuously and significantly both in dollars and in the weighted currency basket of seven large trading partners. In dollar terms a real depreciation at 1985 prices from TL315.4 to TL522.0 was effected from 1980 to 1985. In terms of the G-7 currencies, the real depreciation was from TL432.6 to TL522.0 over that period. After 1985 the lira seems to have been held fairly constant—with adjustments in the nominal exchange rate just about sufficient to offset changes in relative price levels—until 1989. After that year the nominal depreciation of the lira was at a far slower rate than the inflation differential; so a real appreciation of almost 24 percent—in terms of dollars—took place.

Effective Exchange Rates for Import-competing Goods

The total protection conferred on domestic import-competing production depends on the exchange rate, on the level of protection conferred through tariffs and other charges on imports of competing goods, and on the extent to which quantitative restrictions restrain imports.

Removal of Quantitative Restrictions

Table 10 demonstrates the shift in the restrictiveness of import licensing over the 1979–1988 period. The shift from the positive list to the negative list took place between 1983 and 1984—in itself a liberalizing move. In addition, the number of commodities subject to any form of licensing fell sharply: by 1988 only thirty-three items needed prior approval before importation, and only three items were expressly prohibited after 1984.

These measures virtually abolished import licensing in Turkey as an effective means of maintaining domestic prices of import-competing goods above international prices. Without careful analysis of detailed data on domestic and foreign prices and duty rates on imported commodities, however, it is impossible to estimate with any degree of confidence the extent to which liberalization reduced the protection afforded to import-competing goods. It would be highly misleading,

Table 10

Number of Commodities on Various Import Lists, 1979–1988

	1979	1980	1981	1982	1983	1984	1985	1986	1987	1988
Positive list system[a]										
Liberalized list 1	1,600	653	942	956	956					
Liberalized list 2		958	835	821	821					
Quota list	345	312	—	—	—					
Fund list[b]	—	—	—	23	35					
Negative list system[c]										
Prior approval list						1,137	638	245	1¯1	33
Fund list						67	153	347	5¯0	784
Prohibited list[d]						459	3	3	3	3

a. Abolished at the end of 1983.
b. Introduced with the 1982 import program.
c. Introduced in January 1984.
d. Virtually abolished in May 1985.
Source: *Resmi Gazete*, various years.

63

however, to estimate effective exchange rates (seen as protection for domestic industry) without recognizing the impact of quantitative restrictions on imports. Somewhat arbitrarily, therefore, it has been assumed that quantititive restrictions imposed an additional fifty-percentage-point wedge between the landed cost of import-competing items and their domestic prices in 1980, 40 percent in 1981, 30 percent in 1982 and 1983, 20 percent in 1984, 10 percent in 1985, and zero percent thereafter.

Quantification of Tariffs and Surcharges on Imports

In addition to tariffs, Turkey has long levied a variety of surcharges on imports. Table 11 presents a schematic representation of these levies and the ways they were calculated. In addition to the customs duty itself, there were a 15 percent municipality tax (charged as a percentage of the customs duty), a stamp duty (charged at a lower rate but as a fraction of the cost, insurance, and freight [c.i.f.] price), taxes

Table 11

Calculation of Total Charges on Imports

Customs duty collected $(cd) = c.i.f. \times t$
Municipality tax $(mt) = cd \times m$
Stamp duty $(sd) = c.i.f. \times s$
Funds (f) = specific rates
Wharf tax $(wt) = (c.i.f. + cd + mt + f + sd) \times w$
Value-added tax $(vat) = (c.i.f. + cd + mt + f + sd) \times v$

where t is the rate of nominal tariff

m = 15 percent through the entire period

s = 1 percent 1980 to May 1985
4 percent June 1985 to December 1986
6 percent January 1987 to October 1988
10 percent November 1988 to date

w = 15 percent throughout

v = 0 until January 1985
10 percent January 1985 to October 1986
12 percent November 1986 to October 1988
10 percent November 1988 to date

Total charges against imports = $cd + mt + sd + f + w + vat$

for funds, a wharf tax, and a value-added tax (VAT). For example, an item subject to a 10 percent customs duty and a 6 percent funds tax would have been subject to a total charge, at the end of 1988, of 59.6 percent.[1]

The duty rates were so specific and changed so frequently that the only way to provide an estimate of their effect was to take a sample of commodities and trace the evolution of their treatment through time. The results for customs duties and other charges listed in Table 11 are given in Table 12. Appendix Table 20 provides a breakdown of the charges underlying the calculation of the total rate for each commodity for each year. If one were to examine duty rates alone, it is not clear that there was a strong trend toward a reduction in rates: a wide variety of commodities was subject to increases in total rates charged. Motor car imports, for example, were subject to charges amounting to 112 percent of the c.i.f. price in 1980; the rate fluctuated somewhat and rose to 145 percent by 1986 before falling to 96 percent in 1987 and 74 percent in 1989.

Once it is recognized that quantitative restrictions against many imports were removed, however, the downward trend in protection rates is more evident. Table 13 gives the annual means for each commodity group covered, when the estimated impact of quantitative restrictions on imports is taken into account. Detailed data on the composition of the total protection may be found in Table 20 for a sample of specific commodities.

Even at a two-digit level, however, it is apparent that total protection was extremely high in 1980, with total charges equivalent to nominal protection rates ranging from 29 percent on minerals to 135 percent on glass and ceramic products. When account is taken of the existence of quantitative restrictions, these were probably equivalent to protection to domestic import-competing producers of 79 percent and 185 percent respectively.[2]

It is evident from Table 13 that the variance in protection rates among types of economic activity was very great in the early 1980s. This was true of tariffs as well as other charges on imports. When it is recognized that quantitative restrictions on imports also skewed the variation in rates of protection, it can be seen that the system was discriminatory indeed.

In the early 1980s, it is likely that the chief source of reduction in protection was the gradual move away from quantitative restrictions

Table 12

Import Duties and Other Charges, 1980–1989

	1980	1981	1982	1983	1984	1985	1986	1987	1988	1989	Change (1980 to 1989)
Food and beverages											
Soy oil	60.1	66.3	66.3	9.0	12.5	7.4	25.4	41.4	16.5	70.6	10.5
Whiskey	226.7	232.9	232.9	205.8	731.6	263.6	247.4	257.8	264.9	323.9	97.2
Tomato paste	72.2	78.4	78.4	75.4	76.2	31.6	37.5	42.6	50.5	67.7	-4.5
Minerals											
Calcium-phosphate	5.8	27.0	12.0	24.0	24.8	17.2	12.6	19.0	23.1	41.0	35.2
Cement	57.0	63.2	63.2	60.2	15.8	25.0	22.0	19.0	23.1	27.8	-29.2
Asbestos	44.9	51.1	51.1	48.1	48.9	44.8	35.2	41.9	49.0	54.2	9.3
Copper ore	17.8	24.0	24.0	21.0	9.8	25.0	22.0	28.5	35.6	41.0	23.2
Aluminum ore	17.8	24.0	24.0	21.0	9.8	25.0	22.0	28.5	35.6	41.0	23.2
Mineral fuels											
Coal	84.3	90.5	90.5	87.5	88.3	26.3	31.2	40.2	36.9	38.2	-46.1
Lignite	84.3	90.5	90.5	87.5	88.3	26.3	12.6	19.0	44.3	45.9	-38.4
Coke	84.3	90.5	90.5	87.5	15.8	26.3	23.3	29.8	36.9	25.0	-59.3
Chemicals											
Phosphoric acid	47.9	54.1	54.1	51.1	39.9	38.2	35.2	41.9	49.0	47.6	-0.3
Sodium hydroxide	66.0	72.2	72.2	81.3	52.0	51.4	103.9	97.5	38.8	26.8	-39.3
Sodium sulphurate	66.0	72.2	72.2	81.3	141.3	106.4	94.7	98.6	116.4	120.4	54.3
Teraflatic acid	66.0	72.2	72.2	69.2	39.9	38.2	45.3	39.2	46.3	39.2	-26.8

(continued on next page)

Ftalic anhydrite	66.0	72.2	72.2	69.2	52.0	67.2	70.3	70.0	74.5	82.5	16.5
Ammonium sulphate	36.0	42.2	42.2	39.2	40.0	51.4	60.5	57.6	48.5	41.6	5.7
Organic dyes	51.0	57.2	57.2	54.2	37.9	38.2	35.2	41.9	49.0	54.2	3.3
Rubber and plastic											
Polyester chips	97.2	103.4	103.4	100.4	57.6	54.7	49.8	56.9	65.5	54.2	−43.0
Silicons	97.2	103.4	103.4	52.1	45.9	38.2	35.2	41.9	49.0	54.2	−43.0
Latex	54.9	61.1	61.1	58.1	39.8	31.6	28.6	35.2	36.9	25.0	−29.9
Tires (truck)	68.1	74.3	74.3	71.3	103.2	82.2	60.8	68.0	75.1	54.2	−13.9
Leather, hides, and fur											
Hides	23.9	30.1	30.1	21.0	15.8	25.0	12.6	19.0	23.1	25.0	1.1
Sole leather	132.6	138.8	138.8	135.8	136.6	44.8	33.5	19.0	43.9	36.0	−96.6
Leather wear	192.9	199.1	199.1	196.1	196.9	223.3	132.4	82.3	111.2	128.4	−64.5
Paper and products											
Wood pulp	29.9	36.1	36.1	48.1	9.8	25.0	12.6	19.0	23.1	25.0	−4.9
Newsprint	20.8	27.0	27.0	60.2	27.0	67.7	53.9	47.3	35.6	42.3	21.5
Kraft paper	74.1	80.3	80.3	77.3	67.0	73.4	71.1	74.7	68.3	58.0	−16.0
Textiles, clothing											
Polyester yarn	84.2	90.4	90.4	87.4	54.0	44.3	37.3	42.0	49.1	44.3	−39.8
Cotton	23.9	30.1	30.1	135.8	28.2	17.5	12.7	19.0	23.1	25.0	1.1
Long fiber cotton	23.9	30.1	30.1	27.1	27.9	38.2	35.2	41.9	49.0	25.0	1.1
Cotton textiles	114.3	120.5	120.5	117.5	52.0	51.4	48.5	55.4	62.5	45.6	−68.7
Cotton T-shirts	150.6	156.8	156.8	183.9	76.1	77.9	74.9	82.3	89.4	74.6	−75.9
Glass, ceramic											
Tiles	152.6	158.8	158.8	155.8	156.6	64.6	35.2	41.9	49.0	61.0	−91.6
Porcelain	152.6	158.8	158.8	155.8	156.6	64.6	74.9	82.3	89.4	135.1	−17.5

(continued on next page)

Table 12

	1980	1981	1982	1983	1984	1985	1986	1987	1988	1989	Change (1980 to 1989)
Glass, colored	162.6	168.8	168.8	165.8	166.6	77.9	61.7	68.9	75.9	67.5	-95.1
Ordinary glass	72.2	78.4	78.4	75.4	76.2	92.2	61.7	74.0	72.8	51.1	-21.1
Iron and steel											
Blooms, billets	44.9	51.1	51.1	37.1	25.0	26.8	34.8	41.5	48.6	36.0	-8.9
Coils for rerolling	32.8	39.0	39.0	37.1	25.0	26.7	32.5	39.2	37.4	55.6	23.0
Nonferrous metals											
Copper	53.9	60.1	60.1	81.2	37.0	26.3	23.3	29.8	36.9	25.0	-28.9
Aluminum	53.9	60.1	60.1	39.0	9.8	17.2	12.6	19.0	23.1	25.0	-28.9
Alum bottles LPG	73.0	79.2	79.2	51.2	52.0	64.6	74.9	82.3	89.4	65.7	-7.3
Metal products											
Saw blades	82.2	88.4	88.4	85.4	74.1	77.9	74.9	82.3	112.8	103.7	21.5
Drill bits	82.2	88.4	88.4	85.4	86.2	64.6	61.7	68.8	99.3	103.7	21.5
Nonelectric machinery											
Grinders, mills	109.3	115.5	115.5	112.5	113.3	64.6	61.7	68.8	75.9	80.7	-28.6
Electric machinery											
Refrigerators	88.3	94.5	94.5	91.5	116.0	95.1	74.9	82.3	69.2	60.3	-28.0
Dishwashers	56.0	62.2	62.2	53.2	114.1	104.0	87.3	94.9	102.0	60.3	4.3
Transformers	97.2	103.4	103.4	100.4	50.0	51.4	48.5	55.4	62.5	74.6	-22.5

(continued on next page)

Hair dryers	94.3	100.5	100.5	97.5	98.3	77.9	74.9	82.3	89.4	126.7	32.4
Radios	77.2	83.4	83.4	85.4	219.5	192.9	189.9	199.3	206.4	104.1	26.9
Television (color)	92.2	98.4	88.4	100.4	121.9	99.7	96.8	104.5	111.6	84.8	-7.4
Transport equipment											
Motor cars	112.4	118.6	115.6	115.6	119.3	137.1	145.1	95.8	125.4	74.1	-38.3
Buses	112.4	118.6	118.6	115.6	119.3	137.1	144.2	95.8	126.2	67.5	-44.9
Others											
VCR	104.3	110.5	110.5	107.5	121.4	137.1	115.2	123.3	130.3	92.1	-12.1
Magnetic tapes	80.1	86.3	86.3	107.5	62.0	64.6	61.7	68.8	75.9	80.7	0.6

Source: Appendix Table 20.

Table 13

Impact of Import Duties and Quantitative Restrictions, by Commodity Group 1980–1988
(estimated percentage of c.i.f. price)

	1980	1981	1982	1983	1984	1985	1986	1987	1988
Food and beverages[a]	116	112	102	72	64	29	30	41	32
Minerals	79	78	65	65	42	37	22	27	33
Mineral fuels	134	130	120	117	84	36	33	29	38
Chemicals	107	103	93	94	78	63	60	60	56
Rubber and plastic	129	126	116	100	82	60	41	48	54
Leather and hides	166	163	153	148	136	101	56	38	56
Paper and products	92	88	78	92	55	62	43	44	41
Textiles and clothing	129	126	116	140	68	54	40	46	52
Glass, ceramics	185	282	272	268	259	80	55	61	65
Iron and steel	89	85	75	67	45	37	32	38	41
Nonferrous metals	110	106	96	87	53	35	35	41	47
Metal products	132	128	118	115	100	80	64	70	77
Nonelectrical machinery	159	155	145	142	133	71	58	64	71
Electrical machinery	131	130	119	118	140	106	89	95	101
Transport equipment	162	159	147	145	139	131	127	88	88
Other	142	148	138	127	112	103	84	88	91
Unweighted average	129	132	121	119	99	68	54	55	59

Note: For commodities covered and individual tariffs and surcharges, see Appendix Table 20.

a. Whiskey was omitted from the food and beverages group because of its dominance with regard to the total.

Source: Authors' calculations.

on imports. By 1985, however, this move was completed and the average of protection rates still stood at 68 percent. Thereafter, as the data in Table 13 show, there was a further small reduction in average charges on imports, and a tendency for greater uniformity of those charges. In 1986, for example, the range of rates was from 22 to 127 percent. By 1988 that range had fallen to 32 to 101 percent.

The estimates in Table 13 will be used in Table 19 to provide estimates of effective exchange rates for imports, which, along with similar estimates for exports, give an indicator of the change in the bias of the trade regime. Before that is done, however, the changes in export subsidies and incentives must be considered.

Incentives for Industrial Exports in the 1980s

The Turkish trade regime provided strong incentives for import substitution throughout the 1970s (see Chapter 2). The exchange rate was adjusted infrequently and usually by less than the rate of inflation, which by itself made exporting relatively unattractive. In addition, however, the import regime became increasingly restrictive as export earnings lagged and the real appreciation of the lira increased the demand for imports. A highly protected domestic market, in which foreign competition was not permitted and in which demand and prices were rising rapidly, was an irresistible alternative for most producers.

When the Turkish authorities decided to change the system, therefore, they were confronted with a legacy of over thirty years of systematic discrimination against exports. Unlike earlier devaluations, it was stated that the entire orientation of the trade regime would change and that Turkey would henceforth become much more integrated with the world economy. The authorities therefore began dismantling protection and changed exchange rate policy.

The reforms did not stop with exchange rate policy, however, and with a dismantling of protection against imports. They included a variety of measures that provided additional incentives to exports, especially industrial exports. In this chapter we review these incentives for industrial exports and attempt to quantify the extent to which they increased the real return to exporting.

The next subsection provides a survey of the various incentive measures and their relative importance. The following subsection gives estimates of the overall impact of these incentives on the real returns to Turkish exporters. On that basis estimates can be calculated of the evolution of the bias of the Turkish trade regime in the 1980s, which is the subject of the next section.

There were a large number of "incentive schemes." To permit some degree of perspective on these schemes and their relative importance, the text of this chapter contains tables showing the average annual value of each scheme, which usually varied over time. Appendix Tables 21–30 provide estimates of the variations across sectors in the value of each scheme.

The "Export Incentives"

To estimate the bias of a trade regime, a benchmark is needed. Such a benchmark is a "neutral" trade regime, which would occur if producers were confronted with border prices for all their tradable inputs and outputs (and there were no systematic discrimination in the domestic market based on the destination of production).

In Turkey the term "export incentives" was used in a different sense. There were export incentives in place in Turkey throughout most of the two decades preceding the 1980s. Even under the import-substitution regimes, some measures had been taken that it had been hoped would encourage industrial exports. They included rebates on customs duty paid by exporters, which were in reality reductions in the disincentives that exporters would otherwise have faced. Relative to border prices, the removal of customs duties on goods exported simply eliminated further discrimination that would have occurred; simultaneously it permitted Turkish exporters at least a degree of equality with their foreign competitors.

In like manner exporters were exempted from paying the production tax on final goods exported in the 1970s and early 1980s. When that tax was replaced with a VAT in 1985, exports continued to be exempted.[3] This was considered an export incentive in Turkey, although in reality it simply conformed to European practice whereby a VAT is imposed on imports and not on exports.

When the new economic policies were being considered in 1980, therefore, the government inherited a set of policy instruments that had earlier offset some of the disincentives to export that had prevailed and provided some incentives for industrial exports. There had thus been some export credit facilities, some provisions under which exporters could obtain access to a small amount of foreign exchange, and some export subsidies that offset part of the increasing overvaluation of the Turkish lira. In this section we review all the "incentives," although we recognize that some should properly be regarded as necessary to avoid greater disincentives. Later, when the value of incentives is quantified, we do not include these disincentive offsets in our estimates.

The export promotion measures were not discontinued in 1980; indeed, they were seized upon as instruments that could quickly be enhanced to strengthen incentives for exports. Export subsidy rates were increased (see the section "Export Tax Rebates"), provisions for foreign exchange retention were liberalized (see the section "Foreign Exchange Retention"), export credit provisions were enhanced (see the section "Export Credits"), and so on. In the first few years of the new policies, the value of these measures was augmented, and the export regime tended, if anything, to become increasingly complex. By the mid-1980s, however, the government began to reduce the value of incentives provided by tax rebates, and to increase its reliance on the exchange rate and other measures as a means of encouraging export performance.

Within that overall trend, however, there were many twists and turns. In what follows the major instruments used and their value are estimated. In general, the export incentives of the 1980s applied primarily to the same commodities as they had in the 1970s, that is, industrial exports. In this section, therefore, the focus is on these incentives. In general, they did not apply to exports of agricultural or mineral commodities or to tourism or construction services. In those few instances where incentives discussed here were also applicable to those (or other) activities, it is so noted. Otherwise the discussion is confined to incentives for industrial exports.

To assist the reader in understanding the maze of incentives, Table 14 presents estimates of the weighted average value of export subsidies, as a percentage of free-on-board (f.o.b.) price, for 1980 to 1989. The individual items listed are explained in the following subsections. Here it suffices to note that the total value of subsidies as a percentage of export price diminished somewhat over the period and the relative importance of various subsidy components also increased significantly. The first totals in Table 14, the total subsidies, indicate the magnitude of those items that can, to a considerable degree, be regarded as being an additional incentive to exports. The second,

Table 14

Value of Total Export Subsidies, 1980–1989 (weighted average subsidy rates, percentages)

	1980	1981	1982	1983	1984	1985	1986	1987	1988	1989
Subsidies										
Tax rebates	5.9	3.6	9.5	11.8	11.3	3.1	1.90	0.20	-0.90	-3.80
SPSF	0.0	0.0	0.0	0.3	0.3	0.2	0.20	1.60	2.10	12.70
Export credits	5.5	6.4	7.2	7.9	6.0	3.2	3.60	5.90	9.10	9.10
Corporate tax deduction	0.0	0.4	0.6	1.2	1.7	1.6	2.10	2.50	3.00	3.00
Freight subsidy	0.0	0.0	0.0	0.0	0.0	0.0	0.08	0.15	0.15	0.15
Advance payment	0.0	0.0	0.0	0.0	0.0	0.0	0.00	1.10	1.00	0.00
RUSF[a]	0.0	0.0	0.0	0.0	0.0	4.0	2.20	0.00	0.00	0.00
Total subsidies	11.4	10.4	17.3	21.2	19.3	12.1	10.10	11.50	14.50	21.20
Specific offsets										
VAT exemption	0.0	0.0	0.0	0.0	0.0	10.0	10.20	12.00	11.80	10.00
Foreign exchange retention	1.9	1.6	2.5	5.1	0.9	0.5	0.90	1.10	0.80	0.50
Foreign exchange allocation	3.9	3.3	4.2	7.9	3.1	3.4	5.60	6.20	5.50	4.30
Total subsidies and offsets	17.2	15.3	24.0	34.2	23.3	26.0	26.80	30.80	32.60	36.00

Note: Weights are the export shares of manufactured goods in total exports.
a. Resource utilization support fund.
Source: Authors' calculations.

total subsidies and offsets, include the total subsidies and also the VAT exemption and foreign exchange retention and allocation schemes, which were regarded as export incentives in Turkey but which in reality protected exporters from a disadvantage they would otherwise have suffered.

Table 31, in the appendix to this chapter, provides estimates of the values of incentives for a sample of commodities for which the values of each of the items discussed below were calculated over the entire 1980s period. There was some variation in the value of the various export subsidies for different commodities. At first the main source of variation was the inclusion of commodities on different lists. Later, however, other sources of difference also emerged. As the rebates were scaled down, starting in 1984, and phased out in 1989, payments from SPSF were gradually increased to compensate for this elimination.

In what follows we attempt to capture the overall quantitative significance of the various incentive schemes. Any such generalization fails to indicate the full complexity of the arrangements. Nonetheless, it does provide an overview of the relative importance of the different incentive schemes.

Administrative Simplification.

Before delving into the individual items listed in Table 14, we should note that a significant reform of the 1980s was to tilt government policy toward favoring exports. That entailed simplifying and streamlining the procedures exporters had to follow to export.

Despite the variety of export promotion measures that existed in the 1970s, there were considerable barriers to their use. Most of these, of course, were bureaucratic: delays, paperwork, and procedures to be followed. Among the causes of these barriers was the fact that the various incentives—credit, import duty rebates, foreign exchange retention, and so on—were administered by different government agencies. One of the reform measures included in the January 1980 package was a move of all these functions into one agency: a department of the State Planning Organization, the Office of Incentives and Implementation (Teşvik ve Uygulama Dairesi—TUD) was charged with administering all export promotion measures.[4]

There seems to be little question that TUD, and later Teşvik ve Uygulama Başkanlığı (TUB), did simplify and streamline procedures. The basic procedure was for exporters to register their intention to export; TUB/TUD then granted an exporter's certificate on the basis of which exporters were eligible for all incentives—imports without duty for reexport, export credit, and so on. Interviews with exporters in 1989 appeared to show universal agreement that the procedures for obtaining an exporter's certificate were simple and rapid; such a certificate could be obtained within a matter of weeks or even days. This in itself constituted a significant change from the 1970s, when exporters had to confront different agencies with demands for various incentives and had to establish their eligibility anew with each one.[5]

In general, those who had attempted to export in the 1970s and 1980s reported that the bureaucratic attitudes had changed completely; whereas the bureaucracy delayed and generally failed to understand exporters' problems in the 1970s, those interviewed reported no such difficulties in the 1980s.

Export Tax Rebates

Tax rebates started in the 1960s in Turkey and were designed, at least in principle, to provide a refund to exporters for taxes paid at earlier stages of production.[6] There had been significant elements of export encouragement in the rebate rates, especially for nontraditional export commodities.

Before 1975 export rebate rates had been calculated separately for each commodity; government officials would visit individual factories and establish the appropriate rebate rate on inspection of a company's books and discussions with officials. In 1975 a major simplification occurred, as all eligible commodities were divided into eleven lists, with rebate rates established for each list.[7] Table 15 gives the rebate rates in effect for the various lists for the period since 1975.

Rebate rates were altered in line with changes in economic policies. After the March 1978 and June 1979 devaluations of the Turkish lira, rebate rates were substantially reduced in the belief that exchange rate adjustment had provided enough encouragement for exports. After March 1978, however, this did not prove to be the case, and the tax rebate rates were again raised after an interval of only four months. With the June 1979 measures, the reduced rates remained in force for two years (during which there was a large devaluation at the beginning of 1980 and more frequent exchange rate adjustments thereafter). The rates were increased once more in April 1981, however. Thereafter there were eight lists in effect, plus specific rebates for a

Table 15

Tax Rebate Rates for Exports, 1975–1989 (percentage of f.o.b. value exported)

Dates	1	2	3	4	5	6	7	8	9	10	11
September 5, 1975	40	35	30	25	20	15	10	5	s	s	s
March 22, 1978	20	15	10	5	5	5	5	5	s	s	s
July 6, 1978	30	25	20	15	10	5	5	s	s	—	—
June 11, 1979	15	10	5	5	5	5	5	5	0	s	—
April 23, 1981	20	18	15	13	10	8	5	5	0	s	—
April 22, 1982	20	18	15	13	10	8	5	5	0	s	—
April 1, 1984	16	14	12	10	8	6	4	4	0	s	—
September 1, 1984	11	10	8	7	6	4	3	3	0	s	—
March 1, 1986	10	9	8	7	5	4	3	3	0	s	—
July 1, 1986	9	8	7	6	5	4	2	2	0	s	—
November 1, 1986	8	7	6	5	4	3	2	2	0	s	—
January 1, 1987	8	6	4	2	0	—	—	—	—	—	—
April 1, 1988	7	5	4	2	0	—	—	—	—	—	—
June 1, 1988	6	4	3	4	0	—	—	—	—	—	—
October 1, 1988	3	2	2	1	0	—	—	—	—	—	—
January 1, 1989	0	0	0	0	0	—	—	—	—	—	—

Note: See Appendix Table 31 for an indication of which commodities were on each list. Rebate rates are rounded to nearest percentage. In addition to rebates, there was an additional percentage rebate for exporters exceeding specified quantities. s = specific rate of rebate, rather than percentage. " — " means that the list number no longer existed.
Source: *Resmi Gazete*, various issues.

few commodities. Rates were reduced, as indicated in Table 15, until they reached zero in 1989.

Starting in 1984 the tax rebate rates were reduced systematically. The number of lists was reduced from ten to five in 1987. After the policy of maintaining or even depreciating the real exchange rate was firmly established in the mid-1980s, the rebate rates for each list were reduced, and the number of lists was also decreased. Finally, by 1989, export rebates were phased out.[8]

Tables 23, 24, and 31, in the appendix to this chapter, give an indication of the sectoral average rebate and the commodity composition of each list. Some fruits and vegetables were on lists 9 and 10. Most commodities, however, were manufactures. In 1979–80, 527 commodities were enumerated as eligible for a rebate on one of the lists. Chemicals (76 items) and metal products (73 items) were the two commodity categories with the highest number of enumerated items. By 1985 (Table 24), 744 items were enumerated on lists. Again, chemicals predominated with 106 items; food and beverages were second.

As will be seen in the section "The Support and Price Stabilization Fund," export rebates contained an additional incentive for exporters whose volume was large. There was apparently a belief that the government needed to subsidize the establishment of large exporting firms and that special incentives were desirable for this purpose. These firms emerged and were a significant feature of the landscape during the latter 1980s. They and the special incentives that gave rise to them are therefore the subject of a separate discussion below.

Export Credits

Credits have been available to exporters at rates below those prevailing for ordinary loans since the mid-1960s. Credit rationing prevailed in Turkey until the mid-1980s, so that credit availability for local firms was valuable. For exporters, however, access to credit was important because Turkish interest rates were well above world interest rates and the exchange rate was (in the 1960s) fixed.

When the trade and payments regime was reoriented to provide more incentives for exporting in the 1980s, several of the earlier export credit schemes were extended, and new ones were added. It was apparently felt that, with Turkey's high nominal interest rates, exporters would have to be compensated if they were to compete in international markets.

Several funds were used for this purpose. One was the Export Promotion Fund. Established in the 1960s as the Special Export Fund, its name was changed in 1980 to the EPF. It provided credit for exporters of fresh fruit and vegetables, marine products, export trading companies, and construction contractors working overseas.

A second fund was the Interest Differential Rebate Fund. It was intended to compensate exporters for differences in costs attributable to higher interest rates payable in Turkey than in foreign countries. The rebate was paid after exports had been shipped, and the rate was differentiated by product category. Exporters of food products, beverages, and tobacco were eligible for smaller rebate rates than other exporters of manufactured products.

In 1980 the requirements for eligibility for export credits were also relaxed. One consequence in the early 1980s was that export credits were received by individuals who used them to finance activities other than exporting. This resulted in a reduction in the differential in favor of export credits by 3 percent in 1983, but that did not stop the practice. The authorities therefore abolished the entire export credit mechanism in 1985.[9]

In 1986, however, the export credit system was reinstated, and new institutions were created or existing ones restructured to provide export credit.[10] In mid-1987 the Turkish Export Credit Bank (Export-Import Bank) was charged with the responsibility of supplying credits to exporters and of providing insurance for exporters, investors abroad, and contractors. In 1988 a Special Export Credit Facility was established,[11] which was replaced by the Foreign Trade Corporate Companies Rediscount Credit Facility in 1989.[12] It extended credits through the Export-Import Bank to foreign trade companies whose exports exceeded $100 million per year.

Rates of export credits are indicated in Table 16, and an aggregate sectoral breakdown is given in Table 26, in the appendix to this chapter. Nominal interest rates were generally high and, for most of the time, above the rate of inflation. For much of the time export credit rates were significantly below the general interest rate. At first the differential was attributable largely to the exemptions from taxes, but in later years the base interest rate itself was substantially lower for export than for other transactions. In 1989 the general borrowing rate, taking into account taxes and transactions costs, was 96 percent; the export credit rate was about 37 percent. Thus there was a differential of about fifty-nine percentage points.[13]

Table 16

Interest Rates: General, Short-Term, and Export-financing, 1980–1989

	1980		1981		1982		1983		1984	
	Export	General	Export	General	Export	General	Export	General	Export	General
Base rate	27.0	30.2	26.6	35.7	29.5	36.0	28.8	36.0	45.0	55.0
Bank commission	2.0	2.0	2.0	2.0	2.0	2.0	2.0	2.0	2.0	2.0
Expense tax on loans[a]	—	7.6	—	5.4	—	5.4	—	5.4	—	1.7
Expense tax on bank commission	—	0.3	—	0.3	—	0.3	—	0.3	—	0.3
Contribution to the resource utilization support fund[b]	—	3.0	—	3.6	—	3.6	—	3.6	—	4.1
Stamp duty	—	1.0	—	1.0	—	1.0	—	1.0	—	1.0
Effective interest rate	29.0	44.1	28.6	47.9	31.5	48.3	30.8	48.3	47.0	64.1
Rebate[c]	4.1	—	4.0	—	4.4	—	4.3	—	6.8	—
Final cost to borrower	25.0	44.1	24.6	47.9	27.1	48.3	26.5	45.8	40.3	64.1
Interest differential	19.1		23.3		21.2		19.3		23.8	

(continued on next page)

	1985		1986		1987		1988		1989	
Base rate	53.0	62.0	50.8	61.7	38.0	66.0	38.6	87.0	35.0	85.0
Bank commission	2.0	2.0	2.0	2.0	2.0	2.0	2.0	2.0	2.0	2.0
Expense tax on loans[a]	—	1.9	—	1.9	—	2.0	—	2.6	—	2.6
Expense tax on bank commission	—	0.06	—	0.06	—	0.06	—	0.06	—	0.1
Contribution to the resource utilization support fund[b]	—	5.0	—	6.2	—	6.6	—	7.2	—	5.1
Stamp duty	—	1.0	—	1.0	—	1.0	—	1.0	—	1.0
Effective interest rate	55.0	72.0	52.8	72.8	40.0	77.6	40.6	99.9	37.0	95.7
Rebate[c]	—	—	—	—	—	—	—	—	—	—
Final cost to borrower	55.0	72.0	52.9	72.8	40.0	77.6	40.7	64.8	37.1	64.1
Interest differential	17.0		19.9		37.6		24.1		27.0	

a. 25 percent of the base rate until 1981, 15 percent during 1981–1983, and 3 percent thereafter.

b. During 1980–1983 the contribution to the Interest Rate Rebate Fund (IRRF) amounted to 10 percent of the base rate, 7.5 percent in 1984. In December 1984 the Resource Utilization Support Fund replaced the IRRF. The contribution to the RUSF amounted to 7.5 percent until September 1985, 10 percent until August 1988, and 6 percent thereafter.

c. The rebate from the Interest Differential Rebate Fund given to export credits amounted to 15 percent of the base rate.

Sources: Base rates are obtained from various issues of OECD, *Economic Survey-Turkey* and TCMB, *Quarterly Bulletin*, various issues. Bank commission and stamp duty fom Demircelik and Sak 1987.

Export credits were readily available at the lower rates. Until the liberalization of exchange control to permit foreign borrowing, the availability of export credits at preferential rates was regarded as a valuable incentive by exporters. Although many continued to avail themselves of the facility, it lost some of its value with the liberalization of foreign exchange, and some exporters stopped using the Export-Import Bank credits altogether.

Foreign Exchange Retention

During the entire import-substitution period, all exporters were required to surrender their export proceeds to the Central Bank within three months of exportation or ten days after the date at which they received foreign exchange, whichever came first.[14] A foreign exchange retention scheme for exporters was introduced in 1980, however. Under that scheme exporters were permitted to retain up to 5 percent of their proceeds or $40,000, whichever was greater.[15]

In addition, under the incentive schemes exporters were permitted to retain foreign exchange equal in amount to the value of the imported inputs used in exporting and also the amount of their export credits, including interest payments.[16] This was an administrative simplification and was regarded by exporters as being of considerable value.

Beyond that, exporters of industrial and mining products were granted the right to transfer a certain percentage of their export proceeds for financing the importation of goods used in production. Before 1979 this percentage was 25 percent of the net foreign exchange earnings. Thereafter it was raised to 50 percent, and exporters were allowed to transfer their rights to their industrial suppliers. In 1980 the scheme was extended to Turkish construction contractors abroad and exporters of fresh fruit, vegetables, and marine products. In 1980 the retention ratio for that group was initially set at 10 percent, but it was raised to 20 percent in May 1980.[17]

After 1980 the premium on foreign exchange diminished, and exchange regulations were relaxed. Many of these measures therefore became less valuable; they were abolished at the end of 1983, although the foreign exchange retention right was raised to 20 percent for all exporters provided that they surrendered the remaining 80 percent within three months of exporting.[18] The holding time for foreign exchange was raised to six months in 1988, and in 1989 the retention ratio was raised to 30 percent if surrender was within three months.

The foreign exchange retention rights were clearly valuable to exporters in the 1970s and early 1980s, when foreign exchange was scarce and delays in receiving import licenses could disrupt production and delivery schedules. The value of the scheme clearly diminished as the trade regime was liberalized. Finally, in June 1989, it became irrelevant as further liberalization of the payments regime permitted Turkish citizens to purchase and hold foreign exchange, and the surrender provision became inoperative.

Foreign Exchange Allocation Scheme

Although the foreign exchange retention scheme provided exporters with some leeway for obtaining needed imports, it clearly was not adequate to finance all import requirements, especially for exporters with an import content greater than 20 percent and for exporters whose volume of business was expanding rapidly. Two related policies were effected to cover these needs. On one hand, a foreign exchange allocation program was established to provide financing for imports used to produce exports. On the other hand, provisions were made so that exporters could import these commodities without paying duty on their inputs.

Turning first to the foreign exchange allocation scheme, any exporter who had received an exporter's certificate could apply for a foreign exchange allocation to cover imports needed in production of exports. The maximum allowable percentage of the value of exports that could be used for this purpose was 60 percent until 1983, was then changed to 40 percent, and then moved back to 50 percent. In cases where exporters could prove that their import content exceeded the maximum specified rate, they could apply for a higher fraction. Whereas importing up to the specified percentages was relatively simple once an exporter's certificate was in hand, however, obtaining agreement that imports would constitute a higher percentage was a more complex process. Apparently some exporters were deterred from attempting it and chose to use domestically produced components and parts rather than attempt it.

An additional provision of the foreign exchange retention scheme permitted exporters to apply for a foreign exchange allocation to compensate for imported items that had been used in exports. Retroactively, exporters could receive up to 80 percent of the f.o.b. value of their exports to replenish their supplies of imports. The value of the foreign exchange retention scheme obviously declined over time as foreign exchange became more freely available. In the early days of the move toward an outward orientation, however, it facilitated the rapid growth of some exports, whose expansion would otherwise have been inhibited considerably. Estimates of the sectoral value of the foreign exchange retention scheme are given in the appendix to this chapter (Table 27).

In addition to foreign exchange retention, exporters were permitted to import the goods needed for export production duty free. Again the procedures were relatively simple. With an exporter's certificate in hand, all the exporter had to do was declare that his imports were for use in export production (up to the specified percentage of the stated value of the exporter's certificate), and duty was waived. In the event of failure to fill the export order, the exporter then notified the customs authorities and paid the duty. Customs duties were quite high, and the ability to import duty free, rather than paying customs duties and eventually getting them rebated (as had been the practice in earlier years), undoubtedly removed some of the financial costs of exporting. Even in 1989 duties on imports could average more than 50 percent, and the duty exemption—unlike the foreign exchange allocation—remained valuable, though not so much so as it had been in earlier years.

Analytically, however, such a retention scheme should be viewed, at least in part, as an offset to discrimination that would otherwise have taken place against exports. In calculating the real exchange rate confronting exporters below, we therefore deduct the portion of the scheme that reduced the excess costs of importing for reexport.[19]

Corporate Tax Reduction for Exports

Starting in 1981 exporters were permitted to claim an exemption from their corporate profits taxes equal to 20 percent of the value of their exports and to pay a much lower rate of tax on the exempted portion.[20] Initially, export volume had to be at least $250,000 to qualify for the exemption.[21]

Table 17 gives an estimate of the value of these exemptions; the sectoral averages are shown in Table 28. The tax exemption was worth between 6 and 8 percent of the value of exports for a profitable corporation. If, for example, a firm had $1 million of profits and exported $400,000 in 1981, it would normally have paid $500,000

Table 17

Value of Exporters' "Exemption" from Corporate Profits Tax, 1980–1989

Period	Corporate tax rate (%)	Percentage of exports deducted	Tax paid on exempted income (%)	Value to exporter
1980–1981	50	20	2	8.0
1982–1985	40	20	2	6.0
1986–1989	46	20	2	7.2

Note: Exempt income was subject to an alternative tax of 10 percent.
Source: Authors' calculations.

in corporate profits tax, leaving it $500,000 in after-tax profits. With the tax exemption, however, it could take 20 percent of $400,000 and deduct that $80,000 from its tax liability, paying instead 10 percent on that $400,000. Its total tax liability was therefore $440,000 instead of $500,000; each dollar of exports was thus worth eight cents in after-tax profits more than domestic sales of the same amount.

The Support and Price Stabilization Fund

The SPSF was founded in 1980; it was thereafter reorganized several times but has basically retained the same functions. It is regulated by communiqués of the Money and Credit Council, a coordinating body established at the time of the 1980 reforms.[22] Until 1987 the SPSF was relatively minor, providing small subsidy payments to exporters to help finance sales promotion, export-oriented investments, and export insurance schemes. Until the end of 1986, likewise, almost all payments from the SPSF went to subsidize agricultural exports. Starting in 1987, however, an increasing number of export products became eligible for payments from the fund. At the outset 45 products were eligible for SPSF subsidies (of which 24 were manufactured goods). At the beginning of 1988 the number of eligible products rose to 83 (62 manufactured) and in mid-1989 to 122.

During 1986 and 1987 abuses of the SPSF became evident, with overinvoicing of exports and reporting of nonexistent exports.[23] It is difficult to judge how important abuses were quantitatively, but they were featured in the newspapers and became important politically.

Consequently, at the end of 1988 maximum payment rates in percentages of export value were established.

The payments from the fund (which was financed, inter alia, from levies on imports) were important for individual commodities but never constituted more than 2 percent of the value of manufactured exports until 1989 (see Table 14).

Foreign Trade Corporations

The government early in the export drive decreed that large export trading corporations were to be encouraged. Several means of encouragement were decided on. On one hand, export trading corporations meeting specified values of exports were entitled to an additional tax rebate, equal to a percentage of export sales. On the other hand, the government hoped to create large specialized export companies, similar to those that were believed to have accounted for the success of Japan and Korea.

As a consequence, it was decided to provide some incentives available to large and small exporters alike but to provide additional incentives for which only large exporters would be eligible. These large trading companies were to be called foreign trade companies.

To encourage foreign trade companies and provide incentives for small exporters to use them, additional tax rebates were extended to those exporting more than specified amounts (see Table 18). In 1975 exporters exporting more than $1.8 million had been eligible for an additional 5 percent rebate.[24] In 1979 the minimum export requirements for additional rebates were increased to $3.5 million (and $2.5 million for the goods in list 9). In the 1980s these requirements were differentiated not according to the lists but according to the export volume: in 1982 exporters were entitled to a 6 percent rebate for exports in excess of $2 million, and a 12 percent rebate was given for the increment above $10 million to the level of $30 million of exports. Once the $30 million level was reached, an additional 10 percent rate applied to the total value of exports.

These rates remained in place until July 1985, when the 10 percent additional rebate was reduced to 6 percent. Thereafter rates were gradually lowered until January 1989, when they were phased out completely.

In addition to the rebates, which the foreign trade companies typically shared with smaller exporters to entice them to export through

Table 18

Additional Rebates for Foreign Trade Companies, 1975–1989

	Exports (millions of dollars)	Rebate for FTCs (%)	List
September 1975	> $1.8	5	1–8
	> $1.4	5	9
July 1978	> $1.8	5	1–6
	> $1.4	5	7
June 1979	> $3.5	5	1–8
	> $2.5	5	9
April 1981	> $4.0	5	
	> $15	10	
April 1982	$0–2	0	
	$2–10	6	
	$10–30	12	
	> $30	10[a]	
July 1985	$0–2	0	
	$2–10	6	
	$10–30	12	
	> $30	6[a]	
June 1986	$0–2	0	
	$2–10	3	
	$10–30	6	
	> $30	5[a]	
July 1987	$0–2	0	
	$2–10	2	
	$10–30	4	
	$30–50	4	
	> $50	6[a]	
August 1988	$0–2	0	
	$2–10	1	
	$10–30	2	
	$30–50	2	
	> $50	3[a]	
January 1989	$0–2	0	
	$2–10	0	
	$10–30	0	
	$30–50	0	
	> $50	0a	
July 1989	>$100	2	

a. These rates apply total value, not the increments, of exports.
Source: *Resmi Gazete,* various issues.

the larger companies, there were specific measures of encouragement for large trading companies. Starting in 1985 trading companies with a minimum capital of TL500 million (raised to TL2 billion in 1989) and an export volume of at least $15 million (with more than half consisting of manufactures and mineral products) were eligible. For a company to maintain eligibility, its exports had to grow at a rate of at least 10 percent annually. In addition to being eligible for all the incentive measures listed above, those eligible could avail themselves of the following privileges:

- There were preferential credits at the EPF, with more favorable rates than those available to exporters generally and more favorable terms (one-year maturity and 90 percent coverage).

- The requirements for obtaining foreign exchange were simplified even more than those in the foreign exchange allocations described above. In addition, in the early 1980s priority foreign exchange was even allocated for production for the domestic market—a privilege of considerable value at the time.

- Foreign exchange could be allocated for imports of investment goods, materials, and spare parts without regard to their connection to export production.

- Trading companies could sell any good they imported to any domestic industrial producer.

- In principle, trading companies were not supposed to engage in production activities. In fact, however, they were permitted to invest in the development of ancillary export facilities such as packaging, storing, and transportation. Those investments were granted customs duty exemptions and other investment incentives not available to other investors.

In 1984, when incentive measures were gradually being scaled down, the first four specific incentives for the foreign trade companies were also eliminated. An additional incentive was provided, however, that proved to be important. That is, they were the only entities legally entitled to trade with the socialist countries and others where state trading occurred.

When the 1989 export regime was announced, the minimum capital requirement for the foreign trade companies was raised to $5 billion with a yearly minimum export volume of $100 million. As the tax rebate scheme phased out, the companies lost one of their incentives, that is, the additional rebates. As compensation, the Money and Credit Council decreed that a flat 2 percent premium should be extended to trading companies that realized a minimum of $100 million of exports in 1988 and pledged to export the same amount in 1989. This premium was to be paid out of SPSF resources through the Export-Import Bank.

Table 31, in the appendix to this chapter, gives an idea of the value of commodity-specific export incentives for companies exporting $50 million in the years between 1981 and 1989. As can be seen, additional rebates for Foreign Trade Companies provided a significant additional incentive, ranging from 50 percent of the rate for the commodities in List 1 to over 100 percent for others in 1981. As the rates were gradually scaled down, so were the additional payments. However, starting from 1987, payments from the SPSF were gradually increased, to compensate for the reduction of the rebates. In 1989, the year in which all the tax rebates were eliminated, payments from SPSF alone constituted a significant incentive for industrial exporters.

Whether trading companies contributed greatly to Turkey's export expansion is not clear. What is clear is that the incentives were suffi- cient so that many such companies were established, and it paid smaller exporters to export through them. In 1980 there were seven trading companies with exports in excess of $15 million each; they accounted for 7 percent of Turkish exports. In 1983 there were seventeen such companies, with an export share of 17 percent. By the end of 1988 there were thirty-two (six of which were SEEs), with more than half of total Turkish exports. Twenty-six of these companies had export sales in excess of $100 million.

Other Incentives

As the government moved toward a reduction in the importance of some schemes, it introduced others. In 1987 a transportation export incentive was granted. It was assumed that all exports were shipped in Turkish carriers and that Turkish carriers charged $6 more per ton than foreign carriers. Obviously the value of the subsidy was greater for commodities that were heavier per unit of value. Assuming that textiles are worth about $10,000 per ton, the subsidy would have been equivalent to only about $0.06 per $100 of exports. For commodities with a lower value per ton, the number would have been greater. Fairly arbitrarily, we assume that the freight subsidy was worth about 0.15 percent for the average industrial export.

The Resource Utilization Support Fund (RUSF) was another scheme in the form of a direct subsidy, designed to promote exports and reduce the financing cost of investments through subsidized credits. The fund was established in the Central Bank in December 1984 and subsidized exports at the following rates: 4 percent in 1985 and 2 percent between April 1986 and October 1986. After October 1986 support for exports from this fund was eliminated.[25]

Another scheme started in 1987 provided for advance payment of 30 percent of the export tax refund. Thus, if an exporter was entitled to a $100,000 tax reduction because of his exports (see Table 17), he received $30,000 in cash as advance payment. Given that domestic interest rates were about 70 percent, this was probably worth about 2 percent of export value to eligible exporters, in addition to the reduction in tax liabilities.

Effective Exchange Rates for Producers of Exportable and Import-competing Goods

Table 19 provides estimates of the effective exchange rates (EERs) for producers of manufactured exportable goods and for producers of import-competing commodities. Export subsidies appear to have been at best a partial offset to the protection accorded to imports. In general, the average import EER was well above that for exporters of manufactures.[26]

A first observation must be that exporters of agricultural and mineral commodities not subject to the export incentives were subject to a bias introduced by the trade regime even greater than that indicated in Table 19.[27] Even for manufactured exports, the bias of the regime in 1980, immediately after the devaluation (and therefore the presumed large drop in the extent of the bias), is estimated to have been on the order of 95 percent; that is, on average import-competing producers received 1.95 times the liras per dollar of foreign exchange produced as did producers of exportable manufactures.[28]

There is little doubt that there is a reasonably strong downward trend in the bias of the trade and payments regime during the 1980s, especially if one considers the period from 1981 through about 1986 and 1987. It would appear that the momentum for making incentives

Table 19

Effective Exchange Rates for Producers of Import-competing Goods and Manufactured Exports, 1980–1989

	Nominal exchange rate (TL/$) (1)	Export subsidy (2)	Effective exchange rates for exports (3)	Import charges (4)	Effective exchange rates for imports (5)	Bias (5) / (3) (6)
1980	76.0	13.1	89.1	98.1	174.1	1.95
1981	111.2	17.0	128.2	146.8	258.0	2.01
1982	162.6	39.0	201.6	196.7	359.2	1.78
1983	225.5	77.1	300.5	268.3	493.8	1.63
1984	366.7	85.4	452.1	363.0	729.7	1.61
1985	522.0	135.7	657.7	354.9	876.9	1.33
1986	674.5	180.8	855.3	364.2	1,038.7	1.21
1987	857.2	264.0	1,121.2	471.5	1,328.7	1.19
1988	1,422.4	463.7	1,886.1	839.2	2,261.5	1.20
1989	2,121.7	763.8	2,885.5	1,005.0	3,126.7	1.08

Source: Column 1 from Table 9. Column 2 from Table 14 (total subsidies and offsets multiplied by column 1). Column 4 from Table 13 (unweighted average multiplied by column 1).

more nearly equal for exportable and import-competing production was lost, at least for the next year or two, after 1987.

Conclusions

Three trends in the trade and payments regime during the 1980s stand out strongly. First, the real exchange rate was devalued substantially from its level of the 1970s. That in itself made the real return to exporters higher than it had been, especially in contrast with non-tradable goods. Second, there was a strong tendency toward liberalization of the entire trade and payments regime, as import licensing virtually ceased and controls over financial transactions abroad diminished significantly. Third, there was some tendency for the protection accorded to producers of import-competing manufactured goods to decline.

The combination of these three tendencies surely reduced the disincentive for exporting sharply, although it is evident that even in the late 1980s import-competing producers received more liras per dollar of sales than producers of manufactured exportables (and even more so than producers of agricultural and mineral exportables not eligible for export subsidies). It remains for Chapter 5 to provide evidence about the effects of these reforms.

Appendix Tables

Table 20

Import Duties and Other Charges, 1980–1989

1980

	C.D.	M.T.	S.D.	W.T.	P.T.	Guarantee deposits	SPSF	Total protection
Food and beverages								
Soy oil	0.40	0.0600	0.01	0.073	0.00	0.038	0.02	60.10
Whiskey	1.20	0.1800	0.01	0.119	0.70	0.038	0.02	226.70
Tomato paste	0.50	0.0750	0.01	0.079	0.00	0.038	0.02	72.18
Minerals								
Calcium-phosphate	0.00 E	0.0000	0.00	0.000	0.00	0.038	0.02	5.80
Cement	0.25	0.0375	0.01	0.064	0.15	0.038	0.02	56.99
Asbestos	0.15	0.0225	0.01	0.059	0.15	0.038	0.02	44.91
Copper ore	0.05	0.0075	0.01	0.053	0.00	0.038	0.02	17.84
Aluminum ore	0.05	0.0075	0.01	0.053	0.00	0.038	0.02	17.84
Mineral fuels								
Coal	0.60	0.0900	0.01	0.085	0.00	0.038	0.02	84.25
Lignite	0.60	0.0900	0.01	0.085	0.00	0.038	0.02	84.25
Coke	0.60	0.0900	0.01	0.085	0.00	0.038	0.02	84.25
Chemicals								
Phosphoric acid	0.15	0.0225	0.01	0.059	0.18	0.038	0.02	47.91

(continued on next page)

(continued)

Table 20

1980

	C.D.	M.T.	S.D.	W.T.	P.T.	Guarantee deposits	SPSF	Total protection
Sodium hydroxide	0.30	0.0450	0.01	0.067	0.18	0.038	0.02	66.03
Sodium sulphure	0.30	0.0450	0.01	0.067	0.18	0.038	0.02	66.03
Teraflatic acid	0.30	0.0450	0.01	0.067	0.18	0.038	0.02	66.03
Fralic anhidrite	0.30	0.0450	0.01	0.067	0.18	0.038	0.02	66.03
Ammonium sulphate	0.20	0.0300	0.01	0.062	0.00	0.038	0.02	35.95
Organic dyes	0.20	0.0300	0.01	0.062	0.15	0.038	0.02	50.95
Rubber and plastic								
Polyester chips	0.50	0.0750	0.01	0.079	0.25	0.038	0.02	97.18
Silicons	0.50	0.0750	0.01	0.079	0.25	0.038	0.02	97.18
Latex	0.15	0.0225	0.01	0.059	0.25	0.038	0.02	54.91
Tires (truck)	0.40	0.0600	0.01	0.073	0.08	0.038	0.02	68.10
Leather, hides, and fur								
Hides	0.10	0.0150	0.01	0.056	0.00	0.038	0.02	23.88
Sole leather	1.00	0.1500	0.01	0.108	0.00	0.038	0.02	132.55
Leather wear	1.50	0.2250	0.01	0.136	0.00	0.038	0.02	192.93
Paper and products								
Wood pulp	0.15	0.0225	0.01	0.059	0.00	0.038	0.02	29.91

(continued on next page)

Newsprint	0.00 E	0.0000	0.00	0.000	0.15	0.038	0.02	20.80
Kraft paper	0.35	0.0525	0.01	0.070	0.20	0.038	0.02	74.06
Textiles, clothing								
Polyamid yarn	0.50	0.0750	0.01	0.079	0.12	0.038	0.02	84.18
Cotton	0.10	0.0150	0.01	0.056	0.00	0.038	0.02	23.88
Long-fiber cotton	0.10	0.0150	0.01	0.056	0.00	0.038	0.02	23.88
Cotton textiles	0.70	0.1050	0.01	0.090	0.18	0.038	0.02	114.33
Cotton T-shirts	1.00	0.1500	0.01	0.108	0.18	0.038	0.02	150.55
Glass, ceramic								
Tiles	1.00	0.1500	0.01	0.108	0.20	0.038	0.02	152.55
Porcelain tableware	1.00	0.1500	0.01	0.108	0.20	0.038	0.02	152.55
Glass, colored, uncolored	1.00	0.1500	0.01	0.108	0.30	0.038	0.02	162.55
Ordinary glass	0.50	0.0750	0.01	0.079	0.00	0.038	0.02	72.18
Iron and steel								
Blooms, billets	0.15	0.0225	0.01	0.059	0.15	0.038	0.02	44.91
Coils for rerolling	0.05	0.0075	0.01	0.053	0.15	0.038	0.02	32.64
Nonferrous metals								
Blister copper	0.10	0.0150	0.01	0.056	0.30	0.038	0.02	53.88
Aluminum	0.10	0.0150	0.01	0.056	0.30	0.038	0.02	53.88
Alum. bottle for LPG	0.30	0.0450	0.01	0.067	0.25	0.038	0.02	73.03
Metal products								
Saw blades	0.50	0.0750	0.01	0.079	0.10	0.038	0.02	82.18
Drill bits	0.50	0.0750	0.01	0.079	0.10	0.038	0.02	82.18
Nonelectrical machinery								
Grinders, mills	0.60	0.0900	0.01	0.085	0.25	0.038	0.02	109.25

(continued on next page)

(continued)

Table 20

	C.D.	M.T.	S.D.	W.T.	P.T.	Guarantee deposits	SPSF	Total protection
				1980				
Electric machinery								
Refrigerators	0.60	0.0900	0.01	0.085	0.04	0.038	0.02	88.25
Dishwashers	0.30	0.0450	0.01	0.067	0.08	0.038	0.02	56.03
Transformers	0.50	0.0750	0.01	0.079	0.25	0.038	0.02	97.18
Hair dryers	0.60	0.0900	0.01	0.085	0.10	0.038	0.02	94.25
Radios	0.50	0.0750	0.01	0.079	0.05	0.038	0.02	77.18
TV, color	0.50	0.0750	0.01	0.079	0.20	0.038	0.02	92.18
Transport equipment								
Motor cars	0.75	0.1125	0.01	0.093	0.10	0.038	0.02	112.36
Buses	0.75	0.1125	0.01	0.093	0.10	0.038	0.02	112.36
Others								
VCR	0.60	0.0900	0.01	0.085	0.20	0.038	0.02	104.25
Magnetic tapes	0.40	0.0600	0.01	0.073	0.20	0.038	0.02	80.10
				1981				
Food and beverages								
Soy oil	0.40	0.0600	0.01	0.073	0.00	0.1	0.02	66.30

(continued on next page)

Whiskey	1.20	0.1800	0.01	0.119	0.70	0.1	0.02	232.90
Tomato paste	0.50	0.0750	0.01	0.079	0.00	0.1	0.02	78.38
Minerals								
Calcium-phosphate	0.00 E	0.0000	0.00	0.000	0.15	0.1	0.02	27.00
Cement	0.25	0.0375	0.01	0.064	0.15	0.1	0.02	63.19
Asbestos	0.15	0.0225	0.01	0.059	0.15	0.1	0.02	51.11
Copper ore	0.05	0.0075	0.01	0.053	0.00	0.1	0.02	24.04
Aluminum ore	0.05	0.0075	0.01	0.053	0.00	0.1	0.02	24.04
Mineral fuels								
Coal	0.60	0.0900	0.01	0.085	0.00	0.1	0.02	90.45
Lignite	0.60	0.0900	0.01	0.085	0.00	0.1	0.02	90.45
Coke	0.60	0.0900	0.01	0.085	0.00	0.1	0.02	90.45
Chemicals								
Phosphoric acid	0.15	0.0225	0.01	0.059	0.18	0.1	0.02	54.11
Sodium hydroxide	0.30	0.0450	0.01	0.067	0.18	0.1	0.02	72.23
Sodium sulphure	0.30	0.0450	0.01	0.067	0.18	0.1	0.02	72.23
Teraflatic acid	0.30	0.0450	0.01	0.067	0.18	0.1	0.02	72.23
Ftalic anhidrite	0.30	0.0450	0.01	0.067	0.18	0.1	0.02	72.23
Ammonium sulphate	0.20	0.0300	0.01	0.062	0.00	0.1	0.02	42.15
Organic dyes	0.20	0.0300	0.01	0.062	0.15	0.1	0.02	57.15
Rubber and plastic								
Polyester chips	0.50	0.0750	0.01	0.079	0.25	0.1	0.02	103.38
Silicons	0.50	0.0750	0.01	0.079	0.25	0.1	0.02	103.38
Latex	0.15	0.0225	0.01	0.059	0.25	0.1	0.02	61.11
Tires (truck)	0.40	0.0600	0.01	0.073	0.08	0.1	0.02	74.30

(continued on next page)

Table 20

1981

	C.D.	M.T.	S.D.	W.T.	P.T.	Guarantee deposits	SPSF	Total protection
Leather, hides, and fur								
Hides	0.10	0.0150	0.01	0.056	0.00	0.1	0.02	30.08
Sole leather	1.00	0.1500	0.01	0.108	0.00	0.1	0.02	138.75
Leather wear	1.50	0.2250	0.01	0.136	0.00	0.1	0.02	199.13
Paper and products								
Wood pulp	0.15	0.0225	0.01	0.059	0.00	0.1	0.02	36.11
Newsprint	0.00 E	0.0000	0	0.000	0.15	0.1	0.02	27.00
Kraft paper	0.35	0.0525	0.01	0.070	0.20	0.1	0.02	80.26
Textiles, clothing								
Polyamid yarn	0.50	0.0750	0.01	0.079	0.12	0.1	0.02	90.38
Cotton	0.10	0.0150	0.01	0.056	0.00	0.1	0.02	30.08
Long-fiber cotton	0.10	0.0150	0.01	0.056	0.00	0.1	0.02	30.08
Cotton textiles	0.70	0.1050	0.01	0.090	0.18	0.1	0.02	120.53
Cotton T-shirts	1.00	0.1500	0.01	0.108	0.18	0.1	0.02	156.75
Glass, ceramic								
Tiles	1.00	0.1500	0.01	0.108	0.20	0.1	0.02	158.75
Porcelain tableware	1.00	0.1500	0.01	0.108	0.20	0.1	0.02	158.75
Glass, colored, uncolored	1.00	0.1500	0.01	0.108	0.30	0.1	0.02	168.75
Ordinary glass	0.50	0.0750	0.01	0.079	0.00	0.1	0.02	78.38

(continued on next page)

Iron and steel							
Blooms, billets	0.15	0.225	0.01	0.059	0.15	0.1	0.02	51.11
Coils for rerolling	0.05	0.0075	0.01	0.053	0.15	0.1	0.02	39.04
Nonferrous metals							
Blister copper	0.10	0.0150	0.01	0.056	0.30	0.1	0.02	60.08
Aluminum	0.10	0.0150	0.01	0.056	0.30	0.1	0.02	60.06
Alum. bortle for LPG	0.30	0.0450	0.01	0.067	0.25	0.1	0.02	79.23
Metal products							
Saw blades	0.50	0.0750	0.01	0.079	0.10	0.1	0.02	88.38
Drill bits	0.50	0.0750	0.01	0.079	0.10	0.1	0.02	88.38
Nonelectrical machinery							
Grinders, mills	0.60	0.0900	0.01	0.085	0.25	0.1	0.02	115.45
Electric Machinery							
Refrigerators	0.60	0.0900	0.01	0.085	0.04	0.1	0.02	94.45
Dishwashers	0.30	0.0450	0.01	0.067	0.08	0.1	0.02	62.23
Transformers	0.50	0.0750	0.01	0.079	0.25	0.1	0.02	103.38
Hair dryers	0.60	0.0900	0.01	0.085	0.10	0.1	0.02	100.45
Radios	0.50	0.0750	0.01	0.079	0.05	0.1	0.02	83.38
TV, color	0.50	0.0750	0.01	0.079	0.20	0.1	0.02	98.38
Transport equipment							
Motor cars	0.75	0.1125	0.01	0.093	0.10	0.1	0.02	118.56
Buses	0.75	0.1125	0.01	0.093	0.10	0.1	0.02	118.56
Others							
VCR	0.60	0.0900	0.01	0.085	0.20	0.1	0.02	110.45
Magnetic tapes	0.40	0.0600	0.01	0.073	0.20	0.1	0.02	86.30

(continued on next page)

(continued)

Table 20

1982

	C.D.	M.T.	S.D.	W.T.	P.T.	Guarantee deposits	SPSF	Total protection
Food and beverages								
Soy oil	0.40	0.0600	0.01	0.073	0.00	0.1	0.02	66.30
Whiskey	1.20	0.1800	0.01	0.119	0.70	0.1	0.02	232.90
Tomato paste	0.50	0.0750	0.01	0.079	0.00	0.1	0.02	78.38
Minerals								
Calcium-phosphate	0.00 E	0.0000	0.00	0.000	0.00	0.1	0.02	12.00
Cement	0.25	0.0375	0.01	0.064	0.15	0.1	0.02	63.19
Asbestos	0.15	0.0225	0.01	0.059	0.15	0.1	0.02	51.11
Copper ore	0.05	0.0075	0.01	0.053	0.00	0.1	0.02	24.04
Aluminum ore	0.05	0.0075	0.01	0.053	0.00	0.1	0.02	24.04
Mineral fuels								
Coal	0.60	0.0900	0.01	0.085	0.00	0.1	0.02	90.45
Lignite	0.60	0.0900	0.01	0.085	0.00	0.1	0.02	90.45
Coke	0.60	0.0900	0.01	0.085	0.00	0.1	0.02	90.45
Chemicals								
Phosphoric acid	0.15	0.0225	0.01	0.059	0.18	0.1	0.02	54.11
Sodium hydroxide	0.30	0.0450	0.01	0.067	0.18	0.1	0.02	72.23
Sodium sulphure	0.30	0.0450	0.01	0.067	0.18	0.1	0.02	72.23

(continued on next page)

Teraflatic acid	0.30	0.0450	0.01	0.067	0.18	0.1	72.23
Ftalic anhidrite	0.30	0.0450	0.01	0.067	0.18	0.1	72.23
Ammonium sulphate	0.20	0.0300	0.01	0.062	0.00	0.1	42.15
Organic dyes	0.20	0.0300	0.01	0.062	0.15	0.1	57.15
Rubber and plastic							
Polyester chips	0.50	0.0750	0.01	0.079	0.25	0.1	103.38
Silicons	0.50	0.0750	0.01	0.079	0.25	0.1	103.38
Latex	0.15	0.0225	0.01	0.059	0.25	0.1	61.11
Tires (truck)	0.40	0.0600	0.01	0.073	0.08	0.1	74.30
Leather, hides, and fur							
Hides	0.10	0.0150	0.01	0.056	0.00	0.1	30.08
Sole leather	1.00	0.1500	0.01	0.108	0.00	0.1	138.75
Leather wear	1.50	0.2250	0.01	0.136	0.00	0.1	199.13
Paper and products							
Wood pulp	0.15	0.0225	0.01	0.059	0.00	0.1	36.11
Newsprint	0.00 E	0.0000	0.00	0.000	0.15	0.1	27.00
Kraft paper	0.35	0.0525	0.01	0.070	0.20	0.1	80.26
Textiles, clothing							
Polyamid yarn	0.50	0.0750	0.01	0.079	0.12	0.1	90.38
Cotton	0.10	0.0150	0.01	0.056	0.00	0.1	30.08
Long-fiber cotton	0.10	0.0150	0.01	0.056	0.00	0.1	30.08
Cotton textiles	0.70	0.1050	0.01	0.090	0.18	0.1	120.53
Cotton T-shirts	1.00	0.1500	0.01	0.108	0.18	0.1	156.75
Glass, ceramic							
Tiles	1.00	0.1500	0.01	0.108	0.20	0.1	158.75

(continued on next page)

Table 20

| | 1982 | | | | | | | |
	C.D.	M.T.	S.D.	W.T.	P.T.	Guarantee deposits	SPSF	Total protection
Porcelain tableware	1.00	0.1500	0.01	0.108	0.20	0.1	0.02	158.75
Glass, colored, uncolored	1.00	0.1500	0.01	0.108	0.30	0.1	0.02	168.75
Ordinary glass	0.50	0.0750	0.01	0.079	0.00	0.1	0.02	78.38
Iron and steel								
Blooms, billets	0.15	0.0225	0.01	0.059	0.15	0.1	0.02	51.11
Coils for rerolling	0.05	0.0075	0.01	0.053	0.15	0.0	0.02	39.04
Nonferrous metals								
Blister copper	0.10	0.0150	0.01	0.056	0.30	0.1	0.02	60.08
Aluminum	0.10	0.0150	0.01	0.056	0.30	0.1	0.02	60.08
Alum. bottle for LPG	0.30	0.0450	0.01	0.067	0.25	0.1	0.02	79.23
Metal products								
Saw blades	0.50	0.0750	0.01	0.079	0.10	0.1	0.02	88.38
Drill bits	0.50	0.0750	0.01	0.079	0.10	0.1	0.02	88.38
Nonelectrical machinery								
Grinders, mills	0.60	0.0900	0.01	0.085	0.25	0.1	0.02	115.45
Electric machinery								
Refrigerators	0.60	0.0900	0.01	0.085	0.04	0.1	0.02	94.45
Dishwashers	0.30	0.0450	0.01	0.067	0.08	0.1	0.02	62.23

(continued on next page)

1983

Transformers	0.50	0.0750	0.01	0.079	0.25	0.1	0.02	103.38
Hair dryers	0.60	0.0900	0.01	0.085	0.10	0.1	0.02	100.45
Radios	0.50	0.0750	0.01	0.079	0.05	0.1	0.02	83.38
TV, color	0.50	0.0750	0.01	0.079	0.10	0.1	0.02	88.38
Transport equipment								
Motor cars	0.75	0.1125	0.01	0.093	0.07	0.1	0.02	115.56
Buses	0.75	0.1125	0.01	0.093	0.10	0.1	0.02	118.56
Others								
VCR	0.60	0.0900	0.01	0.085	0.20	0.1	0.02	110.45
Magnetic tapes	0.40	0.0600	0.01	0.073	0.20	0.1	0.02	86.30
Food and beverages								
Soy oil	0.00 E	0.0000	0.00	0.000	0.00	0.07	0.02	9.00
Whiskey	1.00	0.1500	0.01	0.108	0.70	0.07	0.02	205.75
Tomato paste	0.50	0.0750	0.01	0.079	0.00	0.07	0.02	75.38
Minerals								
Calcium-phosphate	0.00 E	0.0000	0.00	0.000	0.15	0.07	0.02	24.00
Cement	0.25	0.0375	0.01	0.064	0.15	0.07	0.02	60.19
Asbestos	0.15	0.0225	0.01	0.059	0.15	0.07	0.02	48.11
Copper ore	0.05	0.0075	0.01	0.053	0.00	0.07	0.02	21.04
Aluminum ore	0.05	0.0075	0.01	0.053	0.00	0.07	0.02	21.04

(continued on next page)

(continued)

Table 20

1983

	C.D.	M.T.	S.D.	W.T.	P.T.	Guarantee deposits	SPSF	Total protection
Mineral fuels								
Coal	0.60	0.0900	0.01	0.085	0.00	0.07	0.02	87.45
Lignite	0.60	0.0900	0.01	0.085	0.00	0.07	0.02	87.45
Coke	0.60	0.0900	0.01	0.085	0.00	0.07	0.02	87.45
Chemicals								
Phosphoric acid	0.15	0.0225	0.01	0.059	0.18	0.07	0.02	51.11
Sodium hydroxide	0.40	0.0600	0.01	0.073	0.18	0.07	0.02	81.30
Sodium sulphure	0.40	0.0600	0.01	0.073	0.18	0.07	0.02	81.30
Teraflatic acid	0.30	0.0450	0.01	0.067	0.18	0.07	0.02	69.23
Ftalic anhidrite	0.30	0.0450	0.01	0.067	0.18	0.07	0.02	69.23
Ammonium sulphate	0.20	0.0300	0.01	0.062	0.00	0.07	0.02	39.15
Organic dyes	0.20	0.0300	0.01	0.062	0.15	0.07	0.02	54.15
Rubber and plastic								
Polyester chips	0.50	0.0750	0.01	0.079	0.25	0.07	0.02	100.38
Silicons	0.10	0.0150	0.01	0.056	0.25	0.07	0.02	52.08
Latex	0.15	0.0225	0.01	0.059	0.25	0.07	0.02	58.11
Tires (truck)	0.40	0.0600	0.01	0.073	0.08	0.07	0.02	71.30

(continued on next page)

Leather, hides, and fur								
Hides	0.05	0.0075	0.01	0.053	0.00	0.07	0.02	21.04
Sole leather	1.00	0.1500	0.01	0.108	0.00	0.07	0.02	135.75
Leather wear	1.50	0.2250	0.01	0.136	0.00	0.07	0.02	196.13
Paper and products								
Wood pulp	0.15	0.0225	0.01	0.059	0.15	0.07	0.02	48.11
Newsprint	0.25	0.0375	0.01	0.064	0.15	0.07	0.02	60.19
Kraft paper	0.35	0.0525	0.01	0.070	0.20	0.07	0.02	77.26
Textiles, clothing								
Polyamid yarn	0.50	0.0750	0.01	0.079	0.12	0.07	0.02	87.38
Cotton	1.00	0.1500	0.01	0.108	0.00	0.07	0.02	135.75
Long-fiber cotton	0.10	0.0150	0.01	0.056	0.00	0.07	0.02	27.08
Cotton textiles	0.70	0.1050	0.01	0.090	0.18	0.07	0.02	117.53
Cotton T-shirts	1.25	0.1875	0.01	0.122	0.18	0.07	0.02	183.94
Glass, ceramic								
Tiles	1.00	0.1500	0.01	0.108	0.20	0.07	0.02	155.75
Porcelain tableware	1.00	0.1500	0.01	0.108	0.20	0.07	0.02	155.75
Glass, colored, uncolored	1.00	0.1500	0.01	0.108	0.30	0.07	0.02	165.75
Ordinary glass	0.50	0.0750	0.01	0.079	0.00	0.07	0.02	75.38
Iron and steel								
Blooms, billets	0.10	0.0150	0.01	0.056	0.10	0.07	0.02	37.08
Coils for rerolling	0.10	0.0150	0.01	0.056	0.10	0.07	0.02	37.08
Nonferrous metals								
Blister copper	0.30	0.0450	0.01	0.067	0.30	0.07	0.02	81.23

(continued on next page)

(continued)

Table 20

1983

	C.D.	M.T.	S.D.	W.T.	P.T.	Guarantee deposits	SPSF	Total protection
Aluminum	0.00 E	0.0000	0.00	0.000	0.30	0.07	0.02	39.00
Alum. bortle for LPG	0.30	0.0450	0.01	0.067	0.00	0.07	0.02	51.23
Metal products								
Saw blades	0.50	0.0750	0.01	0.079	0.10	0.07	0.02	85.38
Drill bits	0.50	0.0750	0.01	0.079	0.10	0.07	0.02	85.38
Nonelectrical machinery								
Grinders, mills	0.60	0.0900	0.01	0.085	0.25	0.07	0.02	112.45
Electric machinery								
Refrigerators	0.60	0.0900	0.01	0.085	0.04	0.07	0.02	91.45
Dishwashers	0.25	0.0375	0.01	0.064	0.08	0.07	0.02	53.19
Transformers	0.50	0.0750	0.01	0.079	0.25	0.07	0.02	100.38
Hair dryers	0.60	0.0900	0.01	0.085	0.10	0.07	0.02	97.45
Radios	0.50	0.0750	0.01	0.079	0.10	0.07	0.02	85.38
TV, color	0.50	0.0750	0.01	0.079	0.25	0.07	0.02	100.38
Transport equipment								
Motor cars	0.75	0.1125	0.01	0.093	0.10	0.07	0.02	115.56
Buses	0.75	0.1125	0.01	0.093	0.10	0.07	0.02	115.56

(continued on next page)

Others								
VCR	0.60	0.0900	0.01		0.085	0.20	0.07	0.02	107.45
Magnetic tapes	0.60	0.0900	0.01		0.085	0.20	0.07	0.02	107.45
Food and beverages								
Soy oil	0.00 E	0.0000	0.00	0.027	0.000	0.00	0.078	0.02	12.50
Whiskey	1.00	0.1500	0.01	5.000	0.358	0.70	0.078	0.02	731.55
Tomato paste	0.50	0.0750	0.01		0.079	0.00	0.078	0.02	76.18
Minerals								
Calcium-phosphate	0.00 E	0.0000	0.00		0.000	0.15	0.078	0.02	24.80
Cement	0.00	0.0000	0.01		0.050	0.00	0.078	0.02	15.80
Asbestos	0.15	0.0225	0.01		0.059	0.15	0.078	0.02	48.91
Copper ore	0.00 E	0.0000	0.00		0.000	0.00	0.078	0.02	9.80
Aluminum ore	0.00 E	0.0000	0.00		0.000	0.00	0.078	0.02	9.80
Mineral fuels								
Coal	0.60	0.0900	0.01		0.085	0.00	0.078	0.02	88.25
Lignite	0.60	0.0900	0.01		0.085	0.00	0.078	0.02	88.25
Coke	0.00	0.0000	0.01		0.050	0.00	0.078	0.02	15.80
Chemicals								
Phosphoric acid	0.10	0.0150	0.01		0.056	0.12	0.078	0.02	39.88

(continued on next page)

Table 20

1984

	C.D.	M.T.	S.D.	Fund	W.T.	P.T.	Guarantee deposits	SPSF	Total protection
Sodium hydroxide	0.20	0.0300	0.01		0.062	0.12	0.078	0.02	51.95
Sodium sulphure	0.20	0.0300	0.01	0.851	0.104	0.12	0.078	0.02	141.31
Teraflatic acid	0.10	0.0150	0.01		0.056	0.12	0.078	0.02	39.88
Fralic anhidrite	0.20	0.0300	0.01		0.062	0.12	0.078	0.02	51.95
Ammonium sulphate	0.20	0.0300	0.01		0.062	0.00	0.078	0.02	39.95
Organic dyes	0.10	0.0150	0.01		0.056	0.10	0.078	0.02	37.88
Rubber and plastic									
Polyester chips	0.10	0.0150	0.01	0.140	0.063	0.15	0.078	0.02	57.58
Silicons	0.10	0.0150	0.01		0.056	0.18	0.078	0.02	45.88
Latex	0.05	0.0075	0.01		0.053	0.18	0.078	0.02	39.84
Tires (truck)	0.50	0.0750	0.01	0.210	0.089	0.05	0.078	0.02	103.23
Leather, hides, and fur									
Hides	0.00	0.0000	0.01		0.050	0.00	0.078	0.02	15.80
Sole leather	1.00	0.1500	0.01		0.108	0.00	0.078	0.02	136.55
Leather wear	1.50	0.2250	0.01		0.136	0.00	0.078	0.02	196.93
Paper and products									
Wood pulp	0.00 E	0.0000	0.00		0.000	0.00	0.078	0.02	9.80

(continued on next page)

Newsprint	0.01	0.0015	0.01		0.051	0.10	0.078	0.02	27.01
Kraft paper	0.30	0.0450	0.01		0.067	0.15	0.078	0.02	67.03
Textiles, clothing									
Polyamid yard	0.25	0.0375	0.01	0.003	0.064	0.08	0.078	0.02	53.99
Cotton	0.10	0.0150	0.01		0.056	0.00	0.078	0.02	28.19
Long-fiber cotton	0.10	0.0150	0.01		0.056	0.00	0.078	0.02	27.88
Cotton textiles	0.20	0.0300	0.01		0.062	0.12	0.078	0.02	51.95
Cotton T-shirts	0.40	0.0600	0.01		0.073	0.12	0.078	0.02	76.10
Glass, ceramic									
Tiles	1.00	0.1500	0.01		0.108	0.20	0.078	0.02	156.55
Porcelain tableware	1.00	0.1500	0.01		0.108	0.20	0.078	0.02	156.55
Glass, colored, uncolored	1.00	0.1500	0.01		0.108	0.30	0.078	0.02	166.55
Ordinary glass	0.50	0.0750	0.01		0.079	0.00	0.078	0.02	76.18
Iron and steel									
Blooms, billets	0.01	0.0015	0.01		0.051	0.08	0.078	0.02	25.01
Coils for rerolling	0.01	0.0015	0.01		0.051	0.08	0.078	0.02	25.01
Nonferrous metals									
Blister copper	0.01	0.0015	0.01		0.051	0.20	0.078	0.02	37.01
Aluminum	0.00 E	0.0000	0.00		0.000	0.00	0.078	0.02	9.80
Alum. bottle for LPG	0.30	0.0450	0.01		0.067	0.00	0.078	0.02	52.03
Metal products									
Saw blades	0.40	0.0600	0.01		0.073	0.10	0.078	0.02	74.10
Drill bits	0.50	0.0750	0.01		0.079	0.10	0.078	0.02	86.18
Nonelectrical machinery									
Grinders, mills	0.60	0.0900	0.01		0.085	0.25	0.078	0.02	113.25

(continued on next page)

(continued)

Table 20

	C.D.	M.T.	S.D.	Fund	W.T.	P.T.	Guarantee deposits	SPSF	Total protection
				1984					
Electric machinery									
Refrigerators	0.60	0.0900	0.01	0.226	0.096	0.04	0.078	0.02	115.98
Dishwashers	0.60	0.0900	0.01	0.067	0.096	0.18	0.078	0.02	114.08
Transformers	0.20	0.0300	0.01		0.062	0.10	0.078	0.02	49.95
Hair dryers	0.60	0.0900	0.01		0.085	0.10	0.078	0.02	98.25
Radios	0.30	0.0450	0.01	1.500	0.142	0.10	0.078	0.02	219.53
TV, color	0.40	0.0600	0.01	0.360	0.091	0.20	0.078	0.02	121.90
Transport equipment									
Motor cars	0.60	0.0900	0.01	0.200	0.095	0.10	0.078	0.02	119.25
Buses	0.60	0.0900	0.01	0.200	0.095	0.10	0.078	0.02	119.25
Others									
VCR	0.75	0.1125	0.01		0.093	0.15	0.078	0.02	121.36
Magnetic Tapes	0.30	0.0450	0.01		0.067	0.10	0.078	0.02	62.03
				1985					
Food and beverages									
Soy oil	0.00 E	0.0000	0.000	0.002	0.000	0.00	0.052	0.02	7.40

(continued on next page)

Whiskey	0.50	0.0750	0.025	1.500	0.154	0.31	0.052	0.02	263.58
Tomato paste	0.01	0.0015	0.025	0.046	0.053	0.11	0.052	0.02	31.56
Minerals									
Calcium-phosphate	0.00 E	0.0000	0.000		0.000	0.10	0.052	0.02	17.20
Cement	0.00	0.0000	0.025		0.050	0.10	0.052	0.02	24.95
Asbestos	0.15	0.0225	0.025		0.059	0.12	0.052	0.02	44.79
Copper ore	0.00	0.0000	0.025		0.050	0.10	0.052	0.02	24.95
Aluminum ore	0.00	0.0000	0.025		0.050	0.10	0.052	0.02	24.95
Mineral fuels									
Coal	0.01	0.0015	0.025		0.051	0.10	0.052	0.02	26.27
Lignite	0.01	0.0015	0.025		0.051	0.10	0.052	0.02	26.27
Coke	0.01	0.0015	0.025		0.051	0.10	0.052	0.02	26.27
Chemicals									
Phosphoric acid	0.10	0.0150	0.025		0.056	0.11	0.052	0.02	38.18
Sodium hydroxide	0.20	0.0300	0.025		0.062	0.13	0.052	0.02	51.40
Sodium sulphure	0.20	0.0300	0.025	0.478	0.085	0.17	0.052	0.02	106.37
Teraflatic acid	0.10	0.0150	0.025		0.056	0.11	0.052	0.02	38.18
Fralic anhidrite	0.20	0.0300	0.025	0.137	0.068	0.14	0.052	0.02	67.16
Ammonium sulphate	0.20	0.0300	0.025		0.062	0.13	0.052	0.02	51.40
Organic dyes	0.10	0.0150	0.025		0.056	0.11	0.052	0.02	38.18
Rubber and plastic									
Polyester chips	0.10	0.0150	0.025	0.144	0.063	0.13	0.052	0.02	54.74
Silicons	0.10	0.0150	0.025		0.056	0.11	0.052	0.02	36.18
Latex	0.05	0.0075	0.025		0.053	0.11	0.052	0.02	31.56
Tires (truck)	0.25	0.0375	0.025	0.210	0.075	0.15	0.052	0.02	82.16

(continued on next page)

(continued)

Table 20

1985

	C.D.	M.T.	S.D.	Fund	W.T.	VAT	Guarantee deposits	SPSF	Total protection
Leather, hides, and fur									
Hides	0.00	0.0000	0.025		0.050	0.10	0.052	0.02	24.95
Sole leather	0.15	0.0225	0.025		0.059	0.12	0.052	0.02	44.79
Leather wear	1.50	0.2250	0.025		0.136	0.28	0.052	0.02	223.33
Paper and products									
Wood pulp	0.00	0.0000	0.025		0.050	0.10	0.052	0.02	24.95
Newsprint	0.15	0.0225	0.025	0.199	0.069	0.14	0.052	0.02	67.67
Kraft paper	0.30	0.0450	0.025	0.076	0.071	0.14	0.052	0.02	73.37
Textiles, clothing									
Polyamid yarn	0.10	0.0150	0.025	0.053	0.058	0.12	0.052	0.02	44.27
Cotton	0.00 E	0.0000	0.000	0.003	0.000	0.10	0.052	0.02	17.53
Long-fiber cotton	0.10	0.0150	0.025		0.056	0.11	0.052	0.02	38.18
Cotton textiles	0.20	0.0300	0.025		0.062	0.13	0.052	0.02	51.40
Cotton T-shirts	0.40	0.0600	0.025		0.073	0.15	0.052	0.02	77.85
Glass, ceramic									
Tiles	0.30	0.0450	0.025		0.067	0.14	0.052	0.02	64.63
Porcelain tableware	0.30	0.0450	0.025		0.067	0.14	0.052	0.02	64.63
Glass, colored, uncolored	0.40	0.0600	0.025		0.073	0.15	0.052	0.02	77.85
Ordinary glass	0.50	0.0750	0.025	0.010	0.079	0.16	0.052	0.02	92.23

(continued on next page)

Iron and steel									
Blooms, billets	0.01	0.0015	0.025	0.005	0.051	0.10	0.052	0.02	26.85
Coils for rerolling	0.01	0.0015	0.025	0.004	0.051	0.10	0.052	0.02	26.73
Nonferrous metals									
Blister copper	0.01	0.0015	0.025		0.051	0.10	0.052	0.02	26.27
Aluminum	0.00 E	0.0000	0.000		0.000	0.10	0.052	0.02	17.20
Alum. bottle for LPG	0.30	0.0450	0.025		0.067	0.14	0.052	0.02	64.63
Metal products									
Saw blades	0.40	0.0600	0.025		0.073	0.15	0.052	0.02	77.85
Drill bits	0.30	0.0450	0.025		0.067	0.14	0.052	0.02	64.63
Nonelectrical machinery									
Grinder, mills	0.30	0.0450	0.025		0.067	0.14	0.052	0.02	64.63
Electric machinery									
Refrigerators	0.40	0.0600	0.025	0.150	0.081	0.16	0.052	0.02	95.10
Dishwashers	0.25	0.0375	0.025	0.400	0.084	0.17	0.052	0.02	104.01
Transformers	0.20	0.0300	0.025		0.062	0.13	0.052	0.02	51.40
Hair dryers	0.40	0.0600	0.025		0.073	0.15	0.052	0.02	77.85
Radios	0.40	0.0600	0.025	1.000	0.123	0.25	0.052	0.02	192.85
TV, color	0.40	0.0600	0.025	0.190	0.083	0.17	0.052	0.02	99.70
Transport equipment									
Motor cars	0.50	0.0750	0.025	0.400	0.099	0.20	0.052	0.02	137.07
Buses	0.50	0.0750	0.025	0.400	0.099	0.20	0.052	0.02	137.07
Others									
VCR	0.50	0.0750	0.025	0.400	0.099	0.20	0.052	0.02	137.08
Magnetic tapes	0.30	0.0450	0.025		0.067	0.14	0.052	0.02	64.63

(continued on next page)

Table 20

1986

	C.D.	M.T.	S.D.	Fund	W.T.	VAT	Guarantee deposits	SPSF	Total protection
Food and beverages									
Soy oil	0.00 E	0.0000	0	0.210	0.000	0.02	0.006	0.02	25.42
Whiskey	0.40	0.0600	0.04	1.500	0.148	0.30	0.006	0.02	247.40
Tomato paste	0.01	0.0015	0.04	0.123	0.057	0.12	0.006	0.02	37.47
Minerals									
Calcium-phosphate	0.00 E	0.0000	0.00		0.000	0.10	0.006	0.02	12.60
Cement	0.00	0.0000	0.04		0.050	0.10	0.006	0.02	22.00
Asbestos	0.10	0.0150	0.04		0.056	0.12	0.006	0.02	35.23
Copper ore	0.00	0.0000	0.04		0.050	0.10	0.006	0.02	22.00
Aluminum ore	0.00	0.0000	0.04		0.050	0.10	0.006	0.02	22.00
Mineral fuels									
Coal	0.00 E	0.0000	0.00	0.169	0.000	0.12	0.006	0.02	31.19
Lignite	0.00 E	0.0000	0.00		0.000	0.10	0.006	0.02	12.60
Coke	0.01	0.0015	0.04		0.051	0.11	0.006	0.02	23.32
Chemicals									
Phosphoric acid	0.10	0.0150	0.04		0.056	0.12	0.006	0.02	35.23
Sodium hydroxide	0.20	0.0300	0.04	0.482	0.086	0.18	0.006	0.02	103.88
Sodium sulphure	0.20	0.0300	0.04	0.402	0.082	0.17	0.006	0.02	94.68

(continued on next page)

Teraflatic acid	0.10	0.0150	0.04	0.088	0.060	0.12	0.006	0.02	45.35
Fralic anhidrite	0.20	0.0300	0.04	0.190	0.071	0.15	0.006	0.02	70.30
Ammonium sulphate	0.00 E	0.0000	0.00	0.435	0.000	0.14	0.006	0.02	60.45
Organic dyes	0.10	0.0150	0.04		0.056	0.12	0.006	0.02	35.23
Rubber and plastic									
Polyester chips	0.10	0.0150	0.04	0.127	0.062	0.13	0.006	0.02	49.83
Silicons	0.10	0.0150	0.04		0.056	0.12	0.006	0.02	35.23
Latex	0.05	0.0075	0.04		0.053	0.11	0.006	0.02	28.61
Tires (truck)	0.25	0.0375	0.04	0.050	0.067	0.14	0.006	0.02	60.81
Leather, hides, and fur									
Hides	0.00 E	0.0000	0.00		0.000	0.10	0.006	0.02	12.60
Sole leather	0.00	0.0000	0.04	0.100	0.055	0.11	0.006	0.02	33.50
Leather wear	0.40	0.0600	0.04	0.500	0.098	0.20	0.006	0.02	132.40
Paper and products									
Wood pulp	0.00 E	0.0000	0.00		0.000	0.10	0.006	0.02	12.60
Newsprint	0.15	0.0225	0.04	0.105	0.064	0.13	0.006	0.02	53.91
Kraft paper	0.30	0.0450	0.04	0.082	0.071	0.15	0.006	0.02	71.11
Textiles, clothing									
Polyamid yarn	0.10	0.0150	0.04	0.018	0.057	0.12	0.006	0.02	37.30
Cotton	0.00 E	0.0000	0.00	0.001	0.000	0.10	0.006	0.02	12.71
Long-fiber cotton	0.10	0.0150	0.04		0.056	0.12	0.006	0.02	35.23
Cotton textiles	0.20	0.0300	0.04		0.062	0.13	0.006	0.02	48.45
Cotton T-shirts	0.40	0.0600	0.04		0.073	0.15	0.006	0.02	74.90
Glass, ceramic									
Tiles	0.10	0.0150	0.04		0.056	0.12	0.006	0.02	35.23

(continued on next page)

(*continued*)

Table 20

1986

	C.D.	M.T.	S.D.	Fund	W.T.	VAT	Guarantee deposits	SPSF	Total protection
Porcelain tableware	0.40	0.0600	0.04		0.073	0.15	0.006	0.02	74.90
Glass, colored, uncolored	0.30	0.0450	0.04		0.067	0.14	0.006	0.02	61.68
Ordinary glass	0.30	0.0450	0.04		0.067	0.14	0.006	0.02	61.68
Iron and steel									
Blooms, billets	0.01	0.0015	0.04	0.100	0.056	0.12	0.006	0.02	34.82
Coils for rerolling	0.01	0.0015	0.04	0.080	0.055	0.11	0.006	0.02	32.52
Nonferrous metals									
Blister copper	0.01	0.0015	0.04		0.051	0.11	0.006	0.02	23.32
Aluminum	0.00 E	0.0000	0.00		0.000	0.10	0.006	0.02	12.60
Alum. bottle for LPG	0.40	0.0600	0.04		0.073	0.15	0.006	0.02	74.90
Metal products									
Saw blades	0.40	0.0600	0.04		0.073	0.15	0.006	0.02	74.90
Drill bits	0.30	0.0450	0.04		0.067	0.14	0.006	0.02	61.68
Nonelectrical machinery									
Grinders, mills	0.30	0.0450	0.04	0.000	0.067	0.14	0.006	0.02	61.68
Electric machinery									
Refrigerators	0.40	0.0600	0.04	0.000	0.073	0.15	0.006	0.02	74.90
Dishwashers	0.25	0.0375	0.04	0.280	0.078	0.16	0.006	0.02	87.26

(*continued on next page*)

Transformers	0.20	0.0300	0.04		0.062	0.13	0.006	0.02	48.45
Hair dryers	0.40	0.0600	0.04		0.073	0.15	0.006	0.02	74.90
Radios	0.40	0.0600	0.04	1.000	0.123	0.25	0.006	0.02	189.90
TV, color	0.40	0.0600	0.04	0.190	0.083	0.17	0.006	0.02	96.75
Transport equipment									
Motor cars	0.50	0.0750	0.04	0.496	0.104	0.21	0.006	0.02	145.12
Buses	0.50	0.0750	0.04	0.488	0.103	0.21	0.006	0.02	144.25
Others									
VCR	0.40	0.0600	0.04	0.350	0.091	0.19	0.006	0.02	115.15
Magnetic tapes	0.30	0.0450	0.04		0.067	0.14	0.006	0.02	61.68
1987									
Food and beverages									
Soy oil	0.00 E	0.0000	0.00	0.344	0.000	0.00	0.027	0.043	41.40
Whiskey	0.40	0.0600	0.04	1.500	0.148	0.36	0.027	0.043	257.80
Tomato paste	0.01	0.0015	0.04	0.109	0.056	0.14	0.027	0.043	42.58
Minerals									
Calcium-phosphate	0.00 E	0.0000	0.00		0.000	0.12	0.027	0.043	19.00
Cement	0.00 E	0.0000	0.00		0.000	0.12	0.027	0.043	19.00
Asbestos	0.10	0.0150	0.04		0.056	0.14	0.027	0.043	41.94
Copper ore	0.00	0.0000	0.04		0.050	0.12	0.027	0.043	28.48
Aluminum ore	0.00	0.0000	0.04		0.050	0.12	0.027	0.043	28.48
Mineral fuels									
Coal	0.00 E	0.0000	0.00	0.189	0.000	0.14	0.027	0.043	40.17

(continued on next page)

(continued)

Table 20

1987

	C.D.	M.T.	S.D.	Fund	W.T.	VAT	Guarantee deposits	SPSF	Total protection
Lignite	0.00 E	0.0000	0.00		0.000	0.12	0.027	0.043	19.00
Coke	0.01	0.0015	0.04		0.051	0.13	0.027	0.043	29.83
Chemicals									
Phosphoric acid	0.10	0.0150	0.04		0.056	0.14	0.027	0.043	41.94
Sodium hydroxide	0.20	0.0300	0.04	0.360	0.080	0.20	0.027	0.043	97.51
Sodium sulphure	0.20	0.0300	0.04	0.369	0.080	0.20	0.027	0.043	98.56
Teraflatic acid	0.08	0.0120	0.04		0.055	0.14	0.027	0.043	39.24
Ftalic anhidrite	0.20	0.0300	0.04	0.125	0.068	0.17	0.027	0.043	70.02
Ammonium sulphate	0.00 E	0.0000	0.00	0.345	0.00	0.16	0.027	0.043	57.64
Organic dyes	0.10	0.0150	0.04		0.056	0.14	0.027	0.043	41.94
Rubber and plastic									
Polyester chips	0.10	0.0150	0.04	0.128	0.062	0.15	0.027	0.043	56.91
Silicons	0.10	0.0150	0.04		0.056	0.14	0.027	0.043	41.94
Latex	0.05	0.0075	0.04		0.053	0.13	0.027	0.043	35.21
Tires (truck)	0.25	0.0375	0.04	0.050	0.067	0.17	0.027	0.043	67.97
Leather, hides, and fur									
Hides	0.00 E	0.0000	0.00		0.000	0.12	0.027	0.043	19.00
Sole leather	0.00 E	0.0000	0.00		0.000	0.12	0.027	0.043	19.00
Leather wear	0.40	0.0600	0.04		0.073	0.18	0.027	0.043	82.30

(continued on next page)

Paper products									
Wood pulp	0.00 E	0.0000	0.00	0.000	0.000	0.12	0.027	0.043	19.00
Newsprint	0.14	0.0210	0.04	0.050	0.058	0.14	0.027	0.043	47.34
Kraft paper	0.30	0.0450	0.04		0.070	0.17	0.027	0.043	74.70
Textiles, clothing									
Polyamid yarn	0.10	0.0150	0.04	0.001	0.056	0.14	0.027	0.043	42.04
Cotton	0.00 E	0.0000	0.00		0.000	0.12	0.027	0.043	19.00
Long-fiber cotton	0.10	0.0150	0.04		0.056	0.14	0.027	0.043	41.94
Cotton textiles	0.20	0.0300	0.04		0.062	0.15	0.027	0.043	55.39
Cotton T-shirts	0.40	0.0600	0.04		0.073	0.18	0.027	0.043	82.30
Glass, ceramic									
Tiles	0.10	0.0150	0.04		0.056	0.14	0.027	0.043	41.94
Porcelain tableware	0.40	0.0600	0.04		0.073	0.18	0.027	0.043	82.30
Glass, colored, uncolored	0.30	0.0450	0.04	—	0.067	0.17	0.027	0.043	68.85
Ordinary glass	0.30	0.0450	0.04	0.044	0.069	0.17	0.027	0.043	73.99
Iron and steel									
Blooms, billets	0.01	0.0015	0.04	0.100	0.056	0.14	0.027	0.043	41.53
Coils for rerolling	0.01	0.0015	0.04	0.080	0.055	0.14	0.027	0.043	39.19
Nonferrous metals									
Blister copper	0.01	0.0015	0.04		0.051	0.13	0.027	0.043	29.83
Aluminum	0.00 E	0.0000	0.00		0.000	0.12	0.027	0.043	19.00
Alum. bottle for LPG	0.40	0.0600	0.04		0.073	0.18	0.027	0.043	82.30
Metal products									
Saw blades	0.40	0.0600	0.04		0.073	0.18	0.027	0.043	82.30
Drill bits	0.30	0.0450	0.04		0.067	0.17	0.027	0.043	68.85

(continued on next page)

(continued)

Table 20

	C.D.	M.T.	S.D.	Fund	W.T.	VAT	Guarantee deposits	SPSF	Total protection
				1987					
Nonelectrical machinery									
Grinders, mills	0.30	0.0450	0.04		0.067	0.17	0.027	0.043	68.85
Electrical machinery									
Refrigerators	0.40	0.0600	0.04	0.000	0.073	0.18	0.027	0.043	82.30
Dishwashers	0.25	0.0375	0.04	0.280	0.078	0.19	0.027	0.043	94.88
Transformers	0.20	0.0300	0.04		0.062	0.15	0.027	0.043	55.39
Hair dryers	0.40	0.0600	0.04		0.073	0.18	0.027	0.043	82.30
Radios	0.40	0.0600	0.04	1.000	0.123	0.30	0.027	0.043	199.30
TV, color	0.40	0.0600	0.04	0.190	0.083	0.20	0.027	0.043	104.53
Transport equipment									
Motor cars	0.50	0.0750	0.04		0.079	0.19	0.027	0.043	95.76
Buses	0.50	0.0750	0.04		0.079	0.19	0.027	0.043	95.76
Others									
VCR	0.40	0.0600	0.04	0.350	0.091	0.22	0.027	0.043	123.25
Magnetic tapes	0.30	0.0450	0.04		0.067	0.17	0.027	0.043	68.85
				1988					
Food and beverages									
Soy oil	0.00 E	0.0000	0.00	0.023	0.000	0.03	0.043	0.068	16.47

(continued on next page)

Whiskey	0.40	0.0600	0.0667	1.500	0.148	0.36	0.043	0.068	264.89
Tomato paste	0.01	0.0015	0.0667	0.116	0.056	0.14	0.043	0.068	50.49
Minerals									
Calcium-phosphate	0.00 E	0.0000	0.00		0.000	0.12	0.043	0.068	23.10
Cement	0.00 E	0.0000	0.00		0.000	0.12	0.043	0.068	23.10
Asbestos	0.10	0.0150	0.0667		0.056	0.14	0.043	0.068	49.03
Copper ore	0.00	0.0000	0.0667		0.050	0.13	0.043	0.068	35.57
Aluminum ore	0.00	0.0000	0.0667		0.050	0.13	0.043	0.068	35.57
Mineral fuels									
Coal	0.00 E	0.0000	0.00	0.123	0.000	0.13	0.043	0.068	36.88
Lignite	0.00 E	0.0000	0.00	0.189	0.000	0.14	0.043	0.068	44.27
Coke	0.01	0.0015	0.0667		0.051	0.13	0.043	0.068	36.92
Chemicals									
Phosphoric acid	0.10	0.0150	0.0667		0.056	0.14	0.043	0.068	49.03
Sodium hydroxide	0.01	0.0015	0.0667	0.016	0.051	0.13	0.043	0.068	38.79
Sodium sulphure	0.20	0.0300	0.0667	0.461	0.085	0.21	0.043	0.068	116.42
Teraflatic acid	0.08	0.0120	0.0667		0.055	0.14	0.043	0.068	46.33
Fralic anhidrite	0.20	0.0300	0.0667	0.103	0.067	0.17	0.043	0.068	74.53
Ammonium sulphate	0.00 E	0.0000	0.0000	0.227	0.000	0.15	0.043	0.068	48.52
Organic dyes	0.10	0.0150	0.0667		0.056	0.14	0.043	0.068	49.03
Rubber and plastic									
Polyester chips	0.10	0.0150	0.0667	0.141	0.063	0.16	0.043	0.068	65.52
Silicons	0.10	0.0150	0.0667		0.056	0.14	0.043	0.068	49.03
Latex	0.01	0.0015	0.0667		0.051	0.13	0.043	0.068	36.92
Tires (truck)	0.25	0.0375	0.0667	0.050	0.067	0.17	0.043	0.068	75.06

(continued on next page)

Table 20

1988

	C.D.	M.T.	S.D.	Fund	W.T.	VAT	Guarantee deposits	SPSF	Total protection
Leather, hides, and fur									
Hides	0.00 E	0.0000	0.0000		0.000	0.12	0.043	0.068	23.10
Sole leather	0.00 E	0.0000	0.0000	0.186	0.000	0.14	0.043	0.068	43.93
Leather wear	0.40	0.0600	0.0667	0.186	0.082	0.21	0.043	0.068	111.15
Paper and products									
Wood pulp	0.00 E	0.0000	0.0000		0.000	0.12	0.043	0.068	23.10
Newsprint	0.00	0.0000	0.0667		0.050	0.13	0.043	0.068	35.57
Kraft paper	0.20	0.0300	0.0667	0.050	0.064	0.16	0.043	0.068	68.33
Textiles, clothing									
Polyamid yarn	0.10	0.0150	0.0667	0.001	0.056	0.14	0.043	0.068	49.13
Cotton	0.00 E	0.0000	0.0000		0.000	0.12	0.043	0.068	23.10
Long-fiber cotton	0.10	0.0150	0.0667		0.056	0.14	0.043	0.068	49.03
Cotton textiles	0.20	0.0300	0.0667		0.062	0.16	0.043	0.068	62.48
Cotton T-shirts	0.40	0.0600	0.0667		0.073	0.18	0.043	0.068	89.39
Glass, ceramic									
Tiles	0.10	0.0150	0.0667		0.056	0.14	0.043	0.068	49.03
Porcelain tableware	0.40	0.0600	0.0667		0.073	0.18	0.043	0.068	89.39

(continued on next page)

Glass, colored, uncolored	0.30	0.0450	0.0667		0.067	0.17	0.043	0.068	75.94
Ordinary glass	0.20	0.0300	0.0667	0.088	0.066	0.17	0.043	0.068	72.79
Iron and steel									
Blooms, billets	0.01	0.0015	0.0667	0.100	0.056	0.14	0.043	0.068	48.62
Coils for rerolling	0.01	0.0015	0.0667	0.004	0.051	0.13	0.043	0.068	37.38
Nonferrous metals									
Blister copper	0.01	0.0015	0.0667		0.051	0.13	0.043	0.068	36.92
Aluminum	0.00 E	0.0000	0.000		0.000	0.12	0.043	0.068	23.10
Alum. bottle for LPG	0.40	0.0600	0.0667		0.073	0.18	0.043	0.068	89.39
Metal products									
Saw blades	0.40	0.0600	0.0667	0.200	0.083	0.21	0.043	0.068	112.79
Drill bits	0.30	0.0450	0.0667	0.200	0.077	0.19	0.043	0.068	99.34
Nonelectrical machinery									
Grinders, mills	0.30	0.0450	0.0667		0.067	0.17	0.043	0.068	75.94
Electric machinery									
Refrigerators	0.25	0.0375	0.0667	0.000	0.064	0.16	0.043	0.068	69.21
Dishwashers	0.25	0.0375	0.0667	0.280	0.078	0.20	0.043	0.068	101.97
Transformers	0.20	0.0300	0.0667		0.062	0.16	0.043	0.068	62.48
Hair dryers	0.40	0.0600	0.0667		0.073	0.18	0.043	0.068	89.39
Radios	0.40	0.0600	0.0667	1.000	0.123	0.30	0.043	0.068	206.39
TV, color	0.40	0.0600	0.0667	0.190	0.083	0.21	0.043	0.068	111.62
Transport equipment									
Motor cars	0.50	0.0750	0.0667	0.193	0.088	0.22	0.043	0.068	125.37
Buses	0.40	0.0600	0.0667	0.316	0.089	0.22	0.043	0.068	126.36

(continued on next page)

(continued)

Table 20

	C.D.	M.T.	S.D.	Fund	W.T.	VAT	Guarantee deposits	SPSF	Total protection
1988									
Others									
VCR	0.40	0.0600	0.0667	0.350	0.091	0.23	0.043	0.068	130.34
Magnetic tapes	0.30	0.0450	0.0667		0.067	0.17	0.043	0.068	75.94
1989									
Food and beverages									
Soy oil	0.30	0.05	0.1	0.0000	0.07	0.04	0.05	0.10	70.56
Whiskey	0.40	0.06	0.1	2.0000	0.17	0.36	0.05	0.10	323.90
Tomato paste	0.20	0.03	0.1	0.0020	0.06	0.13	0.05	0.10	67.68
Minerals									
Calcium-phosphate	0.00	0.00	0.1	0.0000	0.05	0.11	0.05	0.10	41.00
Cement	0.00 E	0.00	0.0	0.0250	0.00	0.10	0.05	0.10	27.75
Asbestos	0.10	0.02	0.1	0.0000	0.06	0.12	0.05	0.10	54.23
Copper ore	0.00	0.00	0.1	0.0000	0.05	0.11	0.05	0.10	41.00
Aluminum ore	0.00	0.00	0.1	0.0000	0.05	0.11	0.05	0.10	41.00
Mineral fuels									
Coal	0.00 E	0.00	0.0	0.1200	0.00	0.11	0.05	0.10	38.20

(continued on next page)

Lignite	0.00 E	0.00	0.0	0.1900	0.00	0.12	0.05	0.10	45.90
Coke	0.00 E	0.00	0.0	0.0000	0.00	0.10	0.05	0.10	25.00
Chemicals									
Phosphoric acid	0.05	0.01	0.1	0.0000	0.05	0.12	0.05	0.10	47.61
Sodium hydroxide	0.00 E	0.00	0.0	0.0160	0.00	0.10	0.05	0.10	26.76
Sodium sulphure	0.20	0.03	0.1	0.4600	0.08	0.18	0.05	0.10	120.35
Teraflatic acid	0.00 E	0.00	0.0	0.1290	0.00	0.11	0.05	0.10	39.19
Ftalic anhidrite	0.20	0.03	0.1	0.1310	0.07	0.15	0.05	0.10	82.52
Ammonium sulphate	0.00 E	0.00	0.0	0.1510	0.00	0.12	0.05	0.10	41.61
Organic dyes	0.10	0.02	0.1	0.0000	0.06	0.12	0.05	0.10	54.23
Rubber and plastic									
Polyester chips	0.10	0.02	0.1	0.0000	0.06	0.12	0.05	0.10	54.23
Silicons	0.10	0.02	0.1	0.0000	0.06	0.12	0.05	0.10	54.23
Latex	0.00 E	0.00	0.0	0.0000	0.00	0.10	0.05	0.10	25.00
Tires (truck)	0.10	0.02	0.1	0.0000	0.06	0.12	0.05	0.10	54.23
Leather, hides, and fur									
Hides	0.00 E	0.00	0.0	0.0000	0.00	0.10	0.05	0.10	25.00
Sole leather	0.00 E	0.00	0.0	0.1000	0.00	0.11	0.05	0.10	36.00
Leather wear	0.40	0.06	0.1	0.3000	0.09	0.19	0.05	0.10	128.40
Paper and products									
Wood pulp	0.00 E	0.00	0.0	0.0000	0.00	0.10	0.05	0.10	25.00
Newsprint	0.01	0.00	0.1	0.0000	0.05	0.11	0.05	0.10	42.32
Kraft paper	0.12	0.02	0.1	0.0100	0.06	0.12	0.05	0.10	58.02
Textiles, clothing									
Polyamid yarn	0.01	0.00	0.1	0.0175	0.05	0.11	0.05	0.10	44.34

(continued on next page)

(*continued*)

Table 20

1989

	C.D.	M.T.	S.D.	Fund	W.T.	VAT	Guarantee deposits	SPSF	Total protection
Cotton	0.00 E	0.00	0.0	0.0000	0.00	0.10	0.05	0.10	25.00
Long-fiber cotton	0.00 E	0.00	0.0	0.0000	0.00	0.10	0.05	0.10	25.00
Cotton textiles	0.01	0.00	0.1	0.0286	0.05	0.11	0.05	0.10	45.61
Cotton T-shirts	0.25	0.04	0.1	0.0050	0.06	0.14	0.05	0.10	74.64
Glass, ceramic									
Tiles	0.05	0.01	0.1	0.1160	0.06	0.13	0.05	0.10	60.95
Porcelain tableware	0.20	0.03	0.1	0.5880	0.09	0.19	0.05	0.10	135.07
Glass, colored, uncolored	0.20	0.03	0.1	0.0000	0.06	0.13	0.05	0.10	67.45
Ordinary glass	0.00	0.00	0.1	0.0880	0.05	0.12	0.05	0.10	51.12
Iron and steel									
Blooms, billets	0.00 E	0.00	0.0	0.1000	0.00	0.11	0.05	0.10	36.00
Coils for rerolling	0.10	0.02	0.1	0.0140	0.06	0.12	0.05	0.10	55.84
Nonferrous metals									
Blister copper	0.00 E	0.00	0.0	0.0000	0.00	0.10	0.05	0.10	25.00
Aluminum	0.00 E	0.00	0.0	0.0020	0.00	0.10	0.05	0.10	25.00
Alum. bottles for LPG	0.10	0.02	0.1	0.1000	0.06	0.13	0.05	0.10	65.73
Metal products									
Saw blades	0.30	0.05	0.1	0.2000	0.08	0.16	0.05	0.10	103.68
Drill bits	0.30	0.05	0.1	0.2000	0.08	0.16	0.05	0.10	103.68

(*continued on next page*)

Nonelectrical machinery								
Grinders, mills	0.30	0.05	0.1		0.07	0.14	0.05	0.10	30.68
Electric machinery								
Refrigerators	0.10	0.02	0.1	0.0000	0.06	0.18	0.05	0.10	60.30
Dishwashers	0.10	0.02	0.1		0.06	0.18	0.05	0.10	60.30
Transformers	0.20	0.03	0.1	0.0625	0.06	0.14	0.05	0.10	74.64
Hair dryers	0.30	0.05	0.1	0.4000	0.09	0.18	0.05	0.10	126.68
Radios	0.20	0.03	0.1	0.2500	0.07	0.24	0.05	0.10	104.10
TV, color	0.20	0.03	0.1	0.0890	0.07	0.21	0.05	0.10	84.78
Transport equipment								
Motor cars	0.20	0.03	0.1		0.06	0.20	0.05	0.10	74.10
Buses	0.20	0.03	0.1		0.06	0.13	0.05	0.10	67.45
Others								
VCR	0.20	0.03	0.1	0.1500	0.07	0.22	0.05	0.10	92.10
Magnetic tapes	0.30	0.05	0.1		0.07	0.14	0.05	0.10	80.68

Note: C.D.: customs duty; M.T.: municipality tax; S.D.: stamp duty; W.T.: wharf tax; P.T.: production tax (VAT after 1985); E: Exempt. When C.D. = 0, M.T. is also 0, but P.T., W.T., and S.D. are charged on imports. When exempt, no duties and taxes are charged except P.T. (VAT.).
Source: Authors' calculations.

Table 21

Total Subsidies by Individual Manufacturing Sector, 1980–1989

	1980	1981	1982	1983	1984	1985	1986	1987	1988	1989
Subsidies										
Manufacturing	11.40	10.40	17.30	21.20	19.30	12.10	10.10	11.50	14.50	21.20
Food and beverages	3.86	3.09	8.09	7.89	10.47	3.54	5.28	5.99	4.40	5.35
Textiles	10.39	4.14	11.73	15.25	13.27	2.44	-3.18	-1.49	-0.60	-3.02
Wood products	6.97	10.46	36.15	37.49	37.87	8.17	7.80	14.64	4.17	-3.30
Paper products	7.92	-3.41	32.12	37.54	3.73	3.07	0.42	0.78	11.60	-0.68
Leather products	3.89	8.61	14.01	19.77	16.52	3.74	-0.49	5.54	0.88	-0.23
Chemicals	2.93	7.34	10.12	19.18	16.69	6.19	7.32	7.90	6.19	2.25
Glass, ceramics	5.07	2.13	11.08	5.74	9.41	3.05	3.55	4.65	2.69	-0.95
Iron and steel	0.26	3.67	12.71	20.84	25.74	14.08	14.97	15.58	12.64	14.48
Nonferrous metals	20.46	-3.20	3.36	1.34	3.27	-6.47	-6.59	-7.93	-8.98	-13.81
Metal products	6.34	25.16	82.87	105.26	69.71	10.92	14.68	5.10	11.01	0.46
Nonelectrical machinery	5.21	7.27	13.70	26.96	19.53	4.43	3.55	3.46	4.46	-0.36
Electrical machinery	5.07	2.95	12.39	14.46	15.76	5.57	6.28	4.81	4.19	2.58
Transport vehicles	12.99	7.82	12.37	4.80	6.49	0.72	-2.55	-1.17	0.29	-7.59
Cement, clay	4.22	13.82	21.73	19.79	17.67	13.43	11.27	27.94	10.31	-2.94
Rubber products	4.91	1.62	11.55	8.04	9.21	4.74	2.25	-0.07	0.13	-2.06
Others	1.29	-0.22	1.48	5.77	3.84	2.33	17.02	7.45	2.16	-0.59
Subsidies and offsets										
Manufacturing	17.20	15.30	23.9	34.20	23.30	26.00	26.80	30.80	32.60	36.00

(continued on next page)

Food and beverages	5.30	4.20	9.10	10.60	11.20	5.80	8.90	13.00	7.00	7.80
Textiles	13.60	7.10	15.20	21.30	14.90	7.40	3.70	11.40	6.30	3.70
Wood products	40.50	20.20	44.00	44.10	40.50	9.20	9.70	23.10	23.30	9.30
Paper products	7.90	-1.70	39.40	48.70	4.40	4.10	7.90	12.00	32.10	4.20
Leather products	5.30	9.80	15.00	23.00	17.20	5.50	2.70	12.10	4.40	3.20
Chemicals	4.90	11.10	14.40	28.10	22.60	11.70	14.10	18.00	12.00	9.10
Glass, ceramics	8.90	3.60	12.80	7.40	11.00	4.40	4.60	12.80	4.00	10.40
Iron and steel	3.30	7.90	18.30	29.80	29.40	19.60	20.00	22.60	17.30	20.20
Nonferrous metals	43.70	17.00	19.90	13.50	7.90	0.80	4.90	5.40	2.30	-0.30
Metal products	10.20	39.20	91.40	125.90	75.50	13.90	20.10	12.20	59.00	25.60
Nonelectrical machinery	14.40	9.20	17.60	29.50	20.40	7.20	5.40	10.50	6.50	2.30
Electrical machinery	20.60	22.90	25.20	37.90	19.10	12.60	17.30	14.80	19.40	15.50
Transport vehicles	35.10	21.10	23.90	18.60	14.50	18.80	8.70	7.50	15.90	4.70
Cement, clay	4.90	14.20	22.30	29.90	18.80	15.40	12.40	31.60	18.10	1.70
Rubber products	12.40	9.10	19.30	12.50	13.00	10.00	6.80	11.30	3.40	2.50
Others	1.50	0.70	2.30	6.80	16.30	12.10	57.40	16.50	27.00	12.20

Source: Authors' calculations.

Table 22

Tax Rebates, Subsidy Element, 1980–1989 (weighted averages)

	1980	1981	1982	1983	1984	1985	1986	1987	1988	1989
Manufacturing	5.9	3.6	9.5	11.8	11.3	3.1	1.9	0.2	-0.9	-3.8
Food and beverages	3.1	2.2	6.8	6.7	9.5	2.9	4.6	4.2	0.8	-2.0
Textiles	8.0	1.5	9.5	12.4	10.8	0.7	-5.0	-4.5	-4.9	-7.4
Wood products	6.9	10.3	36.0	37.4	37.8	8.1	7.7	14.5	4.0	-3.5
Paper products	7.9	-3.5	32.0	37.5	3.7	3.0	0.4	-0.9	6.0	-4.4
Leather	3.8	8.5	13.8	19.5	16.3	3.5	-0.7	-3.3	-3.4	-3.7
Chemicals	2.8	7.1	10.0	19.0	16.3	6.1	7.1	6.4	5.4	1.2
Glass, ceramics	4.9	1.9	10.6	5.3	9.3	2.9	3.4	3.5	0.4	-3.1
Iron and steel	0.2	3.4	12.5	18.1	21.3	12.6	12.9	10.2	9.3	7.4
Nonferrous metal products	20.3	-3.4	2.3	-0.1	3.0	-6.9	-6.7	-11.0	-12.2	-16.5
Metal products	6.2	25.0	82.6	105.0	69.6	10.8	14.6	4.9	10.7	0.2
Nonelectrical machinery	4.9	6.7	13.4	26.8	19.0	4.2	3.2	2.7	1.3	-2.8
Electrical machinery	4.9	2.8	12.2	14.1	15.6	5.5	6.1	4.4	-0.1	-3.0
Transport equipment	12.7	7.6	12.0	4.5	6.1	0.5	-2.8	-3.9	-4.0	-11.3
Cement, clay	4.2	13.8	21.7	19.7	17.6	13.4	11.2	27.8	10.3	-3.0
Rubber, plastic	4.6	1.4	11.3	7.6	8.9	4.6	2.1	-1.3	-1.5	-3.5
Others	1.1	-0.4	1.4	5.5	3.6	2.1	16.8	7.0	1.7	-1.0

Note: 1980 rebates are taken as real tax return. Weighted by manufactures' share in total exports.
Source: Authors' calculations.

130

Table 23

Sectoral Breakdown of Products in Tax Rebate Lists, 1979–1980
(number of occurrences)

	1	2	3	4	5	6	7	8	9	10	Total
Manufacturing											
Food and beverages	—	8	10	13	5	22	1	—	—	—	59
Textiles	1	6	5	4	4	—	1	1	—	3	25
Wood products	—	—	—	—	—	—	—	—	—	—	0
Paper products	—	—	—	2	10	2	—	—	—	3	17
Leather	—	—	1	2	—	—	—	1	—	—	4
Chemicals	—	—	3	12	31	19	7	4	—	—	76
Glass, ceramics	—	—	1	22	7	4	—	1	—	1	36
Iron and steel	—	—	—	17	6	—	—	—	—	—	23
Nonferrous metal products	—	—	11	2	8	3	2	1	—	—	27
Metal products	—	—	16	24	23	10	—	—	—	—	73
Nonelectrical machinery	3	5	20	16	8	—	—	—	—	—	52
Electrical machinery	4	3	4	2	18	6	—	—	—	—	37
Transport equipment	6	9	11	—	—	2	—	—	—	—	28
Cement, clay	—	—		3	3	1	1	—	—	—	8
Rubber, plastic	—	—	8	14	5	1	—	1	—	—	29
Others	—	—	1	1	4	19	5	3	—	—	33
Total	14	31	91	134	132	89	17	12	0	7	527

Source: Decree no. 9 Concerning Tax Rebates in Exports, *Resmi Gazete,* 7–11, 1979.

Table 24

Sectoral Breakdown of Products in Tax Rebate Lists, 1985
(number of occurrences)

	1	2	3	4	5	6	7	8	9	10	Total
Manufacturing											
Food and beverages	6	10	13	11	8	20	1	—	26	—	95
Textiles	—	—	5	6	11	—	2	—	5	2	31
Wood products	7	34	—	—	—	—	—	—	—	1	42
Paper products	—	—	6	15	1	—	—	—	—	1	23
Leather	1	—	1	—	2	—	—	—	2	—	6
Chemicals	—	2	6	12	41	27	9	9	—	—	106
Glass, ceramics	—	6	1	17	6	4	—	1	—	—	35
Iron and steel	19	4	—	2	—	—	—	—	—	—	25
Nonferrous metal products	—	13	2	12	3	2	2	—	4	—	38
Metal products	—	25	44	7	1	1	—	—		—	78
Nonelectrical machinery	27	12	23	5	6	—	—	—	1	—	74
Electrical machinery	15	10	1	21	—	—	—	—	—	—	47
Transport equipment	16	8	2	—	1	—	—	—	—	—	27
Cement, clay	—	6	2	1	2	—	—	—	—	—	11
Rubber, plastic	1	8	4	16	2	7	—	1	—	—	39
Others	1	1	18	10	2	20	8	3	—	4	67
Total	93	139	128	135	86	81	22	14	38	8	744

Source: IGEME, Ekonomik İstikrar Tedbirleri, December 1985.

132

Table 25

(number of occurrences)

	1	2	3	4	5	Total
Manufacturing						
Food and beverages	17	19	35	2	4	77
Textiles	—	2	1	2	20	25
Wood products	40	1	—	—	1	42
Paper products	—	24	1	—	—	25
Leather	1	1	1	—	1	4
Chemicals	2	25	79	34	—	140
Glass, ceramics	—	24	9	1	—	34
Iron and steel	25	2	—	—	—	27
Nonferrous metal products	13	17	5	2	4	41
Metal products	25	55	1	—	2	83
Nonelectrical machinery	37	30	6	—	—	73
Electrical machinery	23	28	—	—	2	53
Transport equipment	19	2	1	—	—	22
Cement, clay	6	3	2	—	—	11
Rubber, plastic	9	18	9	1	1	38
Others	2	36	28	11	—	77
Total	219	287	178	53	35	772

Source: IGEME, Dış Ticaret ve Yatırım Mevzuatı, 1988.

Table 26

Value of Export Credits, 1980–1989 (percentage of value of manufactured exports)

	1980	1981	1982	1983	1984	1985	1986	1987	1988	1989
Manufacturing	5.5	6.4	7.2	7.0	6.0	3.2	3.6	5.9	9.1	9.1
Food and Beverages	0.7	0.8	1.2	0.9	0.7	0.4	0.5	0.8	1.2	1.2
Textiles, clothing	2.4	2.5	2.0	2.2	1.8	1.1	1.2	2.1	3.1	3.1
Wood products	0.1	0.2	0.2	0.1	0.0	0.1	0.1	0.1	0.2	0.2
Paper products	0.0	0.0	0.1	0.1	0.0	0.0	0.0	0.0	0.1	0.1
Leather and products	0.1	0.1	0.2	0.2	0.1	0.1	0.1	0.1	0.2	0.2
Chemicals	0.1	0.2	0.1	0.3	0.3	0.1	0.2	0.3	0.2	0.2
Glass, ceramics	0.2	0.3	0.4	0.2	0.0	0.1	0.1	0.2	0.4	0.4
Iron and steel	0.1	0.3	0.2	1.3	1.4	0.1	0.4	0.7	0.2	0.2
Nonferrous metals	0.2	0.2	1.0	0.3	0.2	0.4	0.1	0.2	1.1	1.1
Metal products	0.2	0.2	0.2	0.3	0.1	0.1	0.1	0.2	0.3	0.3
Nonelectrical machinery	0.4	0.6	0.3	0.2	0.4	0.2	0.2	0.3	0.5	0.5
Electrical machinery	0.2	0.1	0.2	0.4	0.1	0.1	0.1	0.2	0.2	0.2
Transportation equipment	0.3	0.2	0.4	0.1	0.3	0.2	0.2	0.3	0.4	0.4
Cement, clay	0.0	0.0	0.0	0.1	0.1	0.0	0.1	0.1	0.0	0.0
Rubber and plastic	0.3	0.2	0.3	0.1	0.2	0.1	0.1	0.1	0.3	0.3
Others	0.2	0.2	0.1	0.1	0.1	0.1	0.0	0.1	0.2	0.2

Note: Weighted by share of manufactures in total exports.
Source: Authors' calculations.

Table 27

Estimated Value of Foreign Exchange Allocation Scheme and Foreign Exchange Retention Scheme, 1980–1989
(weighted average rates as percentage of value)

	1980	1981	1982	1983	1984	1985	1986	1987	1988	1989
Allocation scheme										
Manufacturing	3.9	3.3	4.2	7.9	3.1	3.4	5.6	6.2	5.5	4.3
Food and beverages	1.1	0.8	0.6	1.8	0.6	1.1	2.3	5.5	1.4	1.4
Textiles	2.5	2.4	2.7	4.2	1.3	1.8	3.0	8.5	2.9	2.7
Wood products	33.5	9.7	7.8	6.6	2.6	0.8	1.8	8.4	19.6	12.5
Paper products	0.0	1.7	7.3	11.2	0.6	0.9	7.4	11.1	20.5	4.8
Leather products	1.3	1.1	0.9	3.0	0.6	0.9	2.5	5.4	2.8	2.7
Chemicals	1.8	3.7	4.1	8.8	5.9	5.0	6.1	9.2	4.8	5.9
Glass, ceramics	3.8	1.4	1.7	1.5	1.5	1.0	0.7	7.8	1.0	11.0
Iron and steel	3.0	4.2	5.4	8.4	3.6	3.8	3.4	5.6	3.1	4.1
Nonferrous metals	23.2	20.2	16.5	12.0	4.6	7.1	11.3	13.2	10.9	13.2
Metal products	3.8	14.1	8.5	20.6	5.8	2.9	5.3	6.9	47.9	25.2
Nonelectrical machinery	9.2	1.9	3.8	2.4	0.8	2.1	1.5	5.9	1.5	2.4
Electrical machinery	15.5	19.9	12.8	23.3	3.3	6.9	10.7	9.5	14.8	12.7
Transport vehicles	22.0	13.2	11.4	13.6	7.9	17.9	11.0	8.5	15.5	12.1
Cement, clay	0.6	0.3	0.5	10.0	1.1	1.9	1.1	3.6	7.8	4.6
Rubber products	7.4	7.4	7.7	4.4	3.7	5.1	4.2	11.0	2.8	4.2
Others	0.1	0.8	0.6	0.6	12.4	8.9	39.7	8.4	24.3	12.3

(continued on next page)

(continued)

Table 27

	1980	1981	1982	1983	1984	1985	1986	1987	1988	1989
				Retention scheme						
Manufacturing	1.9	1.6	2.5	5.1	0.9	0.5	0.9	1.1	0.8	0.5
Food and beverages	0.4	0.3	0.4	0.9	0.1	0.1	0.1	0.1	0.1	0.1
Textiles	0.8	0.6	0.8	1.8	0.3	0.2	0.3	0.4	0.3	0.2
Wood products	0.0	0.0	0.0	0.0	0.0	0.0	0.0	0.0	0.0	0.0
Paper products	0.0	0.0	0.0	0.0	0.0	0.0	0.0	0.0	0.0	0.0
Leather products	0.1	0.1	0.1	0.3	0.1	0.0	0.1	0.1	0.0	0.0
Chemicals	0.1	0.1	0.1	0.2	0.0	0.0	0.1	0.1	0.1	0.0
Glass, ceramics	0.1	0.1	0.1	0.2	0.0	0.0	0.0	0.0	0.0	0.0
Iron and steel	0.1	0.1	0.3	0.6	0.1	0.1	0.1	0.1	0.1	0.1
Nonferrous metals	0.0	0.0	0.0	0.1	0.0	0.0	0.0	0.0	0.0	0.0
Metal products	0.0	0.0	0.0	0.0	0.0	0.0	0.0	0.0	0.0	0.0
Nonelectrical machinery	0.0	0.0	0.1	0.1	0.0	0.0	0.0	0.1	0.0	0.0
Electrical machinery	0.0	0.0	0.1	0.1	0.0	0.0	0.0	0.0	0.0	0.0
Transport vehicles	0.1	0.1	0.1	0.2	0.0	0.0	0.0	0.0	0.0	0.0
Cement, clay	0.1	0.1	0.2	0.1	0.0	0.0	0.0	0.0	0.0	0.0
Rubber products	0.0	0.1	0.0	0.1	0.0	0.0	0.0	0.0	0.0	0.0
Others	0.1	0.1	0.3	0.4	0.1	0.0	0.0	0.1	0.0	0.0

Note: Weighted by manufactures' share in total exports.
Source: Authors' calculations.

Table 28

Value of Corporate Income Tax Deductions, 1981–1989 (weighted averages)

	1981	1982	1983	1984	1985	1986	1987	1988	1989
Manufacturing[a]	0.4	0.6	1.2	1.7	1.6	2.1	2.5	3.0	3.0
Food and beverages	0.07	0.11	0.19	0.32	0.26	0.23	0.32	0.35	0.29
Textiles	0.14	0.22	0.36	0.62	0.59	0.63	0.88	0.99	1.06
Wood products	0.00	0.01	0.01	0.01	0.01	0.04	0.02	0.01	0.01
Paper products	0.00	0.00	0.00	0.00	0.02	0.02	0.02	0.03	0.02
Leather products	0.02	0.02	0.04	0.09	0.13	0.17	0.16	0.27	0.17
Chemicals	0.03	0.03	0.05	0.06	0.05	0.09	0.17	0.19	0.24
Glass, ceramics	0.01	0.03	0.04	0.05	0.05	0.07	0.07	0.08	0.08
Iron and steel	0.01	0.03	0.12	0.19	0.18	0.34	0.38	0.31	0.48
Nonferrous metals	0.01	0.01	0.02	0.04	0.03	0.04	0.05	0.05	0.08
Metal products	0.00	0.01	0.01	0.01	0.01	0.03	0.03	0.04	0.02
Nonelectrical machinery	0.01	0.02	0.04	0.05	0.04	0.13	0.10	0.25	0.11
Electrical machinery	0.00	0.01	0.03	0.03	0.03	0.04	0.06	0.11	0.10
Transport vehicles	0.02	0.03	0.04	0.06	0.04	0.05	0.04	0.04	0.04
Cement, clay	0.01	0.05	0.07	0.04	0.02	0.02	0.01	0.00	0.00
Rubber products	0.01	0.02	0.02	0.04	0.03	0.04	0.07	0.09	0.12
Others	0.02	0.04	0.14	0.14	0.15	0.18	0.14	0.14	0.16

NOTE: Share of manufacturing exports is multiplied by the subsidy element of exemption rates: 8 percent for 1981, 6 percent for 1982–1985, 5.9 percent for 1986, and 7.6 percent for 1987–1989.
a. Row 1 is multiplied by shares of exports over $250 million in total exports.
Source: Authors' calculations.

Table 29

Subsidy Rates for Exports from Support and Price Stabilization Fund, 1983–1989 (weighted averages)

	1983	1984	1985	1986	1987	1988	1989
Manufacturing	0.3	0.3	0.2	0.2	1.6	2.1	12.7
Food and beverages	—	—	—	—	0.7	2.0	5.9
Textiles	—	—	—	—	0.1	0.2	0.2
Wood products	—	—	—	—	0.0	0.0	0.0
Paper products	—	—	—	—	1.6	5.5	3.6
Leather products	—	—	—	—	8.5	3.8	3.1
Chemicals	—	—	—	—	1.1	0.4	0.6
Glass, ceramics	—	—	—	—	0.9	1.8	1.7
Iron and steel	2.4	2.9	1.2	1.3	4.3	2.8	6.4
Nonferrous metals	—	—	—	—	2.8	2.0	1.5
Metal products	—	—	—	—	0.0	0.0	0.0
Nonelectrical machinery	—	—	—	—	0.4	2.4	1.9
Electrical machinery	—	—	—	—	0.1	3.9	5.2
Transport vehicles	—	—	—	—	2.4	3.8	3.2
Cement, clay	—	—	—	—	0.0	0.0	0.0
Rubber products	—	—	—	—	1.0	1.2	1.0
Others	—	—	—	—	0.2	0.1	0.1

Note: Calculated from actual payments, weighted by shares of manufactures in total exports. Deferred payments are considered for the year in which exports were entitled for the payment.
Source: Central Bank files.

Table 30

Allowable Duty-free Imports, 1980–1989 (percentage of exports committed)

1980	60
1981	60
1982	60
1983	60
1984	50
1985	50
1986	50
1987	80 global
	50 iron-steel products
1988[a]	70 global and project
	50 iron-steel products
1989[a]	60 global and project
	50 iron-steel products

a. Sales considered as exports and other foreign-exchange-earning activities are also granted 50 percent duty-free import right.

Source: Export promotion decrees, *Resmi Gazete,* various issues.

139

Table 31

Specific Commodity Export Payments from SPSF, 1981–1989

	1981	1982	1984 (Apr.)	1985 (Sept.)	1986 (July)	1987	1988 (July)	1989
			For exports of $50 million					
List 1								
Biscuits	30	36	32	23	17	16	12	20
Medical serum	30	36	32	23	16	20	15	15
Wearing apparel	30	36	32	23	0	0	0	10
Leather footwear	30	36	32	23	17	12	46	10
Refrigerators	30	36	32	23	17	25	19	15
Electrical motors	30	36	32	23	17	20	15	0
TV (color)	30	36	32	23	17	20	15	10
Assembly parts	30	36	32	23	17	15	17	10
Furniture	0	0	32	23	17	12	7	0
List 2[a]								
Tomato paste and preserves	28	33	30	21	16	25	30	20
Footwear	28	33	30	21	16	12	97	10
Ceramic medical products	28	33	30	21	16	22	29	20
List 4[b]								
Kraft bags	23	28	26	19	14	20	13	10

(continued on next page)

	1981 Basic Rate	1981 Additional Rebate	1981 Total	1982 Basic Rate	1982 Additional Rebate	1982 Total	1984 Basic Rate	1984 Additional Rebate	1984 Total
Security glass	23	28	26		14	19	20	15	10
Steel ingots	23	28	26		14	19	15	15	15
List 5									
Cotton yarn[c]	15	21	24		12	8	7	6	0
Ground perlit	0	0	0		0	0	0	12	10
List 6									
Soap[d]	18	23	22		16	11	16	12	10
Optic lenses	18	23	22		16	11	4	2	0
Detergents	0	0	0		0	0	10	10	10

For exports in excess of $50 million

	1981 Basic Rate	1981 Additional Rebate	1981 Total	1982 Basic Rate	1982 Additional Rebate	1982 Total	1984 Basic Rate	1984 Additional Rebate	1984 Total
List 1									
Biscuits	20	10	30	20	15.76	35.76	16	15.76	31.76
Medical serum	20	10	30	20	15.76	35.76	16	15.76	31.76
Wearing apparel	20	10	30	20	15.76	35.76	16	15.76	31.76
Leather footwear	20	10	30	20	15.76	35.76	16	15.76	31.76
Refrigerators	20	10	30	20	15.76	35.76	16	15.76	31.76
Electrical motors	20	10	30	20	15.76	35.76	16	15.76	31.76

(continued on next page)

Table 31

| | 1981 | | | 1982 | | | 1984 | | |
	Basic Rate	Additional Rebate	Total	Basic Rate	Additional Rebate	Total	Basic Rate	Additional Rebate	Total
			For exports in excess of $50 million						
TV (color)	20	10	30	20	15.76	35.76	16	15.76	31.76
Assembly parts	20	10	30	20	15.76	35.76	16	15.76	31.76
Furniture	0	0	0	0	0	0	16	15.76	31.76
List 2[a]									
Tomato paste and preserves	17.5	10	27.5	17.5	15.76	33.26	14	15.76	29.76
Footwear	17.5	10	27.5	17.5	15.76	33.26	14	15.76	29.76
Ceramic medical products	17.5	10	27.5	17.5	15.76	33.26	14	15.76	29.76
List 4[b]									
Kraft bags	12.5	10	22.5	12.5	15.76	28.26	10	15.76	25.76
Security glass	12.5	10	22.5	12.5	15.76	28.26	10	15.76	25.76
Steel ingots	12.5	10	22.5	12.5	15.76	28.26	10	15.76	25.76
List 5									
Cotton yarn[c]	5	10	15	5	15.76	20.76	8	15.76	23.76
Ground perlit	0	0	0	0	0	0	0	0	0

(continued on next page)

(continued on next page)

	1985			1986			1987			
	Basic Rate	Additional Rebate	Total	Basic Rate	Additional Rebate	Total	Basic Rate	Additional Rebate	SPSF	Total
List 6										
Soap[d]	7.5	10	17.5	7.5	15.76	23.26	6	15.76		21.76
Optic lenses	7.5	10	17.5	7.5	15.76	23.26	6	15.76		21.76
Detergents	0	0	0	0	0	0	0	0		0
			For exports in excess of $50 million							
List 1										
Biscuits	11	11.76	22.76	9.4	7.88	17.28	8	3.52	4.9	16.42
Medical serum	11	11.76	22.76	8.225	7.88	16.105	8	3.52	8.8	20.32
Wearing apparel	11	11.76	22.76	0	0	0	0	0	0	0
Leather footwear	11	11.76	22.76	9.4	7.88	17.28	8	3.52	0	11.52
Refrigerators	11	11.76	22.76	9.4	7.88	17.28	8	3.52	13.7	25.22
Electrical motors	11	11.76	22.76	9.4	7.88	17.28	8	3.52	8	19.52
TV (color)	11	11.76	22.76	9.4	7.88	17.28	8	3.52	8	19.52
Assembly parts	11	11.76	22.76	9.4	7.88	17.28	8	3.52	3.5	15.02
Furniture	11	11.76	22.76	9.4	7.88	17.28	8	3.52	0	11.52
List 2[a]										
Tomato paste and preserves	9.625	11.76	21.385	8.225	7.88	16.105	8	3.52	13.8	25.32

143

Table 31

	1985			1986			1987			
	Basic Rate	Additional Rebate	Total	Basic Rate	Additional Rebate	Total	Basic Rate	Additional Rebate	SPSF	Total
	For exports in excess of $50 million									
Footwear	9.625	11.76	21.385	8.225	7.88	16.105	8	3.52	0	11.52
Ceramic medical products	9.625	11.76	21.385	8.225	7.88	16.105	8	3.52	10	21.52
List 4[b]										
Kraft bags	6.875	11.76	18.635	5.875	7.88	13.755	6	3.52	10.6	20.12
Security glass	6.875	11.76	18.635	5.875	7.88	13.755	6	3.52	10	19.52
Steel ingots	6.875	11.76	18.635	5.875	7.88	13.755	6	3.52	5.5	15.02
List 5										
Cotton yarn[c]	0	11.76	11.76	0	7.88	7.88	0	3.52	3.9	7.42
Ground perlit	0	0	0	0	0	0	0	0	0	0
List 6										
Soap[d]	4.125	11.76	15.885	3.525	7.88	11.405	4	3.52	8.2	15.72

(continued on next page)

	1988				1989			
	Basic Rate	Additional Rebate	SPSF	Total	Basic Rate	Additional Rebate	SPSF	Total
Optic lenses	4.125	11.76	15.885	3.525	7.88	11.405	0	3.52
Detergents	0	0	0	0	0	0	1.4	10.4
List 1								
			For exports in excess of $50 million					
Biscuits	4.8	1.76	5.8	12.36	0	0	20	20
Medical serum	4.8	1.76	8.8	15.36	0	0	15	15
Wearing apparel	0	0	0	0	0	0	10	10
Leather footwear	4.8	1.76	39.5	46.06	0	0	10	10
Refrigerators	4.8	1.76	12.2	18.76	0	0	15	15
Electrical motors	4.8	1.76	8	14.56	0	0	0	0
TV (color)	4.8	1.76	8	14.56	0	0	10	10
Assembly parts	4.8	1.76	10	16.56	0	0	10	10
Furniture	4.8	1.76	0	6.56	0	0	0	0
List 2[a]								
Tomato paste and preserves	4.8	1.76	23.8	30.36	0	0	20	20
Footwear	4.8	1.76	90.5	97.06	0	0	10	10
Ceramic medical products	4.8	1.76	22	28.56	0	0	20	20

(continued on next page)

(continued)

Table 31

	1988				1989			
	Basic Rate	Additional Rebate	SPSF	Total	Basic Rate	Additional Rebate	SPSF	Total
For exports in excess of $50 million								
List 4[b]								
Kraft bags	3.6	1.76	7.9	13.26	0	0	10	10
Security glass	3.6	1.76	10	15.36	0	0	10	10
Steel ingots	3.6	1.76	9.2	14.56	0	0	15	15
List 5								
Cotton yarn[c]	0	1.76	3.9	5.66	0	0	0	0
Ground perlit	0	0	11.6	11.6	0	0	10	10
List 6								
Soap[d]	2.4	1.76	7.7	11.86	0	0	10	10
Optic lenses	0	1.76	0	1.76	0	0	0	0
Detergents	0	0	9.6	9.6	0	0	10	10

Note: All figures rounded to nearest percentage.
a. Items listed here classified to list 1 from 1987.
b. Items listed here classified to list 2 from 1987.
c. Classified to list 8 prior to 1983.
d. Classified to list 3 from 1987.
Source: Authors' calculations.

5

Response to the Policy
Reform Efforts

In the winter of 1990 the policy reform effort continued, and its outcome was not entirely clear. Liberalization was continuing, and
additional initiatives and reforms, as well as preannounced changes,
were also continuing to take place. Indeed, as this chapter was being
written (late February 1990), a major round of import liberalization
was announced.[1]

The policy reforms have had mixed results thus far. On one
hand, there have been significant changes in the Turkish economy,
especially in its trade orientation. On the other hand, a number of
economic difficulties have not yet been resolved, and failure to grapple
with them satisfactorily could still negatively affect the outcome of the
entire reform process.

In this chapter we do several things. First, we examine the Turkish
trade performance of the 1980s. Without question the major achievement of the entire reform program has been the shift in the structure
of the Turkish economy, linking it more closely with the international
economy. Exports constituted over 15 percent of gross national product
in the late 1980s, up from less than half that figure a decade earlier.
Even if failure to solve the remaining economic problems (especially
inflation) should stalemate or reverse the reform process in the short
run, it is likely that some of the gains realized under the shift in trade
orientation will be lasting.

Second, we trace the evolution of the balance of payments and
Turkish debt and debt-servicing obligations. Third, we provide an overview of other aspects of economic performance in the late 1980s, with

147

emphasis on some of the less satisfactory aspects, especially inflation. Finally, in a postscript we briefly analyze the economic situation in Turkey in late 1989 and early 1990, focusing on the macroeconomic problems that may jeopardize the overall reform program.

Turkish Trade Performance

A central thrust of government policy reforms during the 1980s was to reorient the Turkish economy away from its earlier import-substitution path and toward a more outward-oriented structure of economic activity. To that end exchange rate policy was altered. After 1980 the nominal value of the Turkish lira was adjusted so as to off-set the excess of Turkish inflation relative to Turkey's major trading partners.[2] Thus the real value of the lira either remained relatively constant or depreciated relative to Turkey's major trading partners, at least up to 1989. Furthermore, the export incentive measures discussed in Chapter 4 and documented in Table 19 were instituted, and the import regime was greatly liberalized.

Those measures are quantifiable. In addition, the reforms had some unquantifiable, but nonetheless important, dimensions. Realignment of the exchange rate regime and trade policy were clearly important in themselves. They also served as a signal of the government's commitment to the new policies. Equally important, however, is that policy makers were also generally much more sensitive to the effects of policies on exports and on economic activity than they had earlier been. Thus the entire atmosphere within which producers' decisions were made changed remarkably.

The extent of the transformation in governmental attitudes and commitments became clear to us during our interviews with businessmen in Istanbul in November 1989. By that time, changes in the nominal exchange rate had been occurring at a rate only about half that of inflation for almost a year.[3] Nonetheless, when questioned about export prospects in light of that real appreciation, every interviewee responded in a way which expressed confidence in the government's commitment to supporting exports and which indicated his belief that relief would be forthcoming shortly.

It is difficult to convey the extent of the transformation of the economy, and of attitudes toward exporting. Historically, Turks have held a deep-seated distrust of foreign trade and have been highly pessimistic about the capabilities of Turkish businessmen. In the late 1970s, exports had constituted only about 7 percent of GNP.[4] This was an amazingly small number for a country geographically proximate both to Europe and to the Middle East, with an abundance of fertile, temperate land and unskilled labor relative to European neighbors and with a complete dependence on foreign countries for imports of oil and many other commodities.

By 1987, the share of exports in GNP had risen to 20.4 percent. This constituted a tripling of export share in GNP in less than eight years. That increase was accomplished with an average annual rate of growth of export earnings (in U.S. dollars) of 18.9 percent over the 1980–1988 period. By the standards of any decade that export growth rate was impressive. Because there was a severe slowdown in the growth of world trade in the first half of the 1980s, Turkish performance is even more outstanding.

Accompanying the increase in export earnings was an increase in the share of imports in GNP. Imports increased from a range of 15–17 percent of GNP in the late 1970s to over 22 percent in every year after 1984. Thus the increase in exports constituted a structural shift as both exports and imports increased in relative and absolute importance.

In this section we first analyze that export growth, focusing on both the commodity composition of exports and the differential growth rates of different commodity groups. We then examine some of the questions that have arisen with regard to that growth—How much was attributable to special trading ties with the Middle East and how much to other special trading arrangements? How much "faked exporting" to collect incentives was there? What was the role of the real exchange rate? How efficient was the export thrust? Next we attempt to convey a sense of the substance of our interviews with exporters in the fall of 1989. Finally we consider the behavior of imports and other components of the balance of payments over the 1980s.

Commodity Composition of Exports

Table 32 gives summary data on the growth of exports by major commodity group.[5] All major categories of exports grew, although exports of industrial goods grew much more rapidly than exports of agricultural commodities, and exports of mineral products grew very little after a short-lived burst in the mid-1980s. Thus, whereas

Table 32

Export Earnings by Major Commodity Category, 1975, 1976, and 1980–1989 (millions of U.S. dollars)

Commodity Group	1975	1976	1980	1981	1982	1983	1984	1985	1986	1987	1988	1989
Agriculture and livestock	793 (57)	1,254 (64)	1,672 (57)	2,219 (47)	2,141 (37)	1,881 (33)	1,749 (25)	1,719 (22)	1,886 (25)	1,853 (18)	2,341 (20)	2,127 (18)
Mining and quarrying	106 (8)	110 (6)	191 (7)	193 (4)	175 (3)	189 (3)	240 (3)	244 (3)	247 (3)	272 (3)	377 (3)	413 (4)
Industrial goods	503 (36)	596 (30)	1,047 (36)	2,290 (49)	3,430 (60)	3,658 (64)	5,145 (72)	5,995 (75)	5,324 (71)	8,065 (79)	8,944 (77)	9,088 (78)
Processed agricultual commodities	129	98	209	412	568	670	808	647	667	954	885	919
Manufactures	338	481	800	1,772	2,517	2,756	3,928	4,976	4,479	6,879	7,728	7,915
Total	1,402	1,960	2,910	4,703	5,746	5,728	7,134	7,958	7,457	10,190	11,662	11,627

Note: Numbers in parentheses indicate percentages of total exports.
Source: Data Appendix Table 14.

agricultural commodities constituted 57 percent of exports in 1975 and 57 percent in 1980, their share of total exports had fallen to about 18 percent by 1989. Conversely, the share of industrial goods in total exports rose rapidly, reaching more than three quarters of total exports by the latter 1980s.

Export earnings from agricultural commodities rose only at an average annual rate of 2.7 percent over the 1980–1989 period. Nonetheless, the growth rate of earnings exceeded that of earlier years. Moreover, exports of processed agricultural commodities rose from $209 million in 1980 to $919 million in 1989; to the extent that these commodities might otherwise have been exported in crude, or unprocessed, form, the growth of agricultural exports is understated by examining only exports of unprocessed commodities.

Table 33 provides a breakdown of the commodity composition of manufactured exports. It should first be noted that, in addition to the commodities covered in that table, exports of processed agricultural commodities increased greatly during the 1980s (see Table 31). It is arguable whether those exports should be classified as manufactured or not: industrial value added was obviously a smaller fraction of export value for some of those commodities, but there was nonetheless a substantial increase in economic activity associated with the handling and processing of exportable agricultural commodities.

Virtually all categories of manufactured exports grew rapidly. Over the course of the decade, however, growth rates differed enough among commodity groups so that the relative concentration of different commodities in exports changed markedly. In 1975 and in 1980 textiles constituted about half of manufactured exports. Although export earnings measured in U.S. dollars from textiles grew at the very rapid average annual rate of 30 percent over the first nine years of the 1980s, that rate was well below the overall growth rate of manufactured exports, which increased almost tenfold during that period.[6]

As contrasted with 1980, all categories of manufactured exports listed in Table 33 grew at rates greater than 10 percent. The more detailed the commodity classification, of course, the greater the variation in growth rates across individual industries, and not all commodity exports grew within two-digit categories. Cement exports, for example, rose sharply from 1980 to 1982 but fell thereafter; by 1988 they were only $6.5 million, down from $39.6 million in 1980 and $206.6 million in 1982. At the two-digit level the most rapidly growing export

Table 33

Commodity Composition of Manufactured Exports, 1975, 1976, and 1980–1989 (thousands of U.S. dollars)

Commodity group	1975	1976	1980	1981	1982	1983	1984	1985	1986	1987	1988	1989
Textiles and clothing	128	265	424	803	1,056	1,299	1,875	1,790	1,851	2,707	3,201	3,508
Hides, leather products	65	60	50	82	111	192	401	484	345	722	514	605
Rubber, plastic	5	3	16	72	60	77	97	108	141	258	352	313
Chemicals	33	44	76	94	148	120	173	266	350	527	734	774
Glass, ceramics	18	21	36	102	104	108	146	190	158	205	233	258
Nonferrous metal products[a]	37	33	58	228	251	160	142	159	138	141	233	300
Iron, steel	20	22	34	100	362	407	576	969	804	852	1,458	1,349
Metal products	4	4	8	20	27	19	16	73	60	107	52	23
Others[b]	29	28	99	271	397	373	502	938	632	1,362	952	788
Total	338	481	800	1,772	2,517	2,756	3,928	4,976	4,479	6,879	7,728	7,915

a. Includes cement.
b. Includes forestry products, electrical and nonelectrical machinery, motor vehicles, instruments, and miscellaneous manufactures not classified elsewhere.
Source: Data Appendix Table 14.

sectors were iron and steel, which grew at an average annual rate of 51 percent. There was rapid growth of exports of hides and leather (32 percent annually), electrical appliances (40 percent annually), and rubber and plastics (39 percent annually).

In the late 1970s and early 1980s Turkish manufactured exports of individual manufacturing sectors were relatively small and scattered across a large number of items except for processed food and textiles and clothing. By 1989 export production was significant in a much larger number of two-digit industries. In the late 1970s only hides and leather products (in addition to the two main exporting activities) accounted for more than 5 percent of manufactured exports. By 1988 hides and leather, chemical products, iron and steel products, and miscellaneous manufactures all constituted more than that percentage.

Manufacturing production was somewhat lower in 1980 than it had been in 1975. By 1985, however, it had increased substantially (see Data Appendix Table 4 for data after 1981), with rapid increases in most sectors. Since domestic demand grew only slowly over the first several years after 1980, it is a reasonable inference that the growth of manufacturing output was in large part the consequence of the expansion of exports.

The Organization for Economic Cooperation and Development performed an extensive analysis of manufacturing exports for a number of countries, classifying exports into five broad categories: resource-intensive industries, labor-intensive industries, scale-intensive industries, differentiated goods, and science-based industries.[7] On that basis Turkish exports were analyzed and classified for 1987 (see Table 34).

Industries classified by the OECD as labor-intensive constituted 46 percent of total exports in 1987. Exports based on Turkish raw materials accounted for another 17 percent. Iron and steel and chemicals accounted for an additional 18 percent of exports. Iron and steel and industrial chemicals were the only two industries classified as scale intensive that were sizable. Even there, a great deal of iron and steel exports consisted of reexported processed scrap metal—the product of a labor-intensive process. If iron and steel were reclassified as labor intensive, that would imply that more than three quarters of Turkish exports in 1987 were either directly labor intensive or based on the availability of natural resources. Clearly, the quality and availability of Turkey's labor force played a significant role

Table 34

Classification of Exports by Nature of Commodity, 1987

Categorization of exportable commodity	Percentage of total manufacturing exports
Resource-intensive industries	17.2
Manufactures of food, beverages, and tobacco	11.1
Manufactures of leather except footwear and wearing apparel	0.3
Manufactures of wood, wood and cork products, except furniture	0.4
Manufactures of pulp, paper and paperboard	0.5
Petroleum products	2.9
Miscellaneous products of petroleum and coal	0.0
Other nonmetallic mineral products	0.5
Nonferrous metal basic industries	1.5
Labor-intensive industries	45.9
Textiles	15.6
Wearing apparel	26.9
Footwear	0.3
Furniture and fixtures (except primary metal)	0.2
Metal scrap	2.4
Other manufacturing	0.5
Scale-intensive industries	23.4
Paper, paper products, printing, and publishing	0.6
Manufacture of industrial chemicals	8.0
Rubber products	0.8
Plastic products not elsewhere classified	0.4
Manufacture of pottery, china, and earthenware	0.4
Manufacture of glass and glass products	1.7
Iron and steel basic industries	9.7
Transport equipment	1.8
Differentiated goods	12.0
Engines and turbines	0.1
Agricultural machinery and equipment	0.3
Metal and woodworking machinery	0.9
Special industrial machinery and equipment excluding metal and woodworking machinery	4.5
Machinery and equipment except electric not elsewhere classified	2.5

(continued on next page)

Table 34

(continued)

Categorization of exportable commodity	Percentage of total manufacturing exports
Electrical machinery, appliances, and supplies	3.6
Photographic and optical goods and watches	0.1
Science-based industries	1.5
Manufacture of other chemical products	1.3
Office, computing, and accounting machinery	0.0
Professional, scientific, measuring, and controlling equipment	0.2

Source: OECD, *OECD Economic Surveys, Turkey 1989/90*, p. 39.

in the development of export industries, although other factors were involved as well.

Destinations of Exports

Table 35 provides data on the distribution of Turkey's exports among major trading destinations during the 1980s. During the 1976–1980 period Turkey's exports were increasingly destined for bilateral trading partners in Eastern Europe and elsewhere; exports to the OECD were roughly constant from 1976 to 1979 and then increased somewhat in 1980.

In the first half of the 1980s, exports to Eastern Europe fell, while those to the OECD and the Middle East countries rose sharply. Indeed, from 1980 to 1985 exports to the Middle East accounted for half of the entire increment of exports, rising by almost US$2.5 billion, out of an increase in total exports of $5 billion. Exports to the OECD rose by an almost equal amount—from US$1.7 billion in 1980 to $4.1 billion in 1985.

After 1985, however, exports to the Middle East fell, dropping from their peak of $3.0 billion to $2.0 billion in 1989. This reflected the reduced buying power of the oil-exporting countries after the price of oil, and therefore the oil exporters' export earnings, began to decline in 1986. From 1985 to 1989 exports to the OECD rose from $4.1 billion to $7.1 billion, accounting for $3.1 billion of an

Table 35

Geographic Distribution of Turkish Exports, 1976 and 1980–1989 (millions of U.S. dollars)

	1976	1980	1981	1982	1983	1984	1985	1986	1987	1988	1989
OECD	1,483	1,680	2,264	2,556	2,760	3,740	4,106	4,293	6,443	6,707	7,176
European Community	959	1,242	1,503	1,755	2,010	2,732	3,133	3,263	4,868	5,098	5,408
Other Western Europe	289	264	447	495	468	579	398	333	633	553	451
United States	191	127	268	252	232	368	506	549	713	761	971
Japan	36	37	35	43	37	37	43	99	156	209	233
Other OECD	7	10	11	11	13	24	27	48	73	86	113
Eastern Europe	178	516	353	333	245	284	334	311	334	609	1,029
Middle East[a]	208	542	1,373	2,159	2,182	2,540	3,042	2,095	2,570	2,688	2,069
Other countries	91	172	714	699	540	570	476	759	841	1,658	1,352
Total exports	1,960	2,910	4,702	5,746	5,728	7,134	7,958	7,457	10,190	11,662	11,627

a. Excludes Israel and Egypt.

Note: Columns may not add to total because of rounding.

Source: SIS, *Monthly Summary of Foreign Trade*, December 1989 and earlier issues; SIS, *Statistical Yearbook of Turkey*, 1989 and earlier issues. SPO, *Main Economic Indicators*, June 1990 and earlier issues.

increase in total exports of $3.7 billion. By 1989 the OECD accounted for 62 percent of Turkey's exports, a reduction from the 75 percent destined for the OECD in the mid-1970s. Exports were thus diversified both geographically and by commodity.

Within the OECD countries most exports were destined for Germany and the other members of the European Community. The Japanese share of Turkey's exports has remained very small, and the United States is far less important as a customer for Turkey than it is for many other developing countries.

Skepticism about Exports

Especially in the early years of the export drive, there was a great deal of skepticism concerning its apparent success. In part because of the historical distrust of exports but in part because there were some legitimate questions, critics of the Turgut Özal reforms suggested that a significant part of the statistical increase in exports was apparent rather than real.

Their suspicions were based on a number of factors. In the early 1980s, immediately after the reforms were announced, it was suggested that the Turkish economy was in a recession and that the incremental export growth would reverse as soon as economic growth resumed. Then and continuing through the mid-1980s, concern was expressed that Turkey's exports depended on its special relationship with oil-exporting Middle Eastern trading partners and had benefited especially from the Iran-Iraq war. Finally, the institution of export trading houses encouraged some "false exports" undertaken to collect the incentives. This was a highly publicized issue in the Turkish press, and critics questioned whether false exporting might account for a significant fraction of the apparent success of the export drive. Here we consider each of the articulated concerns in turn.

Turning first to the issue of excess capacity in the early 1980s, there seems to be little doubt that it was the presence of excess capacity that permitted export growth. The reduction in domestic demand was in large measure the factor that permitted the rapid expansion of exports. Exports of manufactures more than doubled between 1980 and 1981, increasing from $800 million to $1.8 billion, and tripled between 1980 and 1982 (Table 33). Since there is little evidence of any expansion of capacity at that time, there can be little doubt that most of the initial surge of exports came from a diversion of existing capacity to exportable products.

The diversion took place both because of low levels of domestic demand, at least contrasted with the late 1970s, and because of improved incentives for exports. As reported in interviews with the authors, previously existing equipment was often adapted to new functions. In some instances this involved reducing the number of products sold and concentrating production on those lines that were exportable. In other cases firms had been exporting small amounts in earlier years and could profitably increase their exports substantially once the real exchange rate had been altered.

It is probably natural that the incremental exports that occur in the first several years after a change in the trade regime are produced with capacity built under the earlier incentive structure. In part this is inevitable since new capacity takes time to be built once it is perceived that exporting has become profitable. In part, however, some companies had earlier found that exporting a small part of their output was marginally profitable given the special export incentives. It is not surprising that those companies would find it profitable to increase the share of their output going to the export market significantly once incentives for exporting had been enhanced.

To the extent that critics of the trade regime reforms pointed to the excess capacity and recession-induced export expansion, they were largely correct. It is not obvious, however, why this should have been a criticism of the regime. Had exports begun to diminish as soon as domestic economic activity again began to expand at real rates of 4–6 percent a year, the critics might have had a point. As it was, however, subsequent events demonstrated that the initial increase in exports was only a harbinger of further increases that would occur later. Thus, with hindsight, the criticism of the export drive was probably an accurate description; it was not, however, correct to infer that exports were transitory phenomena that would disappear as soon as economic activity once again began to increase more rapidly.[8]

There is also truth in the second contention—that Turkey's proximity to and affinity with her Middle Eastern neighbors helped stimulate exports. This stood in sharp contrast to the 1973–1977 period, when other countries, notably Korea, were able to increase their exports to the Middle East oil-exporting countries while Turkish exports grew only slowly.[9] As the data in Table 35 and the discussion of the section "Destination of Exports" demonstrate, exports to the Middle Eastern countries were important as a source of export growth, especially during the Iran-Iraq war. Much of the Iraqi trade, especially, took place under bilateral trading arrangements. By 1986 Iraq had fallen well behind in financing its imports, and the trade began to diminish.

While it is certainly true that Turkey benefited in the early 1980s from its proximity to a rapidly growing market, equally Turkey was disadvantaged when that market shrank after the mid-1980s. OECD calculations suggest that the "regional composition effect," which reflects the more rapid growth of Turkey's trading partners than of world trade as a whole, was large in 1980–81 relative to 1978–79 and in 1981–82 relative to 1979–80. For the former period the OECD estimates that the regional composition effect accounted for 11.3 percentage points of export growth (of a total of 29.4 percent) and for the latter period for 9.6 percentage points (of a total of 42.1 percent). What is noteworthy, however, is that the use of the constant-market-shares analysis suggested that, even after taking into account the Turkish product composition and other factors, there was still a residual, "unexplained" growth of Turkish exports of 10.5 percent in 1980–81, 34.6 percent in 1981–82, 25.5 percent in 1982–83, 12.7 percent in 1983–84, 15.3 percent in 1984–85, and so on. Indeed, after 1982–83 (in which year the regional composition effect was estimated to be 0.5 percent), the regional composition effect was negative for all subsequent years, reaching a negative 8.3 percent in 1986 and a negative 5.4 percent in 1987—the last year for which the calculations were made.[10]

Thus it may be concluded that the Middle East did constitute an important and rapidly expanding market for Turkish exports in the early 1980s. That Turkish exporters were able to take advantage of that market was a function of the changes in the trade regime. In this regard it is significant both that the residual in the constant-market-shares analysis was positive and that Turkish exports continued to grow rapidly even after the Middle East market stagnated.

This leaves the third source of concern: that Turkish exports did not grow as much as indicated by the statistics because of false invoicing to take advantage of the strong export incentives. When the Turkish authorities wanted to encourage exports, they provided special incentives for export trading corporations.[11] In response to these incentives, a number of such corporations were established. There was some faking of exports to be eligible for incentives. The newspapers were able to document faked consignments, and it was generally believed that the practice of faking exports was widespread.

To examine the probable quantitative importance of this phenomenon, we undertook a comparison of Turkish with partner-country trading statistics for 1982 to 1985. The results are given in Table 36.

There were wide disparities between trading partner and Turkish figures in the individual commodity category statistics for exports in the early 1980s, with a maximum of 21 percent average apparent overstatement in 1984. It is, of course, not possible to estimate the extent to which disparities arise because of overinvoicing in Turkey or because of other statistical problems. Estimated exports to the United States appear to be systematically underreported by the United States, and those to Europe tend to be overreported. Since export incentives appear to have applied equally regardless of destination, this apparent discrepancy raises questions about the validity of the comparison.[12]

The numbers presented in Table 36 are consistent with those obtained by Dani Rodrik. He deflated partner-country trade figures by 1.08 to adjust for the difference between free-on-board (f.o.b.) and cost, insurance, and freight (c.i.f.) figures and compared Turkish statistics with those for the OECD as a whole. He calculated overinvoicing as the percentage by which Turkish export figures were greater than the trading partner deflated figure for imports. Interestingly, his results showed underinvoicing in the late 1970s, averaging about 4.2 percent a year. For the 1980s he found overinvoicing amounting to 1.9 percent of exports in 1981, 11 percent in 1982, 13 percent in 1983, and 28 percent in 1984. The numbers in Rodrik's calculation then drop off sharply, falling to 8.3 percent in 1985 and showing underinvoicing of 5.8 percent in 1986. For the period 1981 through May 1987, Rodrik's calculations suggest cumulate overinvoicing of 11.4 percent.[13]

By the mid-1980s the public outcry over the reported cases of overinvoicing of exports and accession to the Subsidies Code of the General Agreement on Tariffs and Trade led the authorities to begin reducing some of the special incentives for exports.[14] As a consequence, by 1989 it was generally believed that faked invoicing of exports had diminished substantially, if it had not entirely disappeared.

Table 36

Comparison of Turkish and Partner-Country Export Statistics, 1982–1985

	1982			1983			1984			1985		
	OECD	United States	Europe	OECD	United States	Europe	OECD	United States	Europe	OECD	United States	Europe
Food and live animals	-1	-1	-1	3	1	4	4	-17	6	-3	-6	-2
Beverages and tobacco	-7	-11	-1	-25	-31	-6	-34	-36	-27	4	8	2
Crude materials, inedible	-4	-12	-3	-12	-13	-11	-13	5	-15	-23	-29	-23
Mineral fuels	-33	-100	-31	-29	0	-29	-23	-77	-19	-69	-80	-66
Animal and vegetable fats/oil	-24	104	-24	22	34	21	60	68	59	41	-92	64
Chemicals and products	10	34	7	-4	-41	3	20	66	14	27	-62	87
Manufactured goods	39	-18	41	19	27	19	31	1	36	49	3	59
Machinery and transport	90	318	82	114	-52	116	253	-10	262	599	585	614
Miscellaneous manufacture	39	-39	41	47	-77	64	101	14	2,000	56	-10	67
Total exports	6	-13	8	5	-31	11	21	-21	30	6	-22	13

Notes: Disparities are expressed as a percentage of the export value reported by the OECD. A positive sign indicates that Turkish records show more exports than the OECD partner-country records claim. A small negative sign would be consistent with the imports being c.i.f. and the exports f.o.b.

Source: OECD, *Foreign Trade by Commodities*, Series C, vol. 1, *Exports*, various years.

It seems clear that faked invoicing may have resulted in an overstatement of Turkish exports, especially in the period before 1985. Even if faked invoicing was 8–10 percent of the true export value, however, that would result in downward adjustment in the estimated growth rate of Turkish exports of about 1 percent annually. While this would make Turkish export performance during the 1980s a little less impressive, it would not significantly alter the conclusion that Turkish export growth was very rapid, especially against the backdrop of a worldwide recession in the early 1980s and the adversities suffered by some of Turkey's Middle Eastern trading partners in the mid-1980s.

The Role of the Real Exchange Rate

The real exchange rate in the 1980s was significantly more attractive for exporters than it had been in earlier years. An important question is how important this change was in spurring the growth of exports.

To address this question, a simple model of export determination was estimated as follows:

$$X_t = b_0 + b_1 PPP_t + b_2\, LagX_t + e_t$$

where X_t is the log of annual export volumes,[15] PPP_t is the log of the purchasing-power-parity (PPP) exchange rate between the dollar and the Turkish lira, and $LagX_t$ is the log of the volume of exports lagged one period.

Annual observations were used over the period 1975 through 1989. The results are as follows:

$$X_t = 1.29 + 0.43\ PPP_t + 0.57\ lagX_t$$
$$\quad\ \ (8.14)\ \ (2.14)\qquad\quad (3.15)$$

$R^2 -$ adj $= 0.80$
Degrees of freedom $= 12$
Figures in parentheses are t-statistics.

Real export volumes appear to have been responsive to the real exchange rate. A 1 percent increase in the real return from exporting appears on average to have generated an increased supply of exports of about 0.43 percent. On that estimate the change in the real exchange rate between 1979 and 1985 (see Chapter 4, Table 9) would have accounted for an increase in exports of 101 percent, of a total increase of 158 percent. While other factors—including the change in attitude on the part of government officials, special export incentives, and the reduction in domestic excess demand—all undoubtedly contributed to the rapid growth of exports, the change in the real exchange rate was clearly a major factor.

Impressionistic Evidence

By the fall of 1990 the authors had largely completed their collection and analysis of data on changes in the trade regime and on the behavior of exports and imports and deemed it desirable to enrich interpretation of that evidence with interviews of those who had been affected by the changes in the regime. To that end, interviews were arranged in Istanbul in the early part of November. A list of those interviewed is given in the appendix to this chapter, and the authors wish to express their appreciation for the time and efforts given to them and the hospitality received from those interviewed. The results of the interviews have informed many of the judgments made throughout this volume, but there remain some aspects on which interviews provided information not otherwise available. In this section we briefly summarize some of the phenomena that emerged as a consequence of interviews, especially those that had not previously been as clearly evident to us.

Interviews were loosely structured along three general lines: (1) an effort to ascertain the history of the enterprise and, in particular, the motives for exporting; (2) an effort to ascertain the ease or difficulty of negotiations with government officials for incentives or, in other words, to find out how the system actually worked; and (3) an effort to assess current economic policies and prospects. Here each is discussed in turn.

Turning first to how entry into exporting occurred, a surprise was that a very large fraction of exports took place through foreign trade companies (FTCs) and that interviews were therefore almost exclusively with managers of those companies. They had come into existence in the 1980s in response to the law providing for additional incentives for those exporting through them. The reason for the concentration of interviews, it turned out, was that over 50 percent of Turkey's reported exports in 1988 had been effected through these organizations. Since some major primary commodity exports went through other channels, this implies that a very high fraction of manufactured exports left the country in consignments shipped by the FTCs.[16]

It was clearly the intent of the government, in passing the legislation encouraging FTCs, to encourage the development of large export houses that might handle the commodity exports of many smaller firms. The theory, repeated to us frequently by those whom we interviewed, was that large trading houses would be able to afford multiple overseas offices and to acquire information on markets that would be too expensive for individual manufacturing companies to acquire.

Because FTCs were eligible for an additional 5 to 12 percent export subsidy, varying over time, there was a strong inducement for exporters to export through them. (See Chapter 4, Table 29 for an indication of subsidy rates.) In some instances existing concerns had simply established an additional company within their group that legally became the FTC for the group. In these instances small staffs of the export trading house carried on the export trade for the entire industrial group. For example, Enka Holding Company, a major industrial group, followed this route.

In other cases an independent group established an FTC and attempted to establish itself as a middleman between domestic producers and foreign buyers. In some instances these independent groups specialized, but in other cases their exports consisted of a cross section of the entire range of Turkish manufactured exports. One FTC listed its export commodities in 1989 as "foodstuffs, consumer goods, fresh fruit and vegetables, chemicals, construction materials, durable household appliances, textiles, ready to wear cloths [sic], industrial goods, automotive components." The same enterprise listed its imports as "iron and steel, textiles, chemicals, foodstuffs, consumer goods, industrial goods, automotive components."[17]

In some instances an FTC would simply seek out existing exporters and offer to do their exporting for them. In return they offered a split, not necessarily fifty-fifty, of the additional incentive applicable to FTC exports.[18]

In a number of instances export producers reported dissatisfaction with the services of FTCs. In at least two instances the person interviewed reported that it had been decided to develop an in-house FTC because the conglomerate FTCs simply did not have enough information on the business to do an adequate job of representation.

It also appeared that by 1989 there was a regrouping of FTCs so that each would become somewhat more specialized in particular commodity groups. Even so some producers expressed discontent with FTC arrangements, indicating that FTCs were not entirely satisfactory.

Anecdotal evidence of what were felt to be unsatisfactory arrangements included the following episodes. One manufacturer reported that he had had phone calls from two FTCs within a day, each indicating that it could land contracts for him if he simply lowered his price by a specified amount. He did so, only to discover that he had been bidding against himself, as two FTCs were each trying to land business. Another manufacturer reported that there had been significant difficulties when orders had been accepted without proper technical knowledge and that an FTC had taken an order with a regular customer that could not possibly be filled in the time agreed upon. More frequently heard were complaints that FTC representatives abroad did not have enough knowledge of their products to be effective salesmen.

It is difficult to judge how much of a contribution FTCs made to the Turkish export drive. On one hand, FTCs clearly had an incentive to seek out domestic producers and acquaint them with export opportunities. On the other hand, FTCs first sought existing producers and attempted to win their business. Although we interviewed managers of firms that had commenced operations or started exporting after 1980, in no instance was the presence of an FTC willing to undertake exports reported as a reason for startup. Indeed, there appeared in general to be more dissatisfaction with FTCs among those who felt that they had no choice but to export through them (to receive the additional 1, 2, or 3 percent) than a feeling that FTCs had played a constructive role.

Inspection of the list of FTCs operating in 1989 suggested that several (Etibank, Sümerbank, Tariş, the Turkish Iron and Steel Works [TDCI], Tekel, and Toprak Mahsülleri Ofisi [TMO]) were large state economic enterprises (SEEs) that had earlier exported in any event.[19] Many more—Cam, Çolakoğlu, Çukurova, Diler, Edpa, Ekinciler, Enka, Exsa, Fepaş, İzdaş, Kibar, Meptaş, Okan, Ram, Süzer, Tekfen, and Yaşar—were associated with large holding companies. While these FTCs would accept business from individual exporters, they were primarily concerned with the exports of their own group. In many instances the FTC was explicitly created to take advantage of the incentives provided and simply undertook functions formerly carried out under a different organizational structure.

In the future FTCs may develop that provide exporting services to groups of small, independent producers, but only a few of these had sprung up by 1989. Most prominent among them was the Textile Manufacturers' Foreign Trade Company, established in 1987 by nineteen textile manufacturers.

It was difficult, on the basis of interviews conducted primarily with managers of FTCs, to ascertain the extent to which various incentives had contributed to decisions to enter into or expand exporting. Several new firms had been established after 1980, and those were clearly export-oriented from the outset. Firms engaged in importing metal scrap to produce and export iron and steel were the most prominent group, judging from the interviews. In general, however, it appeared that those new or greatly expanded activities that had emerged had done so largely in the existing large industrial houses.

One other feature regarding the initial line of inquiry of the interviews should be mentioned. Contrasted with earlier years and interview experience, the 1989 interviews were especially impressive in one regard: managers were generally well informed about international market conditions and their competitive situation in the world market. In earlier periods Turkish businessmen naturally focused primarily on prospects in the domestic market and were often only vaguely aware of developments in major producer and consumer countries. In 1989, however, that situation had changed dramatically. Even for products for which exports had just begun, knowledge of the intricacies of the various national and regional markets was impressive. While it is naturally impossible to form a judgment about the accuracy or completeness of information, the contrast with earlier indications of lack of interest and unawareness was striking.

Turning then to the questions regarding the administration of export incentives, those interviewed uniformly reported ease in obtaining access to the various incentives. In some instances managers indicated that they simply did not bother to attempt to take advantage of some of the incentives, but these were usually the new and very small incentives. In general, managers reported that, for established houses that had built a reputation of reliability with government officials, paperwork was fairly simple and straightforward, and responses from government officials were rapid. For example, to be able to import free of duty, would-be exporters had to file an export pledge for the coming year. In return they received an exporter's certificate. When they imported, this certificate simply had to be presented, and exports were later recorded against it. There was no reported instance of bureaucratic delays or of other difficulties with this mechanism. One exporter presented us with a list, however, which had been prepared for government officials, of thirty-three steps and procedures that exporters had to go through to export, claiming that paperwork was still very excessive.[20]

When it came to receipt of rebates and other payments of subsidy amounts, there were reports and complaints of delays. In part these were attributable to the high cost of borrowing money when the real interest rate was positive with an inflation running at about 70 percent annually.

Many managers noted the difficulties they were encountering because of the real appreciation of the lira since the beginning of 1989. Those who did not mention the problem were asked about it. In a few instances managers volunteered or responded that they were already experiencing lowered export orders or shipments. In most instances, however, managers indicated concern about the real appreciation of the lira but also voiced their conviction that the authorities would soon correct the problem. When questioned about the authorities' actions and what they might do, the virtually universal response was to suggest that a significant exchange rate correction would be forthcoming.[21]

The degree of conviction that the government would adhere to its export and market-oriented policies was impressive. Although some managers expressed the view that the authorities might be surprised by the negative export response if the real appreciation continued while other export incentives were being reduced, none provided the slightest suggestion that the commitment to exporting had diminished. When asked whether the government might decide to sacrifice export performance to contain inflation, the response was unanimous that the commitment to exports would not be compromised.

If interviews had been the only basis on which to form a judgment about short-term economic prospects in Turkey late in 1989, one would have come away fairly optimistic. Insofar as credibility is an important component of a reform of a trade and payments regime, the

Turkish government had certainly made its commitment to the new, outer-oriented policies completely credible.

Imports during the 1980s

In most regards Turkish import performance during the 1980s is much less remarkable and requires much less analysis than export behavior. Although imports had accounted for as much as 28 percent of GNP in 1976 (while exports were only 9 percent), they had fallen to 14.9 percent in 1979 and 15.1 in 1980. One of the characteristics of Turkey's economic performance during the 1980s that differentiates it strongly from that of most developing countries is that in Turkey, both imports and exports increased in relative importance throughout the period. By 1982 imports were equal to 17.7 percent of GNP, and by 1986 and 1987 they had reached 23.9 and 26.2 percent of GNP. By 1989 imports had reached $15.8 billion, up from $7.9 billion in 1980.

Thus the change in trade policy in Turkey was mirrored by a structural change. Both exports and imports grew as a percentage of GNP, although imports did not increase their share nearly as much as exports, with an average annual rate of growth of 8 percent in dollar terms from 1980 to 1989.[22] Except for the general liberalization of imports, there is little to be noted about the commodity composition of imports. The dollar value of imports of petroleum and petroleum products fell during the interval, reflecting the decline in the price of oil. Whereas these imports had accounted for $3.86 billion of imports in 1980 (of total imports of $7.9 billion), by 1989 they were only $2.95 billion (of total imports of $15.8 billion).

The big structural shifts, therefore, were the increase in the overall share of imports and the reduced relative and absolute importance of petroleum and petroleum products. The growth rates of individual two-digit import categories show little that is remarkable (see Data Appendix Table 15). The most rapidly growing import categories were hides and leather (84.1 percent annually), cement (50 percent), non-ferrous metals (19.1 percent), and iron and steel (19.3 percent). This last undoubtedly reflects the imports of scrap iron and steel for purposes of reforging and reexporting. All other two-digit import categories increased at annual rates in excess of 10 percent except for petroleum and petroleum products, mining and quarrying products, and chemical products. The low overall rate of growth of imports—8 percent—masks the true increase because of the decline in petroleum imports.

The Balance of Payments and Foreign Debt

The Balance of Payments

To a considerable degree the Turkish experience of the 1980s with the balance of payments must be deemed a success. Not only did exports and imports increase rapidly, but the exchange regime was substantially liberalized. The premium in the black market over the official exchange rate had virtually disappeared by the mid-1980s (Data Appendix Table 19). The restrictions governing transfers of foreign exchange were sharply reduced, and full convertibility was announced as a goal.

Table 16 in the Data Appendix gives data on the balance of payments from 1975 to 1988. The most striking feature is the simultaneous growth of both exports and imports: the trade balance was a negative $4.6 billion in 1980, fell to minus $2.6 billion by 1982, and was in the range of minus $2.9 to $3.1 billion in every subsequent year, until 1988, when it fell to a deficit of $1.8 billion.

Regarding other items in the current account, tourism expenditures by Turks abroad increased sharply as restrictions were reduced. Tourist expenditures in Turkey also increased, however, so that the balance on tourist account turned more positive as the 1980s progressed. As with exports and imports, the major effect was a structural change, with more tourism in both directions.

Among the nontrade components of the current account, however, the biggest change was in interest payments to foreigners on debt-service account. These rose from $1.1 billion in 1980 to $2.8 billion in 1988. This reflected both rescheduled debt-servicing obligations in the early 1980s and the large and growing Turkish debt, to which we return below.

Turning to transfers and factor payments, workers' remittances to Turkey increased sharply after 1978, peaking at $2.5 billion in 1981. Thereafter they fell off. In part this was because some part of the 1981 figure reflected delayed remittances that were effected once the exchange rate was altered. In part, too, the number of Turkish workers abroad was declining as the major West European countries that had been employing Turkish workers were experiencing high levels of unemployment.

The net effect of exports, imports, and other current account trans-actions is reflected in the current account balance, given in Data Appendix Table 16. From a maximum deficit of $3.4 billion in 1980, the deficit fell to $935 million in 1982 but thereafter increased, averag-ing about $1.4 billion in the years 1983 through 1986. It fell in 1987 and again in 1988, when the Turkish current account reached a positive $1.5 billion. Although 1989 balance-of-payments figures are not yet available, Turkish reserves increased once again in 1989, suggesting that there may once again have been a current account surplus.

For present purposes what is important is to note that the 1980 devaluation and liberalization package resulted in a fairly immediate and sharp drop in the current account deficit but that thereafter Turkey maintained a fairly constant current account balance for the next several years. After 1984 the noninterest current account was positive, as other receipts were sufficient to cover current account noninterest payments and a portion of the interest on the debt. By 1988, of course, the non-interest current account surplus was large enough to cover all interest charges and to reduce debt somewhat.

The Role of Borrowing and Debt Service

For present purposes the significant fact is that the required financ-ing for the external deficit from 1980 to 1987 necessarily originated primarily from new borrowing. Indeed, accumulation of foreign exchange reserves in 1986 and 1987 implied that borrowing in those years exceeded the amount that would have financed the current account deficit.

Some observers have suggested that Turkey's very successful macroeconomic growth performance of the 1980s was attributable to the increased imports that were financed in part by accumulation of additional debt.[23] It is important, therefore, to consider two issues. On one hand, there is a question about how much borrowing (or equivalent means of financing a current account deficit) there was. On the other hand, there is a question about the importance of the current account deficit in permitting a resumption of economic growth during the 1980s.

A first step is to consider how much new borrowing there was.[24] The evolution of Turkish debt is shown in Table 37. From $19.0 billion in 1980, Turkish debt rose by less than $1.0 billion by the end of 1982. Even in 1984, it grew by only $1.3 billion. Thereafter, however,

Table 37

Turkish Debt and Debt Service, 1980–1988

	1980	1981	1982	1983	1984	1985	1986	1987	1988
Magnitude of debt (billions of U.S. dollars)									
Total debt	19.0	19.2	19.7	20.3	21.6	26.0	32.8	40.8	38.7
Long-term	15.5	15.7	16.5	16.4	16.9	19.9	24.8	31.3	30.7
Short-term	2.5	2.3	1.8	2.3	3.2	4.8	6.9	8.7	7.7
IMF	1.1	1.3	1.5	1.6	1.4	1.3	1.1	.8	.3
Debt service indicators (ratios)									
Debt/exports	6.54	4.08	3.34	3.44	2.92	3.15	4.32	3.95	3.27
Debt service/exports	0.38	0.38	0.40	0.40	0.32	0.45	0.46	0.48	0.56

Source: Data Appendix Table 17.

it rose $6.8 billion in 1986 and $8.0 billion in 1987 and then declined $2 billion in 1988 (reflecting the current account surplus of that year).[25] In analyzing the role of new borrowing in Turkish economic developments during the 1980s, therefore, it seems clear that a sharp distinction should be made between the period 1980–1983, when new loans received by Turkey were negligible, and the period 1985–1987, when borrowing on a fairly large scale recommenced.

Considering the former period first, there does not seem to be any basis on which to conclude that Turkish receipts of new money were quantitatively more important than those obtained by other heavily indebted countries. Although Turkey had restored credit worthiness by the mid-1980s, the additional borrowing that took place between 1980 and 1983 is less, relative to exports or to outstanding debt, than that received (involuntarily) by Mexico, Chile, and a number of other heavily indebted countries. Thus the numbers are simply not there to indicate that foreign borrowing was significant in the early years after the 1980 reforms.

After 1984, however, the situation changed markedly, as Turkish borrowing and outstanding debt service accelerated rapidly. Not by coincidence, this also marked the turning point in public sector behavior: until 1984 public consumption and investment as a percentage of GNP were declining (from 25.8 percent in 1980 to 21.7 percent in 1984). Thereafter, however, the trend was reversed. Public sector expenditures on consumption and investment rose from their 1984 low to 23.9 percent in 1985 and 24.5 percent in 1986.

Thus to a considerable degree additional borrowing financed increased governmental expenditures in the mid-1980s.[26] Clearly, the same level of government expenditures financed by domestic borrowing would have been more inflationary; the question remains whether the increased expenditures resulted in more rapid growth than would otherwise have occurred or whether the inflation tax incurred thereby may not have been greater.[27]

Either way, the fact remains that Turkey was able to borrow in large part because of its export performance. Had exports grown only slowly during the 1980s, it seems clear that Turkey would have faced the same borrowing constraint that afflicted most heavily indebted countries: private creditors would have refused additional credit. Thus it is irrelevant for purposes of the present analysis whether the additional borrowing in the mid-1980s prevented crowding out of private investment and thus permitted accelerated growth or whether it financed an unnecessary and undesirable increase in public sector investment that did not materially affect the growth rate. Turkey's experience was different because Turkish exports grew rapidly. Credit worthiness permitted borrowing because of the trade policy reforms and the boost they gave to export performance.

Overall Macroeconomic Performance

There is little doubt that by the mid-1980s a structural shift of major magnitude, increasing the share of both exports and imports in GNP and opening up the Turkish economy, was taking place. In this respect the policy reforms introduced by the Turkish authorities in 1980 and continued throughout the decade were successful. Even the most severe critics of the Turkish policies recognize the successful reorientation of the economy toward the international economy resulting from liberalizing the trade regime and removing the heavy incentives for import substitution.

It will be recalled, however, that the policy reforms were instituted with several objectives in mind: certainly it was intended to open up the economy and to increase the efficiency of resource utilization by increasing incentives for exports relative to import substitution. Further, it was clearly intended that the relative role of the private sector in the economy should increase and that of the public sector be diminished. Related to that, it was also intended that macroeconomic stabilization would take place and with it a sharp reduction in the rate of inflation. While these were the stated goals of the entire program, there is little doubt that the architects of reforms undertook them because they believed that in the longer term the Turkish economy would grow more rapidly and deliver higher economic well-being to Turks as a result of them.

The focus of this work has been on the policy reforms relating to trade and payments. If the opening up of the economy must be judged, at least to date, however, as having been largely successful, more questions may be asked about the progress of reforms on other fronts.[28] It would not be appropriate, therefore, to reach a verdict with respect to the attainment of structural reforms in the trade sector without at least a cursory examination of the outcome with respect to other objectives.

Such a review must of necessity be briefer and more superficial than our analysis of the trade reforms and their outcomes. It is useful to start by reviewing the growth of real GNP and its major components. Table 38 gives data on the the major macroeconomic variables and their evolution during the 1980s.

The first years of the 1980s witnessed rapid growth of exports but relatively slow growth of real GNP. To be sure, real GNP rose, which was a welcome contrast with the late 1970s, when it was falling. It was also a contrast with many other developing countries in the midst of the worldwide recession. Even on a per capita basis, real incomes were rising in every year after 1980. It was not until 1984, however, that growth accelerated. Thereafter growth rates were highly respectable by any standard.

In the early 1980s observers had been concerned that investment was stagnant and not increasing, even when output growth accelerated. That this was the case is confirmed by the data in Table 38. Real investment was quite sluggish until 1985 but accelerated thereafter. Thus the early years of rapid export growth were accomplished largely out of existing capacity; it would appear that not until the mid-1980s was the reoriented trade regime consistent with an increase in real investment.

Other aspects of the reforms also met with mixed results. Manufacturing employment was generally thought to have grown very slowly, and real wages appear to have fallen.[29] This was at least in part a consequence of the 1980 decree that prohibited employers from laying off workers. To the extent that there was involuntary employment by employers in 1980–1983, that would have permitted later expansion with few new hires.

Even in the early 1980s there was rapid growth of investment and output of utilities and transport. As a result, industrial employment grew considerably faster than manufacturing employment, rising from 2.0 million persons employed in industry in 1981 to 2.3 million in 1985 and to 2.6 million in 1989. The growth in exports over the 1980–1984 period appears to have originated largely out of excess capacity, as little new investment in manufacturing industries for exports appears to have been taking place before about 1985. On one hand, the achievement of the increase in manufacturing output discussed earlier without additional investment or employment attests to the increases in economic efficiency that may have resulted from the policy reforms of the early 1980s.

Table 38

Indicators of Macroeconomic Performance, 1980–1989 (percentages)

	1980	1981	1982	1983	1984	1985	1986	1987	1988	1989
Real GNP growth	-1.1	4.2	4.5	3.3	5.9	5.1	8.1	7.4	3.7	1.7
Growth of real investment[a]	-6.9	1.8	3.2	2.9	-0.1	16.8	11.0	5.5	-1.6	-3.4
Rate of growth of exports	28.7	61.6	22.2	-0.3	24.5	11.6	-6.3	36.7	14.4	-0.3
Increase in consumer price index[b]	110	37	27	31	48	50	37	39	-5	70
Increase in GDP deflator[c]	104	42	28	29	51	41	30	40	66	65

a. In 1988 prices.
b. 1978/79 = 100.
c. 1968 = 100.

Source: See Data Appendix Tables 1, 2, 11, 12, and 14.

175

On the other hand, given the rapid growth of the Turkish labor force, the growth of employment opportunities was disappointing. Manufacturing employment failed to grow rapidly at least before 1985, and the reported unemployment rate rose from 10.7 percent in 1980 (already up from the 7–8 percent range in the mid-1970s) to a peak of 11.8 percent in 1984. These data reflect the failure of the export boom to generate large gains for the labor force in the short run, again in unknown part because of the earlier prohibition against layoffs.[30] Only after 1985 did employment rise rapidly enough to begin bringing down the unemployment rate. Even in 1988 it stood above its 1980 level.

This led to concerns, which still continue, about the impact of the policy reform on income distribution in Turkey. The real wage rose very slowly in the early 1980s, and there was considerable concern about real incomes of the urban poor.[31]

Other areas in which there were mixed results were the rate of inflation and the size of government in the economy. Government expenditures were 25 percent of GNP in 1980. They fell to a low of 18.9 percent in 1985 and rose thereafter to the 21–22 percent range for the following three years. Moreover, the fiscal deficit rose from its low of 1.7 percent of GNP in 1981 to 3.0 percent in 1983 and 5.3 percent in 1984. Thereafter it was once again sharply reduced to 2.8 percent of GNP in 1985 but rose to 3.6 and 4.5 percent of GNP in the following two years. In 1989 it stood at 2.6 percent of GNP.[32] The reasons for this were numerous: interest payments on domestic and foreign debt were a factor, but so, too, were increased government expenditures before each election.

For present purposes the important point is to note how well the rises and falls in the rate of inflation, reported in Table 38, mirror the changes in the fiscal deficit.

To the extent that the large gains achieved by the reorientation of Turkish economic activity toward the international economy are threatened, it is the failure to achieve a lower rate of inflation that constitutes the most visible threat. It is to that subject that we now turn.

Postscript

By 1989 it was clear that the failure of the Özal government to reduce the rate of inflation sufficiently was a major political issue, and the elections of that year showed greatly decreased support for the Motherland party. By that time, too, additional measures were being taken in an attempt to control inflation. As is evident from the 1982 and 1986 declines in the inflation rate, this is not the first such effort. Each inflationary round since 1980 has reached a higher rate of inflation than the preceding one before restrictive monetary and fiscal policies were adopted, and the low, before the next acceleration of inflation, has been successively higher.

Until 1989, however, the exchange rate was managed in such a way that the real value of the Turkish lira was not permitted to appreciate in response to changes in the domestic price level. In 1989, however, the nominal exchange rate changed by approximately half the rate of inflation. There was already a marked slowdown in the rate of growth of exports, although special factors—including reduced exports to Iraq attendant on the end of the Iran-Iraq war and the phasing out of some special export incentives—undoubtedly contributed to the outcome.

Nonetheless, it can hardly be questioned that a real appreciation of over 30 percent between 1988 and 1990 must have made exporting considerably less attractive than it had previously been. Although part of this real appreciation may have been the result of market forces,[33] it is also possible that depreciation of the lira was deliberately slowed down as an anti-inflationary device.

Resolution of the inflation problem for Turkey therefore is not only a political necessity but also essential for achieving a more stable real exchange rate. Should real appreciation continue, even if at a lower rate than in 1989, it is difficult to imagine that exporting will remain profitable, and, of course, importing will become increasingly attractive.[34]

Although the commitment of the authorities to the export orientation and the maintenance of the real exchange rate had achieved impressive credibility by 1989, it is not clear how much longer real appreciation of the currency can continue without a significant shift in expectations and hence in behavior. The outlook, therefore, is uncertain. Should the authorities succeed in greatly reducing the rate of inflation and in stabilizing the real value of the lira at a realistic level, there is every reason to expect continued rapid growth of the Turkish economy based on its new trade orientation and incentive structure. If, however, inflation should accelerate once again after the very small dip experienced late in 1989 and the nominal exchange rate should continue to alter by significantly less than the domestic price level, the policy package would be unsustainable. Should expectations shift toward the latter outcome as the more likely, major difficulties for the Turkish economy could quickly emerge.

Appendix: Persons Interviewed in Istanbul, November 1989

We wish to express our gratitude to all those who assisted us by granting interviews and providing excellent hospitality while patiently answering our many questions in November 1989. A mere listing of them fails to indicate the extent of our appreciation or of the degree to which the analysis of this entire manuscript has benefited by the insights gained through interviews.

Our thanks are extended to the following:

Turhan Alpan, Assistant General Manager, G. S. D. Diş Ticaret, A.Ş.

Latif Anbarlı, General Manager, Ekinciler Diş Ticaret, A. Ş.

Haluk Aral, Assistant General Manager, Exsa Export Sanayi Mamülleri Satiş ve Araştırma, A. Ş.

Farah Aydın, Export Manager, Tamek Gıda Sanayi, A. Ş.

Feyyaz Berker, Head, Board of Managers, Tekfen Holding, A. Ş.

Bedirhan Çelik, General Coordinator, Otomarsan, A. Ş.

Bülent Demircioğlu, Member, Board of Managers, Planning and Sales Coordinator

Murat Dervişoğlu, Assistant General Manager, Gönen Gıda Sanayi, A. Ş.

Nusret Fırıncı, Undersecretariat of Foreign Trade

Günal Eray, Foreign Trade Financing Manager, De-Sa Deri Sanayi ve Ticaret, A. Ş.

Hasan Esen, General Coordinator, EDPA Pazarlama, A. S.

Hüseyin Günes, Export Manager, Ülker, Istanbul, Gıda Diş Ticaret, A. Ş.

Mehmet Kabasakal, Member, Istanbul Hazır Giyim ve Konfeksiyon İhracatçıları Birliği

Ali Haydar Sayıner, Assistant General Manager, Kaleporselen Elektronik Sanayi, A. Ş.

Selim Kalafat, General Manager, Kaleflex-Kale Export, A. Ş.

Çelik Kurdoğlu, Director, DE İ K—Foreign Economic Relations Board of Turkey

Hüsamettin Onanç, General Manager, EKOM Eczacıbaşı Diş
   Ticaret, A. Ş.
İbrahim Öngüt, Assistant General Manager, Türkiye Sinai Kalkınma
   Bankası
Fasih Öven, Board of Managers, Çolakoğlu Diş Ticaret, A. Ş.
Abdullah Pişkin, General Manager, Ekinciler Diş Ticaret, A. Ş.
Murat Toksuz, Foreign Relations Manager, Oyak Renault.
Şafak Türkay, General Manager, Altınel Melamin Sanayi, A. Ş.
Refik Üner, Assistant General Manager, Profilo Holding, A. Ş.
Kamil Uras, Assistant General Manager, Tamek Gıda Sanayi, A. Ş.
Nedim Uzman, General Manager, Cam Pazarlama, A. Ş.

Data Appendix

The tables that follow provide basic data on the Turkish economy, with emphasis on the period from 1975 to 1989.

For several data sets there is no consistent, long-term time series available. Wherever possible, two separate time series have been linked to provide a continuous series. In a few instances (for example, real investment, Table 2), it proved impossible to do so, and two estimates are presented for the year in which the series changed. In other cases two sets of estimates are presented. This is either because a more reliable or later source is available for later years (for example Tables 17 and 18, Turkish debt), or because alternative sources provide breakdowns not available in the other (for example, Tables 5 and 6, where Turkish data provide a breakdown of private and public investment while OECD data provide more information about the role of trade in GNP). In a few instances (Table 3, labor force) earlier data were deemed unreliable, and data are presented only for the 1980s.

It is the practice of most statistics-issuing ministries in Turkey to issue preliminary estimates and then to follow with several revisions. Thus, when we cite "third preliminary" or "third provisional" estimates, the number has been revised twice. In general, almost all data after 1985 were still being revised at the time of writing, although revisions tended, in most instances, to be small.

Table 1

Gross National Product by Kind of Economic Activity, 1975–1989

	1975	1976	1977	1978	1979	1980	1981	1982	1983	1984	1985	1986	1987	1988	1989
(1968 constant prices; billions of Turkish liras)															
Agriculture, forestry, fishing	39.7	42.7	42.2	43.3	44.5	45.3	45.3	48.2	48.1	49.8	51.0	55.1	56.2	60.8	54.0
Industry	35.6	39.2	43.1	46.0	43.4	40.8	43.9	46.0	49.7	54.7	58.1	63.2	69.2	71.4	73.6
Services	84.6	92.2	97.4	101.3	101.6	102.4	106.2	109.9	114.3	120.3	125.1	133.2	142.2	148.0	153.8
GDP (factor cost)	159.9	174.1	182.7	190.6	189.5	188.5	195.3	204.2	212.1	224.9	234.3	251.4	267.7	280.2	281.4
Net income from abroad	3.6	2.5	1.8	1.9	2.9	2.2	1.8	1.0	0.1	0.6	0.6	0.0	0.1	-0.4	1.8
Indirect taxes less subsidies	17.8	19.1	18.9	16.7	16.0	15.4	17.5	19.3	19.7	20.2	23.3	27.6	31.9	31.1	33.1
GNP (market prices)	181.4	195.8	203.4	209.5	208.3	206.1	214.7	224.4	231.9	245.6	258.2	279.0	239.7	310.9	316.3
(real rates of growth)															
Agriculture, forestry, fishing		7.6	-1.2	2.6	2.8	1.8	0.0	6.4	-0.2	3.5	2.4	8.0	2.0	8.2	-11.2
Industry		10.1	9.9	6.7	-5.7	-6.0	7.6	4.8	8.0	10.1	6.2	8.8	9.5	3.2	3.1
Services		9.0	5.6	4.0	0.3	0.8	3.7	3.5	4.0	5.2	4.0	6.5	6.8	4.1	3.9
GNP (market prices)		7.9	4.0	3.0	-0.6	-1.1	4.2	4.5	3.3	5.9	5.1	8.1	7.4	3.7	1.7
(percentages of GDP)															
Agriculture, forestry, fishing	24.8	24.5	23.1	22.7	23.5	24.0	23.2	23.6	22.7	22.2	21.8	21.9	21.0	21.7	19.2
Industry	22.3	22.5	23.6	24.1	22.9	21.6	22.5	22.5	23.4	24.3	24.8	25.1	25.8	25.5	26.2
Services	52.9	53.0	53.3	53.1	53.6	54.3	54.4	53.8	53.9	53.5	53.4	53.0	53.1	52.8	54.7

Source: State Planning Organization, *Main Economic Indicators*, December 1988 and June 1990.

Table 2

Real Fixed Investment, 1979–1989 (1988 prices; billions of Turkish liras)

Industry	1979	1980	1981	1982	1983	1984	1985-1	1985-2	1986	1987	1988	1989	Annual growth (%) 1980–1989	Total investment (%) 1980	Total investment (%) 1989
Private sector															
Agriculture	508	563	718	784	839	857	716	734	644	776	681	490	2.1	3.5	2.1
Mining	101	75	75	82	86	89	112	114	123	166	179	181	10.2	0.5	0.8
Manufacturing	2,772	2,370	2,323	2,337	2,360	2,499	2,652	2,706	3,081	2,953	2,975	2,830	2.6	14.6	12.1
Utilities	47	39	41	43	45	51	46	47	116	108	174	138	18.2	0.2	0.6
Transport	542	729	941	1,061	1,160	1,320	1,441	1,475	1,388	1,438	1,342	1,242	7.0	4.5	5.3
Tourism	42	44	45	47	50	94	172	176	284	421	608	833	34.0	0.3	3.6
Housing	3,170	2,622	1,712	1,794	1,884	2,050	2,355	2,404	3,287	4,754	6,141	6,683	9.9	16.2	28.6
Education	18	12	12	13	13	15	29	30	41	52	55	75	18.9	0.1	0.3
Health	17	13	14	15	15	16	38	39	57	68	56	81	17.3	0.1	0.3
Other	347	272	284	290	297	327	356	365	397	431	447	450	5.7	1.7	1.9
Total private	7,566	6,738	6,165	6,466	6,749	7,318	7,918	8,090	9,417	11,166	12,656	13,002	7.3	41.5	55.7
Public sector															
Agriculture	656	592	915	988	838	792	685	755	858	1,089	1,046	987	6.5	3.6	4.2
Mining	940	775	1,064	879	1,050	1,000	1,298	1,358	985	550	510	375	-4.5	4.8	1.6
Manufacturing	2,566	2,815	2,576	2,166	2,095	1,730	1,851	1,911	1,533	915	678	560	-14.6	17.3	2.4
Utilities	2,305	2,250	2,349	2,621	2,897	2,700	3,003	3,023	3,451	3,151	3,080	2,888	3.6	13.9	12.4

(continued on next page)

Transport	2,049	1,820	1,929	2,251	2,379	2,441	3,539	3,534	4,025	4,495	3,421	3,055	7.3	11.2	13.1
Tourism	73	45	55	49	59	76	128	99	239	226	181	152	16.6	0.3	0.7
Housing	226	157	211	154	156	226	286	289	262	202	208	217	3.2	1.0	0.9
Education	276	280	344	419	371	326	417	471	497	629	654	667	9.9	1.7	2.9
Health	145	132	180	198	142	130	118	134	154	197	205	233	5.0	0.8	1.0
Other	641	628	739	858	809	784	1,225	1,321	1,863	1,941	1,528	1,201	10.4	3.9	5.1
Total public	9,877	9,493	10,362	10,584	10,796	10,205	12,549	12,893	13,864	13,394	11,510	10,333	2.2	58.5	44.3
Total Investment	17,443	16,231	16,527	17,050	17,545	17,523	20,467	20,983	23,281	24,560	24,166	23,335	4.5	100.0	100.0

Note: The series was revised, but earlier years are not available. Therefore 1985-1 gives the data given in 1989 for 1985; 1985-2 gives the data given in 1990 for 1985.
Source: State Planning Organization, *Main Economic Indicators*, April 1989, for 1981 to 1985-1; *Main Economic Indicators*, May 1990, for 1985-2 through 1989.

Table 3

Labor Force, Employment, and Unemployment, 1981–1989 (thousands of persons)

	1981	1982	1983	1984	1985	1986	1987	1988	1989
Labor force									
Civilian labor force	15,959	16,306	16,662	17,024	17,395	17,708	18,027	18,350	18,680
Civilian employment	14,106	14,393	14,649	15,019	15,360	15,845	16,316	16,550	16,773
Unemployed	1,853	1,914	2,014	2,005	2,034	1,866	1,710	1,800	1,947
Employment by sector									
Agriculture	7,673	7,787	7,852	7,975	8,095	8,206	8,321	8,369	8,380
Industry	1,996	2,052	2,117	2,204	2,271	2,388	2,494	2,512	2,561
Mining	190	190	188	192	202	216	219	214	226
Manufacturing	1,705	1,759	1,821	1,902	1,954	2,052	2,151	2,170	2,205
Electricity utilities	100	104	107	111	115	120	124	128	130
Services	4,437	4,554	4,680	4,839	4,995	5,248	5,501	5,669	5,792
Construction	703	706	710	723	743	798	847	866	887
Transport, communications	526	532	541	563	581	604	628	640	700
Commerce	1,298	1,334	1,381	1,440	1,493	1,575	1,658	1,692	1,648
Financial services	308	312	325	336	346	357	367	381	388
Other services	1,601	1,670	1,724	1,777	1,833	1,914	2,000	2,090	2,169
Percentage growth									
Civilian employment		2.0	1.8	2.5	2.3	3.2	3.0	1.4	1.3
Industrial employment		2.8	3.2	4.1	3.0	5.2	4.4	0.7	2.0

Source: State Planning Organization, *Main Economic Indicators*, May 1990, p. 115.

184

Table 4

Indexes of Manufacturing Production, 1981–1989 (1986 = 100)

	1981	1982	1983	1984	1985	1986	1987	1988	1989	Average annual growth (%) 1981–89
Food processing	82.5	94.8	100.6	101.2	98.9	100.0	111.7	114.3	119.1	4.7
Beverages	105.6	102.5	114.9	105.9	94.5	100.0	112.5	127.0	144.9	2.7
Tobacco processing	111.7	105.5	110.7	115.4	115.9	100.0	98.2	102.6	107.8	-1.2
Textiles	70.9	70.2	77.7	85.0	90.9	100.0	109.4	113.3	118.4	6.9
Wearing apparel	69.4	84.4	83.6	84.5	77.0	100.0	108.2	105.6	89.2	6.2
Hides and leather	103.6	96.3	100.5	78.5	76.2	100.0	69.4	70.0	103.1	-5.4
Footwear	136.8	87.3	94.7	98.9	91.2	100.0	118.0	74.9	93.4	-8.2
Wood products	79.9	80.9	88.2	87.8	90.8	100.0	104.4	101.4	103.5	3.5
Paper and products	68.7	76.3	75.0	91.9	94.1	100.0	113.7	112.3	110.7	7.3
Printing	109.1	123.9	108.7	98.8	102.3	100.0	104.0	96.3	84.1	-1.8
Chemicals	57.6	59.6	71.9	74.5	78.4	100.0	115.1	118.2	118.7	10.8
Petrol refining	71.9	85.6	84.7	95.0	94.1	100.0	115.3	119.0	112.9	7.5
Rubber products	63.8	67.5	79.6	95.7	95.5	100.0	103.2	111.5	102.1	8.3
Plastic products	71.9	83.5	79.5	81.7	87.6	100.0	113.9	104.0	118.4	5.4
Pottery and china	62.2	56.5	62.3	79.7	85.5	100.0	119.7	141.8	152.5	12.5
Glass and products	65.1	77.8	79.5	89.8	95.1	100.0	116.9	127.7	134.9	10.1

(continued on next page)

(continued)

Table 4

	1981	1982	1983	1984	1985	1986	1987	1988	1989	Average annual growth (%) 1981–89
Cement and other	70.9	69.7	64.3	74.8	83.4	100.0	107.5	109.8	110.5	6.4
Iron and steel	43.4	50.5	61.7	74.7	81.4	100.0	116.8	121.4	117.9	15.8
Nonferrous metal	53.8	65.3	63.5	81.1	94.7	100.0	97.0	81.3	99.0	6.1
Metal products	67.6	63.0	65.7	81.7	86.1	100.0	113.8	120.4	123.5	8.6
Machinery	92.0	93.8	103.1	109.8	99.4	100.0	122.1	110.9	106.6	2.7
Electric machinery	30.5	31.0	42.3	64.0	83.4	100.0	98.8	80.7	85.8	14.9
Transport equipment	56.5	69.6	87.9	93.6	98.0	100.0	105.8	106.0	97.5	9.4
Total industry	65.1	70.3	76.2	84.5	89.5	100.0	110.5	112.3	116.4	8.1

Source: State Institute of Statistics, *Industrial Production Indexes 1989* (III–IV).

Table 5

GNP by Expenditure Category, 1975–1988 (1987 prices using 1968 relative prices; billions of Turkish liras)

	1975	1976	1977	1978	1979	1980	1981	1982	1983	1984	1985	1986	1987	1988
Consumption	25,946.4	27,501.6	29,898.6	31,078.7	30,882.8	29,628.5	29,572.1	31,287.6	33,350.3	35,458.9	36,008.2	39,769.9	42,628.6	43,797.0
Private	23,224.5	24,588.4	26,835.1	27,569.2	27,511.8	25,710.4	25,430.0	27,861.2	29,207.5	31,316.3	31,654.8	34,887.7	37,373.9	38,375.4
Public	2,721.9	2,913.2	3,063.5	3,509.5	3,371.0	3,918.1	4,142.1	3,426.4	4,142.8	4,142.6	4,343.4	4,882.2	5,254.7	5,421.6
Investment	10,561.1	12,757.9	13,287.0	11,607.4	11,260.2	10,085.3	10,017.3	9,984.6	10,223.4	10,239.9	11,954.7	13,399.9	13,886.2	14,998.8
Private	5,074.5	6,138.5	6,072.3	5,705.2	4,915.7	4,079.9	3,717.0	3,895.5	4,057.5	4,399.5	4,761.8	5,492.4	5,336.1	7,086.9
Public	5,486.6	6,619.4	7,214.7	5,902.2	6,344.5	6,005.4	6,300.3	6,089.1	6,165.9	5,840.4	7,192.9	7,907.5	7,550.1	7,911.9
Stock changes	829.9	988.7	318.2	-1,195.8	-1,086.4	830.2	1,129.0	273.5	474.8	644.9	413.3	705.1	61.2	497.3
GNP	33,963.6	36,659.7	38,082.7	39,168.6	39,000.1	38,588.2	40,198.4	42,014.5	43,418.7	45,983.8	48,342.9	52,199.8	55,757.2	58,545.1
Percentage change														
Consumption		6.0	8.7	3.9	-0.6	-4.1	-0.2	5.8	6.6	6.3	1.5	10.4	7.2	2.7
Private		5.9	9.1	2.7	-0.2	-6.5	-1.1	9.6	4.8	7.2	1.1	10.2	7.1	2.7
Public		7.0	5.2	14.6	-3.9	16.2	5.7	-17.3	20.9	0.0	4.8	12.4	7.6	3.2
Investment		20.8	4.1	-12.6	-3.0	-10.4	-0.7	-0.3	2.4	0.2	16.7	12.1	3.6	8.0
Private		21.0	-1.1	-6.0	-13.8	-17.0	-8.9	4.8	4.2	8.4	8.2	15.3	15.4	11.8
Public		20.6	9.0	-18.2	7.5	-5.3	4.9	-3.4	1.3	-5.3	23.2	9.9	-4.5	4.8
GNP		7.9	3.9	2.9	-0.4	-1.1	4.2	4.5	3.3	5.9	5.1	8.0	6.8	5.0

(continued on next page)

(continued)

Table 5

	1975	1976	1977	1978	1979	1980	1981	1982	1983	1984	1985	1986	1987	1988
Share of GNP														
Consumption	76.4	75.0	78.5	79.3	79.2	76.8	73.6	74.5	76.8	77.1	74.5	76.2	76.5	74.8
Private	68.4	67.1	70.5	70.4	70.5	66.6	63.3	66.3	67.3	68.1	65.5	66.8	67.0	65.5
Public	8.0	7.9	8.0	9.0	8.6	10.2	10.3	8.2	9.5	9.0	9.0	9.4	9.4	9.3
Investment	31.1	34.8	34.9	29.6	28.9	26.1	24.9	23.8	23.5	22.3	24.7	25.7	24.9	25.6
Private	14.9	16.7	15.9	14.6	12.6	10.6	9.2	9.3	9.3	9.6	9.9	10.5	11.4	12.1
Public	16.2	18.1	18.9	15.1	16.3	15.6	15.7	14.5	14.2	12.7	14.9	15.1	13.5	13.5
Stock changes	2.4	2.7	0.8	-3.1	-2.8	2.2	2.8	0.7	1.1	1.4	0.9	1.4	0.1	0.8

Note: GNP growth differs marginally from Table 1 because of different base and sources.
Source: State Planning Organization, *V. Beş Yıllık Plan Destek Çalışmaları: 1, V. Beş Yıllık Kalkınma Plant Öncesinde Gelişmeler, 1972–1983* (pub. no. DPT 1975), January 1985; and State Planning Organization, *VI. Beş Yıllık Kalkınma Plant Öncesinde Gelişmeler 1984–1988*, n.d.

Table 6

Balance between Resources and Expenditures, 1975–1988 (1980 prices using 1982 relative prices; billions of Turkish liras)

	1975	1976	1977	1978	1979	1980	1981	1982	1983	1984	1985	1986	1987
Consumption	3,276.7	3,610.3	3,836.5	3,748.7	3,656.0	3,536.0	3,558.8	3,696.2	3,862.6	4,099,0	4,190,6	4,632,8	4,957,6
Private	2,885.4	3,176.8	3,389.1	3,257.0	3,156.0	2,991.9	3,009.8	3,136.2	3,293.1	3,529.5	3,573.3	3,938.8	4,215.7
Public	391.3	433.5	447.4	491.7	500.0	544.1	549.0	560.0	569.5	559.5	617.3	694.0	741.9
Investment	903.5	1,063.7	1,105.4	995.2	959.5	863.6	878.3	908.7	935.9	936.8	1,094.2	1,228.6	1,290.5
Stock changes	9.9	-9.5	-244.7	-418.2	-368.5	279.6	413.2	250.1	339.1	374.4	327.1	456.5	494.6
Trade deficit	621.1	805.1	847.4	444.5	375.5	351.2	237.6	145.5	201.0	186.1	156.8	338.8	323.6
Exports	276.9	380.9	297.9	336.4	295.2	317.1	514.4	704.3	807.0	972.0	1,081.8	1,075.3	1,340.9
Imports	898.0	1,186.0	1,145.3	780.9	670.7	668.3	752.0	849.8	1,008.0	1,158.1	1,238.6	1,414.1	1,664.5
Statistical discrepancy	203.1	240.5	427.6	581.1	489.0	0.0	-96.1	32.3	-18.9	-24.3	10.2	-58.6	-65.8
GDP	3,772.1	4,099.9	4,277.4	4,462.3	4,360.5	4,328.0	4,516.6	4,741.8	4,917.7	5,199.8	5,465.3	5,920.5	6,353.3
NFI	175.4	121.8	87.7	92.6	141.3	107.2	87.7	48.7	4.9	29.2	29.2	0.0	4.9
GNP	3,947.5	4,221.7	4,365.1	4,554.9	4,501.8	4,435.2	4,604.3	4,790.5	4,922.6	5,229.0	5,494.5	5,920.5	6,358.2
Population (millions)	40.4	40.9	41.8	42.8	43.7	44.7	45.8	46.8	47.8	48.8	49.8	50.9	52.0
GNP/capita (total)	97,711	103,220	104,428	106,422	103,016	99,221	100,531	102,362	102,983	107,152	110,332	116,316	122,273
Consumption/GNP	83.0	85.5	87.9	82.3	81.2	79.7	77.3	77.2	78.5	78.4	76.3	78.3	78.0
Investment/GNP	22.9	25.2	25.3	24.3	21.3	19.5	19.1	19.0	19.0	17.9	19.9	20.8	20.3

Note: NFI: net factor income; GNP growth differs marginally from Tables 1 and 5 because of different base and sources.
Source: OECD, *National Accounts—Main Aggregates: 1960–87.* Division between private and public investment not available from OECD.

Table 7

Consolidated Budget, 1979–1989 (billions of nominal Turkish liras)

	1979	1980	1981	1982	1983	1984	1985	1986	1987	1988	1989
Expenditures[a]	612.7	1,110.0	1,551.7	1,970.6	2,713.7	3,784.1	5,263.0	8,160.2	12,690.9	20,655.9	32,933.4
Current	262.0	497.1	645.1	861.2	1,057.0	1,487.9	2,086.0	3,051.0	4,537.5	7,387.3	11,224.9
Investment	94.7	169.6	310.4	410.1	462.5	676.5	989.0	1,619.1	2,289.9	2,951.4	5,287.6
Transfers	256.0	443.3	596.2	699.3	1,194.2	1,619.7	2,188.0	3,490.1	5,863.5	10,317.2	16,400.9
SEE s	83.4	152.9	229.6	204.9	292.0	274.6	180.7	138.0	445.6	1,013.5	1,108.2
Interest[b]	n.a.	n.a.	n.a.	n.a.	n.a.	375.0	595.0	1,081.5	2,266	4,978	8,259
Revenues[c]	525.6	933.4	1,439.9	1,773.4	2,369.5	2,805.2	4,476.0	6,753.5	10,092.7	17,215.9	28,456.3
Tax	405.5	749.8	1,190.2	1,521.7	1,931.9	2,372.0	3,829.0	5,972.1	9,051.0	14,267.5	24,370.0
Foreign trade tax[d]	69.8	73.3	114.0	145.6	254.7	377.5	585.3	993.2	1,777.7	2,822.1	n.a.
Nontax	120.1	183.6	249.7	251.7	437.6	433.2	647.0	781.4	1,041.7	2,948.4	1,916.3
Deficit	-87.1	-176.6	-111.8	-197.2	-344.2	-978.9	-787.0	-1,406.7	-2,598.2	-3,440.0	-4,477.1
Domestic borrowing	31.0	17.4	22.6	65.2	198.5	668.2	1,167.1	2,194.2	3,313.5	4,480.7	7,835.1
GNP	2,199.5	4,435.2	6,553.6	8,735.0	11,551.9	18,374.8	27,789.4	38,828.6	57,857.1	99,992.3	170,679.9
Percentage of total expenditures:											
Current	42.8	44.8	41.6	43.7	39.0	39.3	39.6	37.4	35.8	35.8	34.1
Investment	15.5	15.3	20.0	20.8	17.0	17.9	18.8	19.8	18.0	14.3	16.1
Transfers	41.8	39.9	38.4	35.5	44.0	42.8	41.6	42.8	46.2	49.9	49.8

(continued on next page)

190

SEEs	13.6	13.8	14.8	10.4	10.8	7.3	3.4	1.7	3.5	4.9	n.a.
Interest	n.a.	n.a.	n.a.	n.a.	n.a.	9.9	11.3	13.3	n.a.	n.a.	n.a.
Percentage of total revenue											
Tax receipts	77.1	80.3	82.7	85.8	81.5	84.6	85.5	88.4	89.7	82.9	85.6
Foreign trade taxes	13.3	7.9	7.9	8.2	10.7	13.5	13.1	14.7	17.6	15.4	n.a.
Nontax revenues	22.9	19.7	17.3	14.2	18.5	15.4	14.5	11.6	10.3	17.1	6.7
Ratios											
Government expenditure/GNP	27.9	25.0	23.7	22.6	23.5	20.6	18.9	21.0	21.9	20.7	19.3
Deficit/revenues	16.6	18.9	7.8	11.1	14.5	34.9	17.6	20.8	25.7	20.0	15.7
Deficit/GNP	4.0	4.0	1.7	2.3	3.0	5.3	2.8	3.6	4.5	3.4	2.6

a. 1989 figures are budget appropriations.

b. Interest figures are from Undersecretariat of Treasury and Foreign Trade, *Main Economic Indicators* (May 1990).

c. 1989 figures are provisional.

d. Source: SIS, *Statistical Yearbook*, various years, to 1989.

Source: 1984–1989, SPO, *Main Economic Indicators*, various issues, to May 1990; 1979–1983, DPT (SPO), *V. Beş Yıllık Kalkınma Planı Öncesinde Gelişmeler* (no. DPT: 1975), Ocak 1985.

Table 8

Money Supply and Credit, 1979–1989 (end of year, billions of Turkish liras)

	1979	1980	1981	1982	1983	1984	1985	1986	1987	1988	1989
Money supply (M4)	610	1,074	2,143	3,178	3,984	5,941	9,209	13,152	19,132	29,736	47,290
Currency and sight deposits (M1)	468	739	1,019	1,407	2,084	2,448	3,420	5,357	8,682	11,312	16,784
Time deposits	88	186	690	1,272	1,393	3,045	5,120	6,919	9,020	15,884	26,554
Total (M2)	556	924	1,710	2,679	3,477	5,493	8,540	12,276	17,702	27,195	43,338
Public deposits	54	150	433	499	507	448	669	876	1,430	2,541.4	3,952
Central bank deposits	144	267	673	867	993	1,279	1,630	1,760	2,371	5,343	8,733
Central bank lending	382	655	926	911	1,234	880	1,300	1,828	3,439	5,142	5,715
Treasury	92	189	262	266	339	528	795	1,052	1,407	2,082	2,038
Public enterprises	123	178	233	257	251	37	122	213	763	1,082	878
Banks	121	240	377	321	569	278	333	479	1,124	1,500	2,072
Other financial institutions	47	48	54	67	76	37	50	84	145	478	727
Commercial bank deposits	445	793	1,619	2,566	3,305	5,246	8,620	12,877	18,349	28,273	40,445
Commercial bank lending	446	790	1,319	1,806	2,418	3,149	5,568	10,053	16,034	22,771	31,412
Industry	156	283	459	557	526	861	1,722	2,517	3,651	4,233	5,330
Agriculture	83	146	266	335	512	530	956	1,782	2,956	4,521	5,113
Foreign trade and tourism	28	61	127	440	596	702	985	1,798	2,315	3,432	5,784
Housing and construction	17	19	42	71	130	250	594	1,330	2,693	4,127	4,820

(continued on next page)

											Average annual growth (%)	
											1976–89	1980–89a
Trade	70	112	211	376	607	725	1,167	2,485	4,141	5,921	9,145		
Unclassified	92	170	213	21	38	64	127	118	240	397	608		
Annual growth rates (percent)													
Money supply (M4)		76.1	99.5	48.3	25.4	49.1	55.0	42.8	45.5	55.4	59.0	39.7	55.6
Currency and sight deposits (M1)		57.9	37.9	38.1	48.1	17.5	39.7	56.6	62.1	30.3	48.4	31.2	43.7
Time deposits		111.4	271.0	84.3	9.5	118.6	68.1	35.1	30.4	76.1	67.2	62.3	87.2
Total (M2)		66.2	85.1	56.7	29.8	58.0	55.5	43.7	44.2	53.6	59.4	39.4	55.2
Public deposits		177.8	188.7	15.2	1.6	-11.6	49.3	30.9	63.2	77.7	55.5	46.3	64.8
Central bank deposits		85.4	152.1	28.8	14.5	28.8	27.4	8.0	34.7	125.3	63.5	40.6	56.9
Central bank lending		71.5	41.4	-1.6	35.5	-28.7	47.7	40.6	88.1	49.5	11.1	25.4	35.5
Treasury		105.4	38.6	1.5	27.4	55.8	50.6	32.3	33.7	48.0	-2.1	27.9	39.1
Public enterprises		44.7	30.9	10.3	-2.3	-85.3	229.7	74.6	258.2	41.8	-18.9	41.7	58.4
Banks		98.3	57.1	-14.9	77.3	-51.1	19.8	43.8	134.7	33.5	38.1	31.2	43.7
Other financial institutions		2.1	12.5	24.1	13.4	-51.3	35.1	68.0	72.6	229.7	52.1	32.7	45.8
Commercial bank deposits		78.2	104.2	58.5	28.8	58.7	64.3	49.4	42.5	54.1	43.1	41.6	58.2
Commercial bank lending		77.1	67.0	36.9	33.9	30.2	76.8	80.5	59.5	42.0	37.9	38.7	54.2
Industry		81.4	62.2	21.4	-5.6	63.7	100.0	46.2	45.1	15.9	25.9	32.6	45.6
Agriculture		75.9	82.2	25.9	52.8	3.5	80.4	86.4	65.9	52.9	13.1	38.5	53.9
Foreign trade and tourism		117.9	108.2	246.5	35.5	17.8	40.3	82.5	28.8	48.3	68.5	56.7	79.4
Housing and construction		11.8	121.1	69.0	83.1	92.3	137.6	123.9	102.5	53.2	16.8	57.9	81.1
Trade		60.0	88.4	78.2	61.4	19.4	61.0	112.9	66.6	43.0	54.5	46.1	64.5
Unclassified		84.8	25.3	-90.1	81.0	68.4	98.4	-7.1	103.4	65.4	53.1	34.5	48.3

a. First eleven months.

Source: TCMB, *Quarterly Bulletin* (1989 IV, October–December) and various issues.

Table 9

Nominal Interest Rates, 1974–1989

	Oct. 1974	Apr. 1978	May 1979	Mar. 1980	July 1980	Feb. 1981	Jan. 1982	July 1983	May 1984	Jan. 1985	Nov. 1986	Jan. 1987	Feb. 1988	Feb. 1989	June 1989
Central Bank															
Short-term credits															
General rate	9.0	10.0	10.8	14.0	26.0	30.3	31.5	31.5	52.0	52.0	48.0	45.0	54.0	54.0	54.0
Agricultural	8.0	8.0	11.5	13.5	13.5	19.5	18.0	18.0	25.0	28.0	28.0	28.0	40.0	40.0	40.0
Industrial	—	9.5	10.4	12.8	25.0	29.3	30.5	—	—	—	—	—	—	—	—
Exports	8.0	10.0	11.0	15.0	17.8	23.5	24.5	30.3	42.0	52.0	48.0	35.0	40.0	35.0	35.0
Medium-term credits															
General rate	10.5	11.5	14.0	15.0	26.0	30.3	31.5	29.5	50.5	50.5	50.5	48.5	60.0	60.0	60.0
Agricultural	8.0	8.0	12.8	14.0	14.0	18.8	17.8	17.8	25.0	28.0	28.0	28.0	—	—	—
Commercial banks															
1-year deposits	9.0	12.0	20.0	20.0	33.0	50.0	50.0	45.0	45.0	45.0	55.0	45.0	65.0	75.0	62.0
Foreign rate	—	16.0	30.0	30.0	—	—	—	—	—	—	—	—	—	—	—
Short-term credits															
General rate	11.5	16.0	19.0	21.0	31.0	36.0	36.0	36.0	53.5	53.5	60.0	66.0	87.0	85.0	85.5
Agricultural	10.5	10.5	14.0	16.0	16.0	22.0	22.0	20.0	28.0	30.0	30.0	36.0	—	—	—
Exports	9.0	14.0	16.0	21.0	22.0	27.0	31.5	30.0	42.0	53.5	38.0	38.0	—	—	—

(continued on next page)

194

Medium-term credits														
General rate	14.0	16.0	20.0	22.0	33.0	38.0	38.0	34.0	62.0	62.0	58.0	62.0	92.5	86.5	86.5
Agricultural	10.5	10.5	16.0	18.0	18.0	24.0	22.0	22.0	28.0	30.0	30.0	30.0	—	—	—

Source: TCMB, *Quarterly Bulletins*, various issues, latest 1989 IV; and OECD, *Economic Surveys*, various issues.

Table 10

Real Interest Rates, 1978–1989

	Apr. 1978	May 1979	Mar. 1980	July 1980	Feb. 1981	Jan. 1982	July 1983	May 1984	Jan. 1985	Nov. 1986	Jan. 1987	Feb. 1988	Feb. 1989	June 1989
Central Bank														
Short-term credits														
General rate	−40.0	−54.5	−101.5	−89.5	−5.2	4.5	1.0	1.7	8.8	18.4	13.0	−14.3	−15.6	−15.6
Agricultural	−35.6	−45.6	−82.0	−82.0	−25.8	−6.5	−13.2	−32.5	−9.4	2.7	−1.6	−11.0	−41.4	−41.4
Industrial	−41.3	−65.0	−113.8	−101.4	2.8	4.0	−3.2	—	—	—	—	—	—	—
Exports	−38.0	−45.7	−86.2	−83.4	−22.9	0.9	−0.5	−8.3	10.1	18.4	3.0	−28.3	−34.6	−34.6
Medium-term credits														
General Rate	−38.5	−51.3	−100.5	−89.5	−5.2	4.5	−1.0	0.2	7.3	20.9	16.5	−8.3	−9.6	−9.6
Agricultural	−35.6	0.0	−81.5	−81.5	−26.5	−6.7	−13.4	−32.5	−9.4	2.7	−1.6	—	—	—
Commercial banks														
1-year deposits	−38.0	−45.3	−95.5	−82.5	14.5	23.0	14.5	−5.3	1.8	−13.3	13.0	−3.3	5.4	−7.6
Foreign rate	−34.0	−35.3	−85.3	—	—	—	—	—	—	—	—	—	—	—
Short-term credits														
General rate	−34.0	−46.3	−94.5	−84.5	0.5	9.0	5.5	3.2	10.3	30.4	34.0	18.7	15.4	15.9
Agricultural	−33.1	−43.1	−79.5	−79.5	−23.3	−2.5	−11.2	−29.5	−7.4	4.7	6.4	—	—	—
Exports	−36.0	−49.2	−94.8	−93.8	−8.5	4.5	−0.5	−8.3	10.3	8.4	6.0	—	—	—

(continued on next page)

Medium-term credits

General rate	−34.0	−45.3	−93.5	−79.8	2.5	11.0	3.5	11.7	18.8	28.4	30.0	24.2	16.9	16.9
Agricultural	−33.1	−41.1	−77.5	−77.5	−21.3	−2.5	−9.2	−29.5	−7.4	4.7	0.4	—	—	—

Note: General rate deflated by all items wholesale price, agriculture by agriculture wholesale price, and industrial by manufactures wholesale prices from Table 13; exports deflated by export wholesale price.

Source: TCMB, *Quarterly Bulletins*, various issues, latest 1988 III.

Table 11

Consumer Price Indexes, 1975–1989 (1978–79 = 100)

	1975	1976	1977	1978	1979	1980	1981	1982	1983	1984	1985	1986	1987	1988	1989
Ankara	33.8	38.9	50.0	74.7	117.0	253.3	344.4	437.7	573.0	850.8	1,279.3	1,752.8	2,447.7	4,219.4	7,171.4
Istanbul	34.2	40.2	51.0	74.2	117.7	247.4	337.8	442.0	586.0	882.7	1,309.3	1,765.7	2,490.1	4,347.0	7,405.1
All Turkey	31.8	37.3	47.4	68.8	109.3	229.6	313.6	410.3	539.1	800.0	1,159.6	1,561.0	2,167.5	3,801.0	6,447.5
Percentage change all-Turkey CPI		17.3	27.1	45.3	58.7	110.2	36.6	30.8	31.4	48.4	44.9	34.6	38.9	75.4	69.6

Source: SIS, *Statistical Yearbook of Turkey* (December 1988); and earlier issues.

Table 12

GNP Deflators, 1975–1989 (annual percentage change; 1968 = 100)

	1976	1977	1978	1979	1980	1981	1982	1983	1984	1985	1986	1987	1988	1989
GNP deflator	16.7	24.5	43.8	71.1	103.8	41.9	27.5	28.0	50.1	43.9	30.9	38.3	5.8	66.8
GDP deflator	17.6	26.5	43.3	70.3	104.4	41.9	28.3	28.9	51.3	41.2	30.1	39.5	5.6	65.3

Source: Calculated from State Planning Organization, *Main Economic Indicators*, December 1988 and June 1990.

Table 13

Wholesale Price Indexes, 1975–1989 (1981 = 100)

	1975	1976	1977	1978	1979	1980	1981	1982	1983	1984	1985	1986	1987	1988	1989
All items	9.7	11.3	13.8	20.7	34.2	73.8	100.0	127.0	165.7	249.1	356.8	462.3	610.4	1,027.3	1,741.9
Agricultural	7.8	13.0	15.6	22.4	35.2	68.8	100.0	124.5	163.4	257.4	353.6	442.9	574.2	866.9	1,572.7
Mining	n.a	n.a	n.a	n.a	n.a	n.a	100.0	149.3	179.9	254.0	416.2	441.4	599.1	1,018.3	1,875.0
Coal mining	3.9	4.2	6.7	16.1	23.7	72.9	100.0	135.1	165.5	219.2	339.0	392.2	496.2	891.1	1,671.4
Metal mining	9.2	9.7	11.7	19.5	41.1	82.9	100.0	151.6	181.9	254.8	493.7	661.4	765.0	1,332.8	2,830.7
Manufacturing	9.4	10.5	13.2	19.9	34.9	79.1	100.0	126.5	166.0	243.2	345.2	457.7	611.3	1,086.6	1,789.2
Textiles	10.2	11.8	13.9	20.7	32.0	65.7	100.0	129.4	179.5	251.1	335.5	470.5	694.0	1,180.3	1,957.8
Nonmetal minerals	7.5	9.9	13.5	18.8	31.5	72.8	100.0	124.9	176.3	244.9	394.5	574.9	822.7	1,329.4	2,089.7
Metals	9.4	9.9	12.1	19.4	36.8	82.7	100.0	124.9	176.3	220.9	297.7	380.4	563.1	1,080.7	1,740.3
Electricity	9.9	10.7	12.9	18.7	26.8	65.7	100.0	148.4	186.1	333.5	665.8	918.8	1,108.6	1,560.4	2,560.0
Gas	9.5	9.6	9.6	14.7	25.8	77.9	100.0	118.4	139.5	208.2	419.3	507.9	550.1	894.1	1,298.3
Percentage change															
All items		16.5	22.1	50.0	65.2	115.8	35.5	27.0	30.5	50.3	43.2	29.6	32.0	68.3	69.6
Agricultural		66.7	20.0	43.6	57.1	95.5	45.3	24.5	31.2	57.5	37.4	25.3	29.6	51.0	81.4
Mining		n.a	n.a	n.a	n.a	n.a	n.a	49.3	20.5	41.2	63.9	6.1	35.7	70.0	84.1
Coal mining		7.7	59.5	140.3	47.2	207.6	37.2	35.1	22.5	32.4	54.7	15.7	26.5	79.6	87.6
Metal mining		5.4	20.6	66.7	110.8	101.7	20.6	51.6	20.0	40.1	93.8	34.0	15.7	74.2	112.4

(continued on next page)

Manufacturing	11.7	25.7	50.8	75.4	126.6	26.4	26.5	31.2	46.5	41.9	32.6	33.6	77.8	64.7
Textiles	15.7	17.8	48.9	54.6	105.3	52.2	29.4	38.7	39.9	33.6	40.2	47.5	70.1	65.9
Nonmetal minerals	32.0	36.4	39.3	67.6	131.1	37.4	24.9	41.2	38.9	61.1	45.7	43.1	61.6	57.2
Metals	5.3	22.2	60.3	89.7	124.7	20.9	24.9	41.2	25.3	34.8	27.8	48.0	91.9	61.0
Electricity	8.1	20.6	45.0	43.3	145.1	52.2	48.4	25.4	79.2	99.6	38.0	20.7	40.8	64.1
Gas	1.1	0.0	53.1	75.5	201.9	28.4	18.4	17.8	49.2	101.4	21.1	8.3	62.5	45.2

Note: New and old indexes are combined to provide continuity.

Source: SIS, *Statistical Yearbook of Turkey*, December 1988 and earlier issues; and SIS, *Wholesale and Consumer Price Indexes*, monthly bulletins.

201

Table 14

Merchandise Exports by Category, 1975–1989 (millions of current U.S. dollars)

	1975	1976	1977	1978	1979	1980	1981	1982	1983	1984	1985	1986	1987	1988	1989	Average annual growth (%)	
																1975–89	1980–89
Agriculture and livestock	792.6	1,254.4	1,041.4	1,542.8	1,343.6	1,671.7	2,219.4	2,141.2	1,880.6	1,749.2	1,719.4	1,885.5	1,852.5	2,341.4	2,126.5	7.3	2.7
Crops	733.8	1,174.1	988.3	1,435.3	1,252.9	1,535.0	1,922.6	1,699.5	1,484.4	1,381.9	1,441.5	1,546.8	1,484.2	1,988.3	1,783.9	6.6	1.7
Cotton	225.2	434.2	210.1	348.4	227.8	322.6	348.3	296.6	196.5	168.1	169.8	138.8	19.9	141.2	160.0	-2.4	-7.5
Tobacco	183.2	251.3	175.8	225.3	177.0	233.7	395.0	348.3	237.8	216.4	330.1	270.2	314.0	266.0	479.8	7.1	8.3
Hazelnuts	154.1	203.2	251.0	330.9	353.0	394.8	301.8	240.7	246.0	304.8	255.4	378.0	390.7	359.4	266.1	4.0	-4.3
Raisins	45.5	52.6	75.0	99.7	114.8	130.3	130.2	100.3	71.4	62.3	74.9	102.9	108.3	139.6	121.3	7.3	-0.8
Others	125.8	232.8	276.4	431.0	380.3	453.6	747.3	713.6	732.7	630.3	611.3	656.9	651.3	1,082.7	756.7	13.7	5.9
Livestock products	41.1	62.7	37.2	77.8	62.0	108.2	258.2	389.7	362.1	323.3	244.2	285.3	310.9	286.0	277.4	14.6	11.0
Fishery products	12.9	12.3	11.6	24.4	21.7	22.7	26.6	24.0	20.3	20.3	21.0	39.7	44.7	51.3	52.7	10.6	9.8
Forestry products	4.8	5.3	4.3	5.3	7.0	5.8	12.0	28.0	13.8	23.7	12.7	13.7	12.7	15.2	12.5	7.1	8.9
Mining and quarrying	105.6	110.0	125.8	124.1	132.5	191.0	193.4	175.3	188.9	239.8	243.8	246.9	272.3	377.2	413.2	10.2	9.0
Industrial products	502.9	595.8	585.8	621.3	785.1	1,047.4	2,290.2	3,429.5	3,658.3	5,144.6	5,994.3	5,324.2	8,065.2	8,943.5	9,087.6	23.0	27.1

(continued on next page)

Processed agri-cultural products	128.6	98.4	136.2	110.2	151.1	209.4	411.7	568.3	669.7	808.2	646.6	666.7	953.9	884.7	918.6	15.1	17.9
Petroleum products	36.1	16.2	0.0	0.0	0.0	38.5	107.0	343.9	232.4	408.8	372.0	178.2	232.2	331.3	254.2	15.0	23.3
Other industrial products	338.2	481.2	449.6	511.1	634.0	799.5	1,771.5	2,517.3	2,756.2	3,927.6	4,976.3	4,479.3	6,879.0	7,727.5	7,914.8	25.3	29.0
Cement	24.2	16.3	9.2	40.5	44.9	39.6	198.5	206.6	80.6	56.0	43.7	26.9	7.0	6.5	34.2	2.5	-1.6
Chemicals	32.8	44.2	33.4	23.7	23.8	75.0	93.8	147.9	120.3	172.6	265.6	350.2	526.5	734.3	774	25.3	29.4
Rubber, plastic	4.9	2.6	2.9	2.4	3.4	15.9	71.8	60.4	76.9	97.4	107.9	140.5	257.5	351.7	312.5	34.6	39.2
Hides, leather	64.9	59.9	52.0	40.1	43.6	49.5	82.1	111.4	192.1	400.7	484.4	345.2	721.9	514.1	604.9	17.3	32.1
Forestry products	2.1	1.4	0.3	0.6	1.6	4.3	19.7	33.4	14.8	23.7	51.7	105.8	31.9	21.6	16.0	15.6	15.7
Textiles	127.5	265.3	259.8	309.1	377.6	424.3	802.8	1,056.3	1,299.2	1,875.4	1,789.5	1,850.7	2,707.1	3,201.4	3,507.8	26.7	26.5
Glass, ceramics	17.9	20.9	27.5	30.1	37.1	35.9	102.1	103.8	108.2	146.0	189.6	157.9	204.7	233.3	258.4	21.0	24.5
Iron, steel	20.3	22.1	14.4	21.2	31.1	33.9	100.2	362.2	407.2	576.4	968.8	803.6	851.8	1,457.5	1,348.8	35.0	50.6
Nonferrous metal	12.7	16.9	20.1	11.5	14.6	18.3	29.8	44.6	78.9	85.5	115.5	111.2	134.0	226.1	265.9	24.3	34.6
Metal products	3.5	4.4	5.2	5.6	5.7	8.1	20.2	27.3	19.4	16.3	72.7	60.4	107.0	51.5	22.7	14.3	12.1
Machinery	10.5	12.1	8.9	12.3	12.4	21.7	64.8	115.7	102.8	118.2	377.7	202.5	680.5	333.0	195.5	23.2	27.7
Electrical appliances	0.8	1.1	3.0	3.7	4.5	11.5	26.1	75.2	69.0	99.6	118.9	129.6	293.3	294.0	234.1	50.0	39.8
Motor vehicles	8.1	9.3	9.2	6.1	26.6	50.3	117.5	110.2	126.3	134.9	146.6	82.4	110.2	118.0	154.3	23.4	13.3
Others	8.0	4.7	3.7	4.2	7.1	10.2	42.1	62.3	60.5	124.9	189.6	166.5	245.6	184.5	185.7	25.2	38.0
Total	1,401.1	1,960.2	1,753.0	2,288.2	2,261.2	2,910.1	4,703.0	5,746.0	5,727.8	7,133.6	7,958.1	7,456.6	10,190.0	11,662.1	11,627.3	16.3	16.6

Source: SPO, *Main Economic Indicators, Turkey*, May 1990 and earlier issues.

Table 15

Merchandise Imports by Category, 1975–1989 (millions of current U.S. dollars)

	1975	1976	1977	1978	1979	1980	1981	1982	1983	1984	1985	1986	1987	1988	1989	Average annual growth (%)	
																1975–89	1980–89
Agriculture and livestock	202.5	78.7	112.6	50.7	36.5	51.1	125.0	176.2	138	418	375	457	782	499	1,041	140.9	215.3
Mining and quarrying	795.2	1,090.3	1,262.4	1,133.9	1,067.6	3,095.9	3,478.0	3,739.0	3,442	3,644	3,626	2,145	3,034	2,861	2,902	18.7	-0.7
Crude oil	718.1	1,002.4	1,151.6	1,043.5	961.6	2,952.2	3,257.5	3,526.6	3,242	3,373	3,321	1,808	2,711	2,434	2,456	17.0	-1.9
Others	77.1	87.9	110.8	90.4	106.0	143.7	220.5	212.4	199	271	305	338	323	427	447	33.6	23.4
Industrial products	3,740.9	3,959.6	4,421.3	3,414.4	3,965.3	4,762.4	5,330.4	4,927.4	5,655	6,695	7,342	8,502	10,341	10,975	11,819	19.6	16.5
Agriculture-based processed products	229.7	146.8	58.7	50.9	116.5	302.8	230.3	176.5	205	434	487	480	720	738	843	59.3	19.8
Petroleum products	88.1	104.1	284.5	351.7	750.4	909.8	620.8	221.0	423	264	290	200	245	343	494	-6.0	-5.1
Other industrial products	3,423.1	3,708.7	4,078.1	3,011.8	3,098.4	3,549.8	4,479.3	4,529.9	5,027	5,998	6,564	7,823	9,377	9,893	10,482	24.4	21.7
Cement	0.3	0.1	0.2	0.1	0.1	0.3	0.4	0.5	0	1	1	3	50	50	12	—	—
Chemicals	580.7	653.8	768.8	762.1	882.8	1,123.0	1,201.2	894.3	1,154	1,340	1,294	1,422	1,937	1,984	2,105	13.9	9.7
Rubber and plastic	152.7	183.5	266.9	154.7	145.7	182.9	240.5	237.3	252	359	343	372	488	525	485	28.9	18.3
Hides and leather	0.6	0.5	0.2	0.2	0.3	0.3	0.6	0.3	2	6	16	25	74	51	73	—	—

(continued on next page)

Wood products	2.0	2.4	2.2	2.2	1.2	2.7	2.3	6.1	3	4	8	6	7	9	9	71.3	27.2
Textiles	66.6	58.4	51.5	50.2	45.8	79.6	78.4	103.5	98	117	146	161	204	260	297	51.9	30.3
Glass and ceramics	26.1	25.2	25.5	17.8	27.9	35.2	40.3	34.3	58	63	63	96	117	141	126	45.1	28.8
Iron and steel	679.8	546.9	693.2	409.8	347.3	451.4	606.8	592.6	677	862	1,060	1,028	1,537	1,655	2,217	41.8	43.5
Nonferrous metals	101.9	89.5	97.0	42.6	54.8	87.2	141.2	122.5	195	220	224	230	418	412	421	72.4	42.5
Metal products	15.2	28.3	15.8	20.4	14.6	23.1	22.7	37.6	34	34	38	51	56	62	57	35.9	16.3
Machinery	998.7	1,090.1	1,082.6	792.1	943.8	871.1	1,246.8	1,323.5	1,449	1,618	1,551	2,304	2,455	2,400	2,188	17.1	16.8
Electric appliances	278.3	278.4	295.8	223.6	259.5	279.9	340.9	378.7	402	573	664	892	940	1,075	1,028	34.9	29.7
Transport vehicles	400.5	615.2	635.1	450.8	283.6	261.0	384.0	611.6	496	517	813	768	550	690	790	15.9	22.5
Others	119.7	136.4	143.3	85.2	91.0	152.1	173.2	187.1	208	283	346	466	545	579	674	59.5	38.2
Total	4,738.6	5,128.6	5,796.3	4,599.0	5,069.4	7,909.4	8,933.4	8,842.6	9,235	10,757	11,343	11,105	14,158	14,335	15,763	20.3	11.0

Source: SPO, *Main Economic Indicators*, June 1990 and earlier issues.

Table 16

Balance of Payments, 1975–1988 (millions of current U.S. dollars)

	1975	1976	1977	1978	1979	1980	1981	1982	1983	1984	1985	1986	1987	1988
Current account														
Merchandise exports f.o.b.	1,401	1,960	1,753	2,288	2,261	2,910	4,703	5,890	5,905	7,389	8,255	7,583	10,322	11,846
Exports f.o.b.	1,401	1,960	1,753	2,288	2,261	2,910	4,703	5,746	5,728	7,134	7,959	7,457	10,190	11,662
Transit trade	0	0	0	0	0	0	0	144	177	255	296	126	132	184
Merchandise imports f.o.b.	−4,502	−4,872	−5,506	−4,369	−4,815	−7,513	−8,567	−8,518	−8,895	−10,331	−11,230	−10,664	−13,551	−13,646
Imports c.i.f.	−4,739	−5,129	−5,796	−4,599	−5,069	−7,909	−8,933	−8,843	−9,235	−10,757	−11,613	−11,199	−14,279	−14,372
Transit trade	0	0	0	0	0	0	0	−112	−134	−193	−227	−105	−88	−96
Freight and insurance	237	257	290	230	254	396	366	437	474	619	610	640	816	822
Trade balance	−3,101	−2,912	−3,753	−2,081	−2,554	−4,603	−3,864	−2,628	−2,990	−2,942	−2,975	−3,081	−3,229	−1,800
Other goods and services and income: credit	617	581	540	533	708	762	1,316	2,038	2,041	2,366	3,148	3,250	4,111	5,945
Tourism	201	181	205	234	281	326	380	373	420	548	1,094	950	1,476	2,355
Other	416	400	335	299	427	436	936	1,665	1,621	1,818	2,054	2,300	2,635	3,590
Other goods and services and income: debit	−601	−818	−1,034	−816	−1,377	−1,738	−1,946	−2,639	−2,734	−2,945	−3,184	−3,646	−4,282	−4,812
Tourism	−143	−194	−253	−71	−83	−104	−103	−149	−128	−277	−324	−313	−448	−358
Interest	−124	−217	−320	−489	−1,010	−1,138	−1,443	−1,565	−1,511	−1,586	−1,753	−2,134	−2,507	−2,799
Other	−334	−407	−461	−256	−284	−496	−400	−925	−1,095	−1,082	−1,107	−1,199	−1,327	−1,655
Total goods and services and income	−3,085	−3,149	−4,247	−2,364	−3,223	−5,579	−4,494	−3,229	−3,683	−3,521	−3,011	−3,477	−3,400	−667

(continued on next page)

Unrequited transfers private credit	1,410	1,118	1,084	1,103	1,818	2,166	2,559	2,189	1,569	1,901	1,782	1,718	2,088	1,825
Workers' remittances	1,312	982	982	983	1,694	2,071	2,490	2,140	1,513	1,807	1,714	1,634	2,021	1,755
Others	98	136	102	120	124	95	69	49	56	94	68	84	67	70
Unrequited transfers private debit	-12	-14	-16	-17	-19	-13	0	0	-20	-16	-20	-15	-22	-19
Unrequited transfers official	39	16	39	13	11	18	16	105	236	229	236	246	352	364
Workers' remittances	0	0	0	0	0	0	0	0	50	74	60	62	81	89
Others	39	16	39	13	11	18	16	105	186	155	176	184	271	275
Balance on current account	-1,648	-2,029	-3,140	-1,265	-1,413	-3,408	-1,919	-935	-1,898	-1,407	-1,013	-1,528	-982	1503
Capital account except reserves														
Private foreign capital	114	10	27	34	75	18	95	55	46	113	99	125	110	352
Portfolio investment	0	0	0	0	0	0	0	0	0	0	0	0	-29	-4
Long- and medium-term capital	173	1,049	650	412	532	656	683	127	-319	387	-439	910	1,573	930
Drawings	382	1,726	864	908	3,719	2,284	1,972	1,730	1,817	1,728	1,159	2,670	3,662	4,308
Dresdner	0	0	0	0	0	0	0	0	0	343	260	385	568	549
Repayments	-209	-677	-214	-496	-3,187	-1,628	-1,289	-1,603	-2,136	-1,684	-1,858	-2,145	-2,657	-3,927
Short-term capital	40	73	968	402	-1,000	-2	104	81	1,033	-460	1,390	1,093	356	-1,979
Assets	0	0	149	-17	-109	85	360	-181	177	-1,625	127	-313	-945	-1,428
Liabilities	40	73	819	419	-891	-87	-256	262	856	1,165	1,263	1,406	1,301	-551
Capital balance	327	1,132	1,645	848	-393	672	882	263	760	40	1,050	2,128	2,010	-701

(continued on next page)

(continued)

Table 16

	1975	1976	1977	1978	1979	1980	1981	1982	1983	1984	1985	1986	1987	1988
Net errors and omissions	-351	-830	-634	-874	676	1,434	649	-75	507	470	-813	-65	-459	347
Exceptional financing	1,035	1,500	1,763	1,269	1,003	1,373	315	902	622	1,002	676	0	0	0
Counterpart items	-40	30	-1	-4	40	19	68	13	161	-171	223	251	424	-261
Balance on capital account	971	1,832	2,773	1,239	1,326	3,498	1,914	1,103	2,050	1,341	1,136	2,314	1,975	-615
Current less capital account	-677	-197	-367	-26	-87	90	-5	168	152	-66	123	786	993	888
Total change in reserves	677	197	367	26	87	-90	5	-168	-152	66	-123	-786	-993	-888
IMF	300	158	39	213	10	423	268	133	77	-138	-103	-241	-344	-467
Official reserves	377	39	328	-187	77	-513	-263	-301	-229	204	-20	-545	-649	-421

Source: Central Bank of Turkey, *Monthly Statistical Bulletin*, various issues.

Table 17

World Bank Estimates of External Debt, 1970–1988 (millions of U.S. dollars)

	1970	1975	1976	1977	1978	1979	1980	1981	1982	1983	1984	1985	1986	1987	1988
Total debt	1,960	3,585	4,258	11,419	14,829	15,889	19,040	19,181	19,677	20,289	21,567	25,977	32,784	40,818	38,700
Long-term debt (LTD)	1,886	3,342	3,867	4,917	7,021	11,660	15,496	15,665	16,458	16,441	16,961	19,892	24,788	31,356	30,697
Public	1,844	3,182	3,619	4,438	6,464	11,030	14,961	15,225	16,064	16,042	16,536	19,533	24,285	30,490	30,162
Private	42	160	248	479	557	630	535	440	394	399	425	359	503	866	535
IMF	74	243	391	409	622	633	1,054	1,322	1,455	1,567	1,426	1,326	1,085	770	299
Short-term debt[a]	—	—	—	6,093	7,186	3,596	2,490	2,194	1,764	2,281	3,180	4,759	6,911	8,692	7,704
Debt ratios															
Debt/export	3.33	2.56	2.17	6.51	6.48	7.03	6.54	4.08	3.34	3.44	2.92	3.15	4.32	3.95	3.27
LTD/exports	3.21	2.39	1.97	2.80	3.07	5.16	5.33	3.33	2.79	2.78	2.30	2.41	3.27	3.04	2.59
Service/exports[b]	0.30	0.21	0.19	0.24	0.25	0.34	0.38	0.38	0.40	0.40	0.32	0.45	0.46	0.48	0.56

Note: The debt figures given by the Central Bank of Turkey (see Table 18) do not coincide exactly with those in Table 17. Central Bank estimates go back only to 1984.

a. Short-term debt estimates are not available before 1977.

b. Service ratio defined as repayments of public and private principal interest payments to total exports.

Source: Debt data from World Bank, *World Debt Tables* and Supplements, 1988–89; exports from IMF, *International Financial Statistics*, 1988 *Yearbook* and May 1989.

Table 18

Central Bank Breakdown of Turkish Debt, 1982–1989 (millions of U.S. dollars)

	1982	1983	1984	1985	1986	1987	1988	1989
Total debt	17,619	18,385	20,659	25,476	32,101	40,228	40,722	41,751
Long-term debt (LTD)	15,855	16,104	17,479	20,717	25,752	32,605	34,305	36,006
Public	14,950	15,264	16,687	19,758	24,668	31,282	32,780	34,400
Private	905	840	792	959	1,084	1,323	1,525	1,606
IMF	1,455	1,572	1,426	1,326	1,085	770	299	48
Short-term debt	1,764	2,281	3,180	4,759	6,349	7,623	6,417	5,745
Debt ratios								
Debt/exports	2.99	3.11	2.80	3.09	4.23	3.90	3.41	3.59
LTD/exports	2.69	2.73	2.37	2.51	3.40	3.16	2.88	3.06
Service/exports	0.56	0.65	0.50	0.51	0.62	0.53	0.60	0.61

Note: After 1984 figures are adjusted for exchange rate variations.
Source: TCMB, *Monthly Statistical and Evaluation Bulletin*, June 1987 and various issues; TCMB, *Balance of Payments Statistics of Turkey*, June 1991.

Table 19

Exchange Rates: Annual Averages for Official and Free (Black) Market, 1975–1990 (Turkish liras per U.S. dollar)

	Official rate	Free rate	Difference (%)
1975	14.36	15.79	10.0
1976	15.92	17.65	10.9
1977	17.92	21.22	18.4
1978	24.04	29.25	21.7
1979	38.14	48.33	26.7
1980	77.78	84.03	8.0
1981	112.42	117.14	4.2
1982	163.66	173.55	6.0
1983	228.14	259.08	13.6
1984	370.87	385.08	3.8
1985	526.18	534.66	1.6
1986	676.53	702.40	3.8
1987	866.09	907.42	4.8
1988	1,447.75	1,499.58	3.6
1989	2,136.77	2,145.33	0.4
1990[a]	2,642.00	2,654.94	0.5

a. June 1990.
Source: Calculated from Data Appendix Table 20.

Table 20

Exchange Rates: Official and Free (Black) Market, 1975–1990 (Turkish liras per U.S. dollar)

	1975				1976				1977			
			Difference				Difference				Difference	
	Official	Free market	Amount	%	Official	Free market	Amount	%	Official	Free market	Amount	%
January	13.85	14.55	0.70	5.05	15.00	17.55	2.55	17.00	16.50	18.65	2.15	13.03
February	13.85	15.80	1.95	14.08	15.00	17.40	2.40	16.00	16.50	18.90	2.40	14.55
March	13.85	15.50	1.65	11.91	15.50	16.85	1.35	8.71	17.50	18.85	1.35	7.71
April	14.00	15.40	1.40	10.00	16.00	17.65	1.65	10.31	17.50	18.45	0.95	5.43
May	14.00	14.60	0.60	4.29	16.00	17.10	1.10	6.88	17.50	19.70	2.20	12.57
June	14.00	14.40	0.40	2.86	16.00	17.45	1.45	9.06	17.50	20.70	3.20	18.29
July	14.25	15.55	1.30	9.12	16.00	17.00	1.00	6.25	17.50	19.05	1.55	8.86
August	14.75	16.00	1.25	8.47	16.00	17.00	1.00	6.25	17.50	21.00	3.50	20.00
September	14.75	16.80	2.05	13.90	16.00	18.50	2.50	15.63	19.25	20.80	1.55	8.05
October	15.00	17.00	2.00	13.33	16.50	18.75	2.25	13.64	19.25	24.90	5.65	29.35
November	15.00	17.00	2.00	13.33	16.50	18.45	1.95	11.82	19.25	27.40	8.15	42.34
December	15.00	16.85	1.85	12.33	16.50	18.10	1.60	9.70	19.25	26.25	7.00	36.36
Average	14.36	15.79	1.43	9.95	15.92	17.65	1.73	10.89	17.92	21.22	3.30	18.44
	1978				1979				1980			
January	19.25	26.60	7.35	38.18	25.00	39.40	14.40	57.60	70.00	73.30	3.30	4.71

(continued on next page)

(continued on next page)

February	19.25	26.50	7.25	37.66	25.00	44.65	19.65	78.60	70.00	73.80	3.80	5.43
March	25.00	27.00	2.00	8.00	25.00	47.85	22.85	91.40	70.00	76.50	6.50	9.29
April	25.00	28.00	3.00	12.00	26.50	49.30	22.80	86.04	73.70	80.00	6.30	8.55
May	25.00	28.50	3.50	14.00	26.50	46.25	19.75	74.53	73.70	79.50	5.80	7.87
June	25.00	28.50	3.50	14.00	47.10	45.75	-1.35	-2.87	78.00	81.00	3.00	3.85
July	25.00	26.65	1.65	6.60	47.10	50.60	3.50	7.43	78.00	85.00	7.00	8.97
August	25.00	28.40	3.40	13.60	47.10	50.90	3.80	8.07	80.00	84.80	4.80	6.00
September	25.00	27.35	2.35	9.40	47.10	50.00	2.90	6.16	80.00	91.00	11.00	13.75
October	25.00	28.75	3.75	15.00	47.10	50.45	3.35	7.11	82.70	92.50	9.80	11.85
November	25.00	36.85	11.85	47.40	47.10	50.75	3.65	7.75	87.95	95.00	7.05	8.02
December	25.00	37.90	12.90	51.60	47.10	54.00	6.90	14.65	89.25	96.00	6.75	7.56
Average	24.04	29.25	5.21	21.66	38.14	48.33	10.18	26.70	77.78	84.03	6.26	8.05

	1981				1982				1983			
January	92.80	96.00	3.20	3.45	138.90	144.60	5.70	4.10	191.15	217.00	25.85	13.52
February	96.90	98.10	1.20	1.24	144.30	147.50	3.20	2.22	194.30	231.00	36.70	18.89
March	96.90	98.00	1.10	1.14	147.40	147.50	0.10	0.07	203.75	239.00	35.25	17.30
April	99.20	100.00	0.80	0.81	149.20	188.00	38.80	26.01	208.00	252.00	44.00	21.15
May	103.60	104.00	0.40	0.39	151.10	155.00	3.90	2.58	213.75	259.00	45.25	21.17
June	111.00	115.00	4.00	3.60	166.10	175.00	8.90	5.36	219.35	249.00	29.65	13.52
July	115.60	120.00	4.40	3.81	166.90	170.00	3.10	1.86	228.90	247.00	18.10	7.91
August	121.70	128.50	6.80	5.59	172.60	181.00	8.40	4.87	238.85	270.00	31.15	13.04

(continued)

Table 20

	1981				1982				1983			
			Difference				Difference				Difference	
	Official	Free market	Amount	%	Official	Free market	Amount	%	Official	Free market	Amount	%
September	122.20	130.00	7.80	6.38	175.90	184.00	8.10	4.60	243.45	269.00	25.55	10.49
October	127.90	136.40	8.50	6.65	178.50	187.00	8.50	4.76	250.00	271.00	21.00	8.40
November	129.50	137.70	8.20	6.33	185.30	190.00	4.70	2.54	266.20	290.00	23.80	8.94
December	131.70	142.00	10.30	7.82	187.70	213.00	25.30	13.48	280.00	315.00	35.00	12.50
Average	112.42	117.14	4.72	4.20	163.66	173.55	9.89	6.04	228.14	259.08	30.94	13.56

	1984				1985				1986			
			Difference				Difference				Difference	
	Official	Free market	Amount	%	Official	Free market	Amount	%	Official	Free market	Amount	%
January	311.40	330.00	18.60	5.97	452.80	454.00	1.20	0.27	581.05	585.00	3.95	0.68
February	310.60	340.00	29.40	9.47	479.80	470.00	-9.80	-2.04	591.00	600.00	9.00	1.52
March	320.20	350.00	29.80	9.31	493.00	491.00	-2.00	-0.41	658.25	683.10	24.85	3.78
April	333.40	360.00	26.60	7.98	513.30	518.00	4.70	0.92	651.65	670.00	18.35	2.82
May	356.20	380.00	23.80	6.68	527.30	535.00	7.70	1.46	682.55	685.00	2.45	0.36
June	368.30	375.00	6.70	1.82	532.20	540.00	7.80	1.47	675.35	750.00	74.65	11.05
July	379.90	383.00	3.10	0.82	535.20	553.90	18.70	3.49	673.15	720.00	46.85	6.96
August	387.20	389.00	1.80	0.46	535.90	550.50	14.60	2.72	676.55	710.00	33.45	4.94
September	409.70	414.00	4.30	1.05	553.20	590.30	37.10	6.71	691.95	740.00	48.05	6.94

(continued on next page)

214

	1987				1988				1989			
October	413.50	430.00	16.50	3.99	553.50	565.00	11.50	2.08	735.70	725.75	-9.95	-1.35
November	423.30	425.00	1.70	0.40	561.00	573.20	12.20	2.17	745.20	785.00	39.80	5.34
December	436.70	445.00	8.30	1.90	576.90	575.00	-1.90	-0.33	755.90	775.00	19.10	2.53
Average	370.87	385.08	14.22	3.83	526.18	534.66	8.48	1.61	676.53	702.40	25.88	3.83
January	753.65	783.00	29.35	3.89	1,117.65	1,375.00	257.35	23.03	1,881.19	1,890.00	8.81	0.47
February	764.30	782.00	17.70	2.32	1,167.45	1,278.00	110.55	9.47	1,927.63	1,948.00	20.37	1.06
March	776.00	785.00	9.00	1.16	1,220.70	1,264.00	43.30	3.55	2,025.44	2,051.00	25.56	1.26
April	795.15	801.00	5.85	0.74	1,266.30	1,280.00	13.70	1.08	2,074.84	2,085.00	10.16	0.49
May	819.00	832.00	13.00	1.59	1,320.10	1,336.00	15.90	1.20	2,094.60	2,101.00	6.40	0.31
June	850.30	863.00	12.70	1.49	1,385.85	1,410.00	24.15	1.74	2,138.08	2,145.00	6.92	0.32
July	877.85	885.00	7.15	0.81	1,440.80	1,460.00	19.20	1.33	2,148.54	2,150.00	1.46	0.07
August	894.80	917.00	22.20	2.48	1,533.21	1,564.00	30.79	2.01	2,210.36	2,212.00	1.64	0.07
September	931.40	979.00	47.60	5.11	1,649.01	1,730.00	80.99	4.91	2,234.28	2,234.00	-0.28	-0.01
October	944.45	1,036.00	91.55	9.69	1,681.61	1,687.00	5.39	0.32	2,294.10	2,304.00	9.90	0.43
November	967.80	1,116.00	148.20	15.31	1,776.46	1,788.00	11.54	0.65	2,303.07	2,310.00	6.93	0.30
December	1,018.35	1,110.00	91.65	9.00	1,813.82	1,823.00	9.18	0.51	2,309.06	2,314.00	4.94	0.21
Average	866.09	907.42	41.33	4.77	1,447.75	1,499.58	51.84	3.58	2,136.77	2,145.33	8.57	0.40

(continued on next page)

215

(continued)

Table 20

| | 1990 | | Difference | |
	Official	Free market	Amount	%
January	2,344.95	2,355.00	10.05	0.43
February	2,405.76	2,418.50	12.74	0.53
March	2,481.54	2,502.00	20.46	0.82
April	2,522.00	2,536.00	14.00	0.56
May	2,590.81	2,607.00	16.19	0.62
June	2,642.00[a]	2,654.94[a]	12.94	0.49

Note: End-of-month rates. Percentage differences are calculated over the official rate.

a. June 22.

Source: 1975–1979: *Pick's Currency Yearbook*; 1980–1986: *Anka Economic Review*; 1987–1989, for official rates: TCMB, *Quarterly Bulletin*, 1988 III and 1989 II; for free market rates: TCMB data files.

Chronological Appendix:
Policy Changes in Turkey,
1980–1989

1980

January 24. Prime Minister Süleyman Demirel announces a major policy reform. The main features of the program are as follows:

A. Organizational changes:

To facilitate economic policy making and coordinating policy implementation, two specific committees and two new departments in the Prime Minister's Office are created:

> Coordination Committee
> Money and Credit Committee
> Department of Foreign Investment
> Department of Investment and Export Promotion and
>   Implementation

B. Policies related to prices:

The Price Control Committee, which was established in 1978, is abolished.

State economic enterprises (SEEs) shall in the future determine their prices freely, and, with few exceptions, they will no longer receive government subsidies. The prices of coal, fertilizers, and electricity used in ferrochrome and aluminum production and tariffs of the state railways and maritime transport remain under government control.

C. Exchange rate and foreign trade and payments policies:

The Turkish lira is devalued vis-à-vis the U.S. dollar by 33 percent from TL47 to TL70 = $1. Multiple-rate practices are abolished except for imports of fertilizers and pesticides; for these the rate is TL55 = $1.

Trade in gold is liberalized.

Banks authorized to hold foreign exchange are permitted to keep up to 80 percent of their foreign exchange receipts (previously only 25 percent). The foreign exchange allocation for Turkish tourists going abroad, as well as for commercial travels, is increased. Exporters are allowed to hold in foreign bank accounts 5 percent or $10,000 (whichever is larger) of export receipts. Exports of goods not falling under the support schemes up to a value of $40,000 are also exempt from foreign exchange repatriation rules.

Import taxes in raw materials and intermediate goods imported for incorporation in Turkish exports are reduced to zero, provided exporters used their own permitted foreign exchange holdings to finance the transactions.

Administrative procedures related to exports are simplified. Exports on credit and prefinancing of exports will be encouraged. Priority will be given in foreign exchange allocations of the Central Bank for raw material requirements of exporters. Fifty percent of import deposits at the Central Bank can be used for extending credits to exporters and related industries.

1980 import regime: Liberalized list I is enlarged (after having been reduced a year earlier). Requirements for advance deposits on imports are eased.

Allocations from the Quota List will be made twice a year instead of once. Imports are no longer subject to systematic price control.

D. Interest rates:

Interest rates for all credits are increased by two percentage points. Central Bank discount rates have also been raised.

E. Foreign investment regulations:

Subject to the provision of the Foreign Investment Law 6224, all foreign investment applications will in future be evaluated and processed by the Foreign Investment Department.

The Foreign Investment Department is empowered to issue investment permission under its authority if the following specific conditions are fulfilled:

- The value of fixed investment falls between $2 million and $50 million.

- The share of the foreign partner is between 10 and 49 percent of total investment.

- The amount of foreign participation is not less than $1 million.

All or part of the limitations above do not apply to investments financed by international institutions or by foreign investors from specific Arab countries or for investment in tourism installations of a certain size.

F. Petroleum exploration policy:

Oil exploration is opened to private Turkish and foreign companies. 65 percent of the oil produced after January 1, 1980, must be sold in Turkey; producers are free to export the remaining 35 percent.

January 25. Export Promotion Decree 8/182 introduces new incentives for exporters. Among the measures are the foreign exchange retention right to finance the imported input requirements of the exporters and the credit system for the trading companies.

April 2. The Turkish lira is again devalued against the U.S. dollar. The new rate is TL73.70 = $1.

May. The right to transfer the export proceeds of Turkish contractors abroad is increased from 10 percent to 20 percent.

June 9. The Turkish lira is devalued. The new parity for $1 is TL78.00.

June 18. Turkey signs a standby agreement with the International Monetary Fund for the release of 1.25 billion special drawing rights over three years.

June. The Foreign Capital Decree of January 24 is amended. Under the new ruling the minimum foreign capital requirement of $1 million is waived. Interest rate regulations in bank's lending and deposits are abolished except for the minimum interest rate on sight deposits, which is fixed at 5 percent. Legal reserve ratios and differential interest rebate rates are amended.

A decree is published to regulate the liquidation of nonguaranteed commercial debt. Suppliers who have claims arising from exports of goods to Turkey made before December 31, 1979, are given different options for repayment in Turkish liras or in foreign exchange. Maturities, interest rates, and other conditions vary depending on the modalities of repayment.

July. Import regulations are eased. Industrial importers can make cash down payments of 10–15 percent in two installments, and no down payment will be required on imports financed by foreign credit. Exporters eligible to receive foreign exchange allocations for their import requirements are allowed to benefit from the scheme retroactively.

July 23. Turkey concludes a major debt rescheduling agreement under which $3.0 billion is rescheduled with a three-year grace period, expiring in 1984.

August 4. The Turkish lira is devalued vis-à-vis the U.S. dollar from TL78 to TL80.

September 12. A military government assumes power and announces that the reform program will be continued. Turgut Özal, the architect of the reform package, is retained as deputy prime minister. Strikes are banned, the labor union D İ SK is closed, and collective bargaining is suspended.

September. Commercial banks are requested to allocate at least 15 percent of total credit engagements to exports of manufactures. Exporters to Socialist bloc countries are also allowed to use part of their foreign exchange earnings for their import requirements.

October. A new export regime is announced. Industrial goods can be exported without a license.

The Turkish lira is devalued vis-à-vis the U.S. dollar from TL80 to TL82.70 on October 11 and to TL84.80 on October 26.

November 9. The Turkish lira is devalued vis-à-vis the U.S. dollar to TL89.25.

The government allows both public and private Turkish companies to sell equity shares to foreign concerns. This will enable foreign suppliers to buy equity in Turkish companies and repatriate the profits.

A system of convertible currency deposits is introduced. Accounts may be opened by workers, the self-employed, and employers abroad for terms of three to twenty-four months. At the end of the term the depositor will be paid in Turkish liras calculated on the basis of the rate of exchange valid on that date, for both the deposit and the accrued interest.

The High Arbitration council is authorized to determine wages in lieu of collective bargaining. The council uses this authority until May 1983, when the Law on Collective Bargaining, Strikes, and Lockout is adopted. Wage increases for 1981 are restrained to 25 percent, and employers are forbidden to lay off workers.

1981

January. The quota list for imports is abolished; most items are transferred to liberalized list 2; many items are transferred from the quota list and list 2 to list 1, thus liberalizing imports very significantly. Guarantee deposit rates for imports are simultaneously reduced.

January 27. The Turkish lira is devalued vis-à-vis the U.S. dollar from TL89.25 to TL91.90.

February 5. The Turkish lira is further devalued to $1 = TL95.95.

An Economic Affairs High Coordination Council is established. The council is headed by the prime minister and composed of the two deputy prime ministers, the ministers of foreign affairs, finance, trade, agriculture/forestry, industry/technology, and energy (the functions of this council are transferred to the High Planning Council in January 1988).

The interest rates on bank's lending and deposit are increased by ten percentage points, and the Central Bank rediscount rates are rearranged.

The government's budget for fiscal year 1981–82 is approved; total appropriations amount to TL1,560 billion. The planned budget deficit is reduced from 11.3 percent of GNP in 1980–81 to 2.9 percent in 1981–82.

March. An Export Promotion Center within the Undersecretariat for Treasury and Foreign Trade is established.

April. The criteria for workers' wage increases are established by the Supreme Arbitration Board (also rendered in English as the High Arbitration Council): wages of workers whose collective contracts expired in 1979 are increased by 170 percent (gross). For contracts that expired in 1980 the rise is 80 percent.

A new export credit system is announced; the formalities are simplified, and limits of borrowing from the Central Bank and commercial banks are abolished.

The export tax rebate system is revised. The rates are increased over those in force since June 1979. Additional rebates for large exporters are also increased.

The Turkish lira is devalued vis-à-vis the U.S. dollar by 2.7 percent. The new rate is $1 = TL98.20.

May. A flexible exchange rate policy is announced under which the exchange rate for the Turkish lira will be adjusted daily. In principle these adjustments are to compensate for fluctuations in purchasing power parity.

Banks are allowed to include foreign currency holdings in their legal reserves.

August. Commercial banks are permitted to process import requests, subject to certain ceilings, without formal import permits.

November. Guidelines on foreign export prefinancing credits are revised. Maximum interest on such credits may not exceed 1.25 percent above LIBOR. Exports must be effected within a period of six months.

1982

January. The 1982 import and export regimes are announced. Liberalized list 1 is further enlarged by transferring forty items from list 2.

Imports of several essential goods will be subject to a new levy to be determined by the Money and Credit Committee. The funds raised will go into the Support and Price Stabilization Fund.

The export regime is further liberalized; the number of items requiring an export license is reduced from twenty-five to just two: tobacco and opium. The number of goods subject to registration is reduced from forty to thirty. Exporters are allowed to import up to 5 percent (maximum TL40,000) of their exports in 1981 and 1982.

February. For exports exceeding $4 million per year, the tax rebate is increased from 5 to 6 percent.

March. New rules concerning export prefinancing credits are introduced. The exchange rate guarantee is abolished, and credits cannot be transferred from one exporter to another.

Foreign exchange regulations are relaxed. Travel abroad can now take place every two years instead of three, and the tourism allowance is increased from $400 to $500.

April. The export tax rebate scheme is revised. Additional rebates for large exporters are differentiated by the volume of exports.

June. A 2 percent levy on imports is introduced, with proceeds going to the Support and Price Stabilization Fund.

A financial crisis, caused by the collapse of the money brokers, results in the departure of Özal from the government.

August. By a new decree the Ministry of Finance is empowered to regulate the legal status and financial structure of the capital market. (This authority, which had originally been vested in the Ministry of Finance, was transferred to the Capital Market Board at the beginning of 1982).

November. The Central Bank is authorized to determine the value of gold on a daily basis.

November 7. The new Constitution is adopted by Parliament.

December. New interest rates for bank deposits are announced. They are lowered on time deposits (from 45–50 to 40–45 percent) and increased for sight deposits (from 5 to 20 percent). The income tax law is changed. Tax rates are lowered by three percentage points. The fiscal balancing tax is abolished.

1983

January. Highlights of the 1983 import regime are as follows:

- Liberalized list 1 is enlarged further by transferring thirteen more items from liberalized list 2.

- Guarantee deposit rates are lowered.

- Administrative formalities are simplified; import permits can be renewed by authorized banks without prior approval by the Ministry of Commerce; imports by exporters with an incentive certificate can be carried out by authorized banks. Exporters, contractors, and others earning foreign currency are allowed to open foreign currency accounts with authorized Turkish banks up to 5 percent of their annual export earnings.

April. Exceptions are introduced in respect of the 2 percent levy on imports. Imports of investment goods by government and by the private sector with incentive certificates, as well as imports of petroleum companies and imports for national defense purposes, are exempted from the levy.

Foreign capital companies are allowed to use blocked funds (in cash or kind) to increase share capital, provided that foreign capital equal to at least half the blocked funds has been imported. Blocked funds will be converted at the current exchange rate and cannot be transferred for five years.

May. A decree law for the reorganization of state enterprises is published. They are divided into the following groups:

- state economic enterprises (SEEs): commercial enterprises whose capital is fully owned by the state

- public economic enterprises: public service enterprises (production of basic goods and services including monopoly goods) whose capital is fully owned by the state

- establishments: enterprises owned by an SEE or a PEE

- Attached participations: enterprises 50 percent or more of whose capital belongs to an SEE or a PEE

- Participations: enterprises between 25 and 50 percent of whose capital belongs to an SEE or a PEE

The Laws on Trade Unions and the Law on Collective Bargaining, Strikes, and Lockout are adopted by Parliament.

August. Banks permitted to hold foreign exchange positions are allowed to extend credits in foreign currency to contractors working abroad.

December. The first national elections since the September 1980 military takeover are held on November 6, and on December 13 the Motherland party forms a government with Özal as prime minister. The government announces its determination to continue policies of integrating Turkey into the world economy.

The new government reorganizes economic ministries. The Treasury Department of the Ministry of Finance and the Foreign Trade Department of the Ministry of Trade are combined to form the Office of the Undersecretary for the Treasury and Foreign Trade; the office is attached to the deputy prime minister and has main responsibility for economic policy.

A major realignment of interest rates take place. Central Bank rediscount rate for short-term credit is increased from 31.5 to 48.5 percent, for medium-term credits from 29.5 to 50.5 percent. Commercial banks' deposit rates for time savings are increased, and the rate for sight deposits is reduced from 20 to 5 percent.

The 1984 import and export regimes are published.

For imports, liberalized lists 1 and 2 are abolished and replaced by two new lists:

1. prohibited imports (some agricultural and textile products, arms, drugs, and so on)

2. goods subject to variable surcharge (mainly consumption goods)

Goods not included in either list may be imported without restriction (former liberalized list 1).

Imports from countries with a state trading regime may be made by trading companies whose exports have exceeded $50 million in 1983. Revenues arising from the surcharge on imports are earmarked for a new housing fund. Average tariff reductions are about 20 percent for customs duties and 8 percent for production tax.

Revenues arising from the surcharge on imports are earmarked for a new housing fund.

For exports, formalities are further simplified. Export price controls are only applied to exports with license.

The government announces its intention to reduce the importance of export subsidies because of their budgetary cost and the abuse of the system through fictitious exports and to rely more on the exchange rate for incentives. The exports tax rebate rates are therefore reduced by 45 percent in two steps on April 1, 1984, and September 1, 1984.

The foreign exchange retention right is increased from 5 percent (or $40,000) to 20 percent of export proceeds if the remaining 80 percent is surrendered within three months.

The government announces its intention to make the Turkish lira a convertible currency. The foreign exchange regulations are made more liberal. Residents and nonresidents are allowed to possess foreign currency and to open foreign exchange deposit accounts in banks with no restrictions on the use of these funds. Currency restrictions on tourists traveling abroad are removed.

Restrictions on importing Turkish liras, notes, securities, bills, and commercial papers are abolished.

Nonresidents are allowed to purchase real estate and participate in investment in Turkey.

Turkish residents are allowed to export capital.

Foreign credits may be contracted directly by authorized banks. Residents in Turkey may extend foreign exchange credits.

Commerical banks may retain 60 percent, and exports up to 20 percent, of their foreign exchange earnings.

The Money and Credit Council set up in 1980 and abolished in 1982 is formed again.

A Support and Price Stabilization Fund is reorganized within the Central Bank, which derives its revenues from a 2 percent levy on the cost, insurance, and freight (c.i.f.) value of imports (with certain exceptions) and a levy on some agricultural exports.

1984

January. A new Export Promotion Decree is published. An Incentives Department, attached to the Prime Minister's Office, is in charge of its implementation.

Trading companies whose exports in 1983 were over $30 million (of which at least 75 percent must have consisted of industrial or mining products) will be given incentive certificates.

Banks are no longer obliged to transfer 20 percent of foreign exchange earnings to the Central Bank. The new regulations permit banks to retain up to 40 percent of foreign currency assets adjusted by foreign exchange liabilities.

February. Central Bank rediscount rates are further increased: for short-term credits from 48.5 to 50 percent; for export credits from 35 to 40 percent; and for medium-term credits from 50 to 52 percent.

March. The Encouragement of Savings and Acceleration of Public Investment Law is approved by Parliament. Under the law the government is authorized to issue revenue-sharing certificates in public works such as dams, power plants, bridges, and highways. Funds raised will be centralized in a Public Partnership Fund.

The Housing Fund Law is approved. The fund will be used to finance the government's low-cost housing scheme.

April. A Foreign Credits Exchange Rate Differential Fund is set up at the Central Bank. The fund makes loans for export-oriented or other foreign exchange–earning projects, assuming the exchange rate risk for these loans and for approved foreign borrowing.

May. Commercial banks are permitted to engage in forward operations.

July. Decree No. 28 for the Protection of the Value of the Turkish Currency and related communiqués are replaced by Decree No. 30, which integrates all regulations concerning foreign exchange transactions, including those relating to exports and foreign investment.

The Fifth Five Year Development Plan 1985–1989 is approved by Parliament. The plan foresees 6.3 percent average annual GNP growth over the plan period.

October. Commercial banks are asked to allocate 20 percent of foreign exchange holdings to reserves (previously 10 percent).

A Central Bank communiqué announces that convertible Turkish lira deposits of nonresidents, including rescheduled credits, may be used for investment projects (Foreign Investment Law 6224) and for oil exploration activities (Petroleum Law). Amounts used for this purpose cannot be transferred abroad before the original repayment dates, which were fixed under the General Debt Rescheduling Agreement signed in 1979 and amended in 1981.

November. Tax privileges granted to SEEs—exemptions on income tax, stamp duty, and banking and insurance tax—are abolished.

December. Two new funds are set up in the Central Bank. The Support and Development Fund encourages investment in agriculture and tourism and small business and provides assistance to students. The Resource Utilization Support Fund replaces the Interest Differential Rebate Fund.

The 1985 export regime and the Export Promotion Decree are published. Upon presentation of an export project to the Department of Incentives and Implementation, exporters may be issued an export incentives certificate, valid for twelve months, which entitles them to use a foreign exchange allocation and duty-free imports for the export production.

The 1985 import regime is published. Guarantee deposit rates remain at 15 percent for importers and 7.5 percent for industrialists but will be reduced to 75 percent of the present level on April 1, 1985, 50 percent on August 1, 1985, and 25 percent on December 1, 1985.

The Central Bank is authorized to buy and sell gold.

1985

January. From January 1, 1985, a value-added tax of 10 percent is levied on products and services in commercial, industrial, agricultural, and private professional activities. The rate for basic foodstuffs is fixed at 6 percent to be effective from April 1, 1985. The VAT replaces the following indirect taxes: all production taxes and tax on sales, transportation, sugar, advertising, and postal services.

Preferential credits for exports are abolished.

February. Turkey signs the General Agreement on Tariffs and Trade subsidies code and agrees to phase out all subsidies on exports by the end of 1989.

Regulations for border trade are published. The value of goods for each transaction shall not exceed $10,000, and 80 percent of export earnings (in foreign currency or Turkish liras) must be repatriated.

March. The withholding tax of 20 percent on dividends paid by foreign capital ventures in Turkey is abolished.

May. The import regime is further simplified. Several commodities from the prohibited list are moved to the list of imports subject to permit, and a number of other commodities are fully liberalized. The list of prohibited imports is thus reduced from 500 items to only 3 items; the list of imports subject to prior permission is reduced from 1,000 to 600 items; simultaneously the list of imports subject to special levies is expanded.

The Banking Law is amended. Banks are required to be in the form of joint stock companies and to have at least 100 shareholders and a minimum capital and reserves of TL1 billion.

June. The Law on the Establishment of Free Zones is approved by Parliament. It aims to promote export-oriented production and investment, particularly foreign investment, by providing specific commercial and financial incentives.

The stamp duty on imports is raised from 1 to 4 percent.

Exporters are allowed to keep their foreign currency up to three months instead of ten days.

July. Bank deposit rates are changed. One-year deposits are made more attractive by increasing the rate from 48 to 56 percent.

Formalities for the export of fresh fruit and vegetables are simplified. Foreign importers are allowed to buy directly from local markets and pay in Turkish liras for a period of three months, starting from July 20, 1985. A 5 percent rebate on exports of fresh fruit and vegetables is reintroduced.

September. The Central Bank announces increases of levies for the Resource Utilization Support Fund.

December. The 1986 import regime is announced. All commodities can be imported without any restrictions, apart from narcotics, arms, and ammunitions, which are subject to special regulations. The number of items in the list of imports subject to license is reduced from 625 to 245. Rates of import duty are adjusted for 1,095 items, the average tariff being somewhat lower than earlier. The number of items subject to levies for extra budgetary funds is increased from 152 to 347. The guarantee deposit rate is reduced from 15 to 3 percent for importers and from 7.5 to 1 percent for industrialists.

The corporation tax rate is raised from 40 to 46 percent.

Commercial banks are obliged to transfer the equivalent of 20 percent of new foreign currency deposits to their reserves with the Central Bank from January 1, 1986. In addition, they must transfer 20 percent of their monthly foreign currency earnings to the Central Bank.

1986

March. Commercial banks are directed to set the buying and selling rates for foreign exchange within a bank at 1 percent below and above the rates announced by the Central Bank.

March 14. The Turkish lira is devalued by 5 percent against the U.S. dollar.

April. The Central Bank introduces a system for interbank lending for periods of one to two weeks (exceptionally twenty-one days).

May. The 1986 import regime is further liberalized. The number of items subject to license is reduced from 245 to 100.

Exemptions granted to public sector entities (such as municipalities and SEEs) in respect of customs duties, some other taxes, and fees on imports are abolished.

With the amendment of the Tobacco Law, the tobacco monopoly is lifted, and production is opened to domestic and foreign firms. Import of tobacco, subject to a surcharge, is also liberalized.

June. A 5 percent surcharge on the c.i.f. value of imports from European Community countries is abolished.

July. Import guarantee deposit rates are increased from 3 to 9 percent and from 1 to 7 percent to be effective from July 1, 1986.

October. The 10 percent surcharge for the Resource Utilization Support Fund on export credits is abolished.

The regulation restricting imports from countries under a state trading regime to trading companies whose exports have exceeded $50 million during the preceding year is altered to cover firms that possess investment incentive certificates.

Surcharges are increased on imports of specific luxury goods.

Rules governing the establishment of nonbank foreign exchange agencies are published. The minimum capital requirement is TL1 billion. Agencies must have at least ten branches. Buying and selling rates may be set at 1 percent above the Central Bank rates, and a commission may be charged.

November. A series of policy measures is introduced in November and December aimed at restricting growth of domestic demand and promoting exports: The government is authorized to raise VAT to 15 percent; as a first step the current rate is increased to 12 percent, to be effective from December 1, 1986; the zero rate for basic foodstuff is maintained, and a rate of 1 percent is introduced for some agricultural goods.

The Central Bank rediscount facility for short-term export credits is made operative.

December. The surcharge earmarked for the Support and Price Stabilization Fund and levied on the c.i.f. value of imports in increased from 2 to 4 percent. The fund's scope for supporting exports is enlarged; customs duties on 163 items are lowered by 50 to 100 percent; moreover, import surcharges on several goods are increased. The import regime is further liberalized. The number of items on the list subject to import permission is reduced from 245 to 111. All the items simultaneously become subject to levies for the special fund. Guarantee deposit rates are fixed uniformly at 7 percent.

The stamp duty on imports is raised from 4 to 6 percent.

1987

January. The interest rate for credits eligible for support by the Exchange Rate Differential Fund (also rendered in English as the Interest Differential Rebate Fund) is reduced from 35 to 32 percent.

February. The Central Bank Law is amended. The bank is authorized to engage in open market operations

March. Subject to government authorization, creditor banks are permitted to swap bad loans against equity in companies in financial difficulties and take control of their boards. The State Investment Bank is authorized to operate as an export-import financing bank.

April. The Wage Negotiations Coordination Board, which was formed in 1982 to set guidelines for collective bargaining agreements, is abolished.

May. Turkish contractors successful in international bidding for public sector projects financed by foreign credits are eligible for a tax rebate of 2 percent of the foreign exchange cost of the contract. Surcharges and customs duty on imports of selected investment goods are lowered.

July. Monetary policy is eased; the legal reserve ratio is reduced from 15 to 10 percent for Turkish lira deposits and raised from 15 to 20 percent for foreign exchange deposits.

The surcharge for the Resource Utilization Support Fund on interest earnings of banks from nonpreferential credits is decreased from 10 to 5 percent.

August. The former State Investment Bank is officially renamed the Turkish Export-Import Bank.

September. The State Industry and Workers' Investment Bank (DESIYAB) takes over the task of the former State Investment Bank to provide finance for SEEs.

October. The 4 percent surcharge for the Support and Price Stabilization Fund on the c.i.f. value of imports is increased to 6 percent.

November. Surcharges on imports of iron and steel, television sets, radios, and passenger cars are lowered.

December. After the general elections on November 21 the second Özal government is formed and receives a vote of confidence from Parliament.

1988

January. A Foreign Debt Strategy Committee is set up. It is chaired by the state minister in charge of economic affairs; members are the minister of finance, the undersecretaries of the State Planning Organization and the Treasury and foreign trade, the governor of the Central Bank, and the head of the Public Participation Fund. The committee determines guidelines for foreign borrowing by public sector entities.

A new fiscal policy package is introduced: civil servants' salaries and income tax brackets are indexed to inflation.

The general VAT rate is maintained at 12 percent, but VAT is increased to 15 percent for specific items, such as, electrical appliances, motor cars, and precious stones. Basic foodstuffs are now taxed at a rate of 3 percent. The VAT rate on books, newspapers, and pharmaceutical products is increased from 5 to 8 percent.

For the first time, interest income on government securities is made subject to 5 percent withholding tax.

1988 import and export regulations are published. The import regime is further liberalized; the number of items on the list subject to permission is reduced from 111 to 33; customs tariffs on 234 items, including basic inputs, are lowered. All tariffs are now below 50 percent. The number of items subject to surcharges is increased from 577 to 787. A new surcharge of 3 percent on the c.i.f. value of imports by the public sector is introduced.

February. Further restrictive economic policy measures, called the 4th of February package, are announced:

- Monetary policy is tightened; the legal reserve ratio for Turkish lira deposits is raised from 14 to 16 percent.

- Interest rates on commercial bank deposits are increased to 65 percent for deposits of over one year and to 36 percent for sight deposits. Official deposits receive 10 percent.

- Central Bank rediscount rates are raised by between eight and twelve percentage points.

- For imports, the guarantee deposit rate is increased from 7 to 15 percent in the period February 4 through March 1, 1988. The rate will be 14 percent in March and 10 percent in April, after which it will again be 7 percent by May 1, 1988.

- Exporters are required to sell their foreign exchange earnings to banks within six months of exporting. If they transfer receipts within three months, exporters are allowed to retain 20 percent.

- Export tax rebates are amended. For foreign exchange earnings turned over within thirty days, exporters are granted an additional premium and receive a tax rebate equal to 120 percent of the regular rate. For transfers within a period of thirty to sixty days, the export rebate rate will be 90 percent of the regular rate, and up to ninety days the rebate will be 50 percent. If export revenues are not transferred within the maximum limit of ninety days, no tax rebate will be granted.

- The 5 percent withholding tax on government securities introduced in January 1988 is abolished.

- Commercial banks are requested to transfer 25 percent of their foreign exchange holdings to the Central Bank.

March. Profit transfers abroad can now be made through commercial banks without prior approval from the Central Bank.

The petroleum consumption tax rate is raised from 9 to 26 percent.

Customs duties and import surcharges are lowered for several items.

The list of imported goods subject to surcharge for the Support and Price Stabilization Fund is changed. Raw materials for export-oriented investments and goods used for investments in development priority regions are excluded.

April. Export incentives are amended. Starting from April 1, rebates are to be scaled down gradually to be terminated by January 1989.

A special export credit facility is created within the Central Bank.

June. A communiqué regulating foreign borrowing is published.

The surcharge in favor of the Resource Utilization Support Fund on the credits and on the imports by acceptance credit is set at 6 percent.

The Multinational Investment Guarantee Agreement and the agreement to join the International Center for Settlement of Investment Disputes are ratified by the Turkish Parliament.

Foreign investors are authorized to use their blocked funds in Turkey for reinvestment under the provisions of the Foreign Investment Law.

July. A decree concerning the establishment of a foreign exchange market within the Central Bank is published.

Imports with incentive certificates for investment in priority development regions are exempted from the 5 percent surcharge earmarked for the Export Encouragement Fund.

Exporters are granted additional tax rebates for foreign currency earnings transferred to Turkey within ninety days after the close of the deal. The additional rebate rate will be 2 percent for exports of $2 to $10 million, 4 percent for exports of $10 to $30 million, and 6 percent for exports exceeding $30 million.

The surcharge on imports of luxury goods earmarked for the Support and Price Stabilization Fund is increased from 6 to 8 percent.

August. Export rebate rates for large exporters are lowered by 50 percent.

October. An interbank market for foreign currency is established.

The minimum amount of exports required for postshipment credits by the Export-Import Bank is reduced from $50 million to $25 million; the credit limit is increased from 10 to 25 percent of the free-on-board (f.o.b.) value of exports.

The stamp duty on imports is increased from 6 to 10 percent.

The import deposit rate is increased from 7 to 15 percent to the end of March 1989. In April 1989 it will be reduced to 12 percent, in May 1989 to 10 percent, and thereafter to 7 percent.

Banks are authorized to determine freely all interest rates on deposits and credits with the exception of official deposits, for which the maximum rate is fixed at 10 percent. Rates can be changed once a month.

The surcharge on imports of luxury goods earmarked for the Support and Price Stabilization Fund is increased from 8 to 10 percent.

December. Several tax laws are amended; an advance tax payment system is introduced for income and corporation taxes; interest earnings on government papers (bonds, Treasury bills, revenue-sharing certificates) held by corporations are made subject to a withholding tax retroactive to January 1988; the rate is 5 percent for 1988 and 10 percent for 1989.

The 5 percent withholding tax on dividends from foreign exchange participation accounts of private finance corporations is raised to 10 percent, and for the first time interest earnings on foreign exchange deposits are subject to a 10 percent withholding tax.

1989

January. All export rebates are eliminated.

The new export credit system is amended. Export companies that have exported at least $100 million in the preceding twelve months are eligible for credit up to 5 percent of the lira equivalent of the value of these exports.

Foreign companies subject to corporation tax are exempted from advance tax payments.

February. New export incentives are announced: manufacturer-exporters are exempted from the surcharge on fuel oil consumption and are granted price reductions for electricity and coal consumed in export-oriented productions (25 percent for coal and one U.S. cent per 100 kilowatt-hours for electricity).

March. A preshipment export credit scheme by the Turkish Export-Import Bank is introduced.

The State Planning Organization announces the list of transactions exempted from stamp duty:

- export credit and credit guarantees, payments against exports, other transactions with an export promotion certificate, and imports for export-oriented projects

- foreign currency–generating activities

- medium- and long-term investment credits for projects with incentive certificates

The 1989 import regime is amended. Customs tariffs are lowered for 40 items and raised for 147 items. Import surcharges are also changed for 62 items.

April. An official gold market is opened.

May. Deposit money banks are permitted to offer floating interest rates for two- to five-year deposits.

June. The export regime is simplified, and the practice of "export licenses" is abolished. Trading companies eligible for various privileges must have a minimum capital of TL5 billion and an annual export volume of $100 million.

A "transport infrastructure duty" replaces the wharf duty on imports to cover imports via customs gates in addition to seaports. It amounts to 4 percent on imports through seaports and 3 percent through other customs gates.

Customs duty on cotton yarn imports is lifted, but the surcharge is raised from $130 to $200 to $300 per ton, except for imports for export-oriented projects with an incentive certificate, which are exempted from the surcharge.

July. Trading companies that have exported at least $100 million in 1988 and aim at the same figure in 1989 are granted a "marketing premium" of 2 percent of their 1988 exports from the Support and Price Stabilization Fund.

Premiums paid from the Support and Price Stabilization Fund for exports of certain items—such as fresh and frozen meat, tractors, transport vehicles, and iron and steel products—are increased, and new items, such as electrical equipment, ceramics and kitchenware, and sanitary fixtures, are added to the list.

August. Foreign exchange transactions are further liberalized under Decree No. 32, Protection of the Value of the Turkish Lira.

Customs duties and surcharges are lowered on 331 items, mostly consumer goods like cars, household appliances, cosmetics, tea, and coffee, and on a number of raw materials.

September. Exports against Turkish liras are permitted.

The Central Bank ceases to carry out foreign exchange transactions concerning invisible export earnings.

Customs duties and surcharges on several goods, including those already lowered in August, are further decreased.

October. Customs duties on several goods, for example, passenger cars, tires, some textile products, and electrical batteries, are lowered, and surcharges on vegetable oils are increased.

November. Özal is elected president of the Turkish Republic by Parliament.

New export incentives are published.

The Central Bank reduces the legal reserve ratio.

With the communiqué of the Money and Credit Council, export premiums are reduced. If 70 percent of the export proceeds are repatriated within ninety days, the total amount will be paid. Previously, if 80 percent of foreign exchange earnings were brought to Turkey, 120 percent of the premium was to be paid.

Notes

Chapter 2

1. See Krueger 1987 for a comparative analysis of Turkish and Korean growth.

2. An interesting feature of the Turkish economy, and one that is not well understood, is that the ratio of urban to rural per capita income is unusually high. See Dervis and Robinson 1980 for further analysis of this phenomenon.

3. The government imposed price controls on a number of commodities and kept the prices of government-provided goods and services low in an effort to contain inflation. Its price indexes had a bias toward using official prices, which failed to reflect actual prices for a number of commodities. The result was a significant downward bias in the price indexes of the time. See Krueger 1974 for a fuller account of this episode.

4. See Krueger 1974, chap. 4; and Sturc 1968 for an analysis.

5. Republic of Turkey, State Planning Organization, *First Five Year Plan, 1963–67,* Ankara, January 1963.

6. This sharp increase was the result of a number of factors, including the increased flexibility of the Turkish economy resulting from the preceding decade's growth, but also importantly the remittances of Turkish workers who had emigrated to northern European countries, predominantly Germany, in large numbers. The government had recognized the sensitivity of these funds to the exchange rate and had provided a special exchange rate and incentives for workers to repatriate their funds. Workers' remittances had already become a major source of foreign exchange earnings by 1968 and continued growing in 1969. It was not recognized, however, that workers were nonetheless depositing large sums in German banks, anticipating that the exchange rate might in the future be altered. Thus after the 1970 devaluation there was a large-scale inflow of funds from Western Europe.

7. See Chapter 5 for a further discussion of effective exchange rates for exports and their evolution over time.

8. The situation was confounded by serious civil unrest. This was manifested both in a large number of labor disputes and in a large number

of politically motivated murders. The latter situation appears to have provided the major impetus for military intervention in the fall of 1980. It is
significant, however, that the reform program began under the elected civilian
government of Prime Minister Süleyman Demirel and then continued under
the military government that assumed power in September 1980. The ruling
group invited Turgut Özal, the architect of the economic reforms of January
1980, to remain in the military government as deputy prime minister in
charge of economic policy.

9. See Krueger and Tuncer 1982 for an analysis of the relative efficiency
of private enterprises and SEEs during the 1960s and 1970s.

10. Baysan and Blitzer 1988, Table 2.5.

11. Balassa 1985.

12. The August 1970 devaluation package had the same three components, although the situation was far less extreme in August 1970 than
it had been in 1958 and there was considerably less emphasis on curbing
inflation. In both those respects the January 1980 program bore a greater
resemblance to the 1958 program than to the 1970 program.

13. Even these were accorded larger premiums over the TL2.80 rate
than they had earlier received.

14. See Chapter 4, Table 9, for estimates of the real exchange rate.

15. The rate for Turkish workers' remittances and for tourism was
significantly above the official rate by 1970.

16. See Chapter 4 for a full discussion.

17. Even these data fail fully to reflect the sharp increase in foreign
exchange availability: in the 1970–1973 period imports of military hard-
ware rose markedly in response to increased foreign exchange receipts.

18. There are several bases for believing that the recorded reduction
in imports—more than 20 percent between 1977 and 1978—may over-
estimate the actual reduction. There probably was a good deal of smuggling.

19. The estimate is Rodrik's (1989, p. 41), and takes into account the
deficits of the SEEs as well as the central government deficit. The latter is
estimated at about 4 percent of GNP.

20. Table 4.3 from Amelung 1988, who used State Institute of Statistics
(SIS) data. In the winter of 1980, when Krueger and Baran Tuncer were

interviewing Istanbul industrialists in connection with a study of Turkish total factor productivity growth, they inquired about sources of low productivity over the preceding years. Despite inflation of more than 100 percent, acute difficulties in obtaining foreign exchange, and other problems, the almost universal response focused on the strikes of the preceding several months and years as having been the most serious problem those employers faced. This response came even in interviews where the offices in which they were held were unheated.

21. See Amelung 1988 for a more detailed discussion.

22. Baysan and Blitzer 1988a, p. 48.

23. Dervis, de Melo, and Robinson 1982, pp. 338–39.

24. OECD 1980, p. 5.

25. Amelung 1988, p. 27.

26. Celasun and Rodrik 1987, pp. 2-6–7.

27. Ibid., p. 2-45.

28. Ibid., p. 2-44.

Chapter 3

1. Banker Kasteli was a prominent financier, whose inability to meet his debt-servicing obligations in the money market led to panic among creditors about their other outstanding obligations.

2. This section draws heavily on the excellent account of Okyar 1983.

3. Ibid., pp. 539–40.

4. Ibid., p. 535.

5. In preference to further devaluation, the Turkish government had increased export "rebates" in July 1978. In the IMF's view these ad hoc supplements to the exchange rate were less attractive to exporters than an exchange rate change would have been, in part because there was no assurance that they would continue.

6. *Economist,* March 17, 1979, p. 13. The *Economist* reported that for 1977 the government's central budget deficit was 5.6 percent of GNP and the financing requirements of the SEEs were 6.8 percent of GNP. Both of these were financed by borrowing from the Central Bank.

7. Barkey reports that there was a meeting of the four chambers of Industry with the Istanbul Chamber of Commerce in January 1979. The participants then submitted proposals to the government with recommendations for a stabilization program. They apparently agreed on all recommendations except for devaluation, to which the Instanbul Chamber of Industry—which represents primarily the large import-substitution industrialists—objected. He concludes, "The significance of this meeting was that, despite the objections of the Istanbul Chamber of Industry, the leading economic groups in the country had finally come to the realization that if the Turkish economy was to escape its paralysis . . . , a new and radical alternative had to be sought." Barkey 1984, p. 61.

8. Heper 1984, p. 80. Demirel did send Özal to Washington for discussion with IMF staff in December 1979, and the IMF was kept informed of the general outlines of the government's program. See Okyar 1983, pp. 542–43, for a description.

9. In addition, it was announced that interest rates for all credits were raised by two percentage points, that foreign investment regulations would be liberalized to encourage the inflow of foreign capital into all sections of the economy, including those from which it had earlier been effectively discouraged, and that policy regarding petroleum exploration would be significantly liberalized. See Chronological Appendix and Organization for Economic Cooperation and Development 1981, pp. 34–35, for details.

10. Legally, special exchange rates continued to apply to Turkish workers' remittances and tourism, but the effective exchange rate for these transactions was unified. For example, there was a 50 percent tax on the sale of foreign exchange for tourism abroad. Some transition measures were taken to buffer the impact of the exchange rate change. Students who had left to study abroad before June 12, 1979, were permitted to receive remittances at TL26.50 until August 31, 1980; for students departing later, the exchange rate effective at the time they departed temporarily applied. See International Monetary Fund 1981, p. 425.

11. See Organization for European Cooperation and Development 1981, p. 33. Levies for 1980 were specific and are thus hard to interpret. Some rates were TL4.1 per kilogram for wheat, TL36–41 per kilogram for cotton, TL400 per kilogram for mohair, and TL110 per kilogram for tobacco.

12. For example, for items on liberalized list I, the advance deposit required of importers fell from 40 to 30 percent and that for industrialists was lowered from 25 to 15 percent. Ibid.

13. The increases in the pricing of commodities produced by SEEs were, however, probably significantly larger than earlier increases had been. It could be argued that it was these increases, which are immediately felt by large segments of the population and are politically difficult to implement, that provided the signal that the government was serious in its intent.

14. Indeed, the fact that it was a minority government that was in power made the prospects for passing legislation to implement many of the government's statements of intent poor indeed. Özal, in an interview late in 1981 in *Yankı,* agreed that the best he could have hoped for in January 1980 would have been the announcement of an early election that could have given the Justice party a majority in Parliament. See Barkey 1984, p. 63.

15. OECD 1981, p. 18. As already noted, these transfers covered operating losses. Central Bank credits to finance investments are not included in these numbers.

16. Increases in prices of SEE products had been important and visible components of earlier stabilization programs in 1958 and 1970. See Krueger 1974 for an account.

17. Okyar 1983, p. 544.

18. This account is based on OECD, *Economic Survey, 1981,* Annex 1. See also Chronological Appendix.

19. When Prime Minister Demirel first announced the program in January 1979, Ecevit and others attacked the program on the grounds that it was foreign supported and even foreign inspired. These attacks lost some of their effectiveness in light of Ecevit's willingness to agree to the two standby programs in 1978 and 1979. The record indicates, however, that the Turkish authorities had kept in contact with the international community but did not approach them for support until after they had developed the program. See Okyar 1983, pp. 546ff.

20. Ibid., p. 547.

21. Ibid., p. 549.

22. Ibid., p. 550.

23. It was believed by many that the financial crisis was anticipated but that the authorities did not think they could act until the liquidity problem became apparent. On the other hand, many believe that the authorities allowed these operations in the expectation of facilitating additional financing for industry.

24. There is no question but that the election was fairly conducted. The government's control over the parties that could contest the election, however, and the fact that many politicians remained who had been forbidden to participate in politics after the 1980 military takeover led many to question the legitimacy of the election.

25. Sachs 1989, p. 23. See also Celasun and Rodrik 1987.

26. See section "The IMF Standbys of 1978 and 1979."

27. Kopits 1987, p. 8. Kopits comments that there was, in effect, a multiyear agreement, which covered a consolidation period of several years beyond the agreement, subject to continued Turkish compliance with policy undertakings reached in the three-year standby.

28. World Bank 1985–86, p. 471.

29. On assuming power in September 1980, the military outlawed strikes. The elimination of strikes was also a factor in the upturn in capacity utilization in Turkish industries.

30. *Economist,* September 21, 1981, "Turkey Survey," p. 8.

31. The rate of inflation has not again reached 100 percent, although there have been sizable swings in the inflationary effects of the government budget and its financing.

32. *Economist,* September 21, 1981, "Turkey Survey," p. 9. There is some dispute about how much of the recorded increase in exports reflected a real increase in export volume and how much reflected a shift from underinvoicing to overinvoicing of exports on the part of exporters. See Chapter 5 for an analysis of the importance of this possibility.

33. Much of the increase was in petroleum imports; at the time it was uncertain whether increased imports were simply restocking and purchases for reexport or whether they constituted inventory accumulation by consumers and others who were skeptical about the durability of the liberalization of the trade regime. Okyar 1983, pp. 554–55.

34. Estimates are from Baysan and Blitzer 1988b, Table 1.

35. See Chapter 4 for an account of the various export incentives and their value during the 1980–1989 period.

36. In May 1986, for example, the number of items subject to license was reduced from 245 to 100. OECD 1987, p. 68. See Chapter 4 for a

quantification of export incentives, and the Chronological Appendix for a more detailed chronology of individual policy changes undertaken.

37. See Chronological Appendix for a chronology of the dates and amounts by which the levies were increased. They were initially imposed at a rate of 2 percent in 1981. See also the discussion in Chapter 4 of the use of SPSF funds for export incentives.

38. Baysan and Blitzer 1988b, p. 11. Estimates from the Central Bank suggest even greater real effective exchange rate depreciation. See also Saracoglu 1987, p. 126.

39. These measures were known as the "4th of February package." See OECD 1990, p. 52 and 116, for a description and analysis.

40. See Chapter 5 for discussion of the impact of these effects on exporters.

41. See OECD 1990, p. 91, for a description.

42. For example, uniform accounting standards were introduced in 1985. In 1987 external auditing of banks' accounts became mandatory.

43. Deregulation was not complete: banks were permitted to change their rates only once a month. See OECD 1990, p. 119.

44. Special funds were established and became additional off-budget sources of revenue. The creation of these funds was perhaps the only major dimension in which tax reforms did not result in simplification and unification of the tax structure.

45. See OECD 1990, p. 100ff., for a fuller discussion. See also the discussion in the June 1987 OECD *Survey,* sec. 4.

46. A major component of the growth in expenditure was expenditures out of the special funds; already in 1987 expenditures by the funds accounted for 10.2 percent of GNP, up from 3.2 percent in 1985 and a negligible fraction in years before that. See OECD 1990, p. 101.

47. See Data Appendix Table 1 for additional data.

48. The data are for the years 1980 to 1988; 1989 was a drought year, and agricultural production fell sharply.

Chapter 4

1. Computed as 10 percent customs duty, plus 1.5 percent municipality tax, plus 10 percent stamp duty, plus 6 percent fund tax, plus 19.1 percent wharf tax, plus 12.95 percent value-added tax.

2. It is likely that the addition of fifty percentage points for all commodities underestimates the true differential in protection rates, as this example demonstrates. Many minerals—especially copper—were exported. It is therefore likely that import restrictions did not affect domestic price for those commodities. For some import-competing commodities, the effect may have been even greater than the 50 percent number.

3. Exports were exempt from production tax under a decree introduced in 1973. *Resmi Gazete,* June 17, 1973.

4. TUD's name was changed in 1984 to Teşvik ve Uygulama Başkanlığı (TUB).

5. Individual exporters in interviews appeared to be very relaxed about the procedures for obtaining exporters' certificates. They simply declared their intention to export a given amount within a specified period—generally three to six months. On the basis of their statement of intent, the certificate was issued. If, for some reason, the export was not realized, they simply notified TUD/TUB that they would not be exporting that amount, and there was no penalty. According to exporters, the authorities followed up and attempted to penalize for providing a statement of intent and failing to deliver only if export incentives were used when there was no intent to export.

6. Law 261, *Resmi Gazete,* May 7, 1963, is the legal basis for the tax rebates. Actual payments started in March 1964 under Decree 6/2453, May 12, 1963.

7. Decree 7/10624, September 9, 1975.

8. Turkey acceded to the GATT subsidies code in 1985, which was the instrumental factor in the decision to eliminate the rebates.

9. In Turkey there is a tax on all financial transactions, in addition to a banking commission and a stamp duty. Exporters were exempted from these charges. There was also an "interest equalization tax"; exporters were charged only half the ordinary rate, which in Turkish jargon was an additional "export incentive." The values of these tax exemptions and reductions are indicated in Table 16.

10. This was apparently in response to the failure of Iraqi importers to pay Turkish exporters for their sales. With Communiqué no. 1 of November 1, 1986, the Central Bank opened its rediscount credit facility for short-term export credits. Later the Turkish Export Credit Bank (Turkish Export-Import Bank) was established under Decree no. 87/11914. *Resmi Gazete,* August 21, 1987.

11. Central Bank Communiqué no. 4. *Resmi Gazete,* April 5, 1988.

12. Central Bank Communiqué no. 6. *Resmi Gazete,* October 28, 1989.

13. Until 1989 the exchange rate was depreciating at a rate at least equal to the rate of inflation. In 1989, however, the nominal exchange rate depreciated at about half the rate of inflation (about 70 percent annual rate).

14. Depending on the availability of credit, however, these limits were tightened or relaxed.

15. The amount was $10,000 for products subject to charges for the Support and Price Stabilization Fund.

16. Incentive certificates were issued to exporters who declared their intention to import for the purposes of reexporting. This mechanism permitted the authorities to monitor the goods entering the country for purposes of reexporting.

17. Communiqué II-5/4, May 6, 1980.

18. Communiqué no. 28, Dec. 29, 1983.

19. If one wants to contrast an existing incentive structure with one that would prevail at free trade, it is evident that the excess cost of imports (because of duties and other charges on imports) should be treated as a disincentive. Insofar as a trade and payments regime removes those disincentives through a duty drawback scheme, it should not be regarded as an export incentive.

20. In addition to corporate profits taxes, firms were assessed taxes for the various special funds. These taxes, however, were paid at the same rate as that on domestic sales, and tax liabilities were thus not affected by the value of exports.

21. Exports of fresh fruit and vegetables, marine products, tourism, and transport services were also accorded the tax exemption. Construction firms were entirely exempted from corporate profits taxes.

22. Statutory Decree no. 86/11282, December 13, 1986.

23. One instance was the payment of $3 per pair for plastic slippers while the domestic market price was about fifty cents per pair. There appear to have been a number of items for which the subsidy exceeded the domestic market price of the item.

24. This export ceiling applied for the goods in lists 1 to 8. For those in list 9 the ceiling was $1.5 million. See Table 18.

25. Decree no. 84/8869, *Resmi Gazete,* December 15, 1986; Decree no. 86/10520, *Resmi Gazete,* April 2, 1986; and Decree no. 86/11085, *Resmi Gazete,* October 9, 1986.

26. The EER for importers would be below that for producers of import-competing goods to the extent that imports were able to obtain import licenses. For in that case they did not have to pay the value of the premium on import licenses, an estimate of which is included in the present computation. For producers of import-competing goods who were able to obtain their imports at below-average import charge rates while selling in the domestic market protected by import licenses of the value estimated here, the effective protection rate would be even higher than that indicated in Table 19.

27. The interested reader can see the bias for himself. For commodities that were exported and not subject to any export subsidies, the bias of the regime was simply one plus the import duty rate (given in Table 13) expressed as a ratio. In 1982, for example, the estimated bias against agricultural commodities not eligible for any export incentives would be 2.21.

28. To the extent that import-competing producers had a higher import content than exportable producers, the estimate is biased downward. There is considerable reason to believe that, on average, there was a higher import content of import-competing goods.

Chapter 5

1. *Financial Times,* March 6, 1990, p. 2. The major motive may have been an attempt to control inflation.

2. See Table 9 for the evolution of the real exchange rate.

3. Compared with 1988, the Turkish lira experienced a real appreciation of 25 percent by 1990. See Table 9.

4. See Table 3 in Chapter 2.

5. More detail may be found in Data Appendix Table 14.

6. Even that rate of growth understates true performance, as can be seen by inspection of Data Appendix Table 14: since the exchange rate was altered in January 1980, there was already considerable growth in exports in 1980 over the very depressed levels of 1979. Use of 1979 as a base year, however, is subject to the opposite error: there is considerable anecdotal evidence (consistent with the incentives provided by the trade regime at that time) that a large volume of exports was shipped through extralegal channels. Hence part of the increase from the late 1970s to 1980 probably reflected the return of exports to official channels, and using 1979 as a year for comparison would overstate export growth after the policy reforms were instituted.

7. See OECD, *Structural Adjustment and Economic Performance, 1987* (Paris, 1987).

8. After the Koreans altered their incentive structure in 1960, the initial rapid increase in exports also originated largely from excess capacity. See Kim and Roemer 1979, chap. 5.

9. See Krueger 1987 for a discussion.

10. OECD, *Economic Surveys. Turkey,* 1989/90, p. 43. The constant-market-shares analysis is essentially a mechanical decomposition of the regional effect and the commodity composition effect of a country's growth—in this case, export—performance. It computes what growth would have been had the country been able to maintain its share in each of its product lines in each of its regional markets. A positive residual indicates an increase in share, and a negative residual indicates a decrease in share, relative to what would have happened had shares held constant. A negative regional effect, therefore, indicates that the country would have experienced a decrease in exports had its share of its regional markets been constant. While no causation can be imputed to this sort of analysis, a positive residual is strongly suggestive of increasing competitiveness of a country's exports, either by virtue of a change in its policies toward exporters or because of shifts in comparative advantage (and consequent reduction in costs) attributable to other factors.

11. See the discussion in Chapter 4.

12. See Bhagwati 1974 and Krueger 1974, chap. 6, for further discussion of the technique of using partner country trade statistics and for comparisons between Turkish and partner country trading statistics in earlier years.

13. Rodrik 1988, p. 31. Rodrik calculated a number for the first five months of 1987—the latest month for which data were available at the time

he was writing. His estimates showed an extraordinary 53 percent for those five months. Note that if the average f.o.b.–c.i.f. differential is smaller than 8 percentage points, Rodrik's estimates overstate overinvoicing by the amount of the differential. Thus, if the true c.i.f.–f.o.b. differential for Turkey were, for example, 5 percentage points, the "best estimate" of overinvoicing by this method would be 8.4 instead of 11.4 percent over the 1981–1987 period. IMF data (*International Financial Statistics*) for 1985 show a worldwide differential between c.i.f. and f.o.b. of 3.8 percentage points. The differential is clearly larger in the case of bulk shipments and longer distances. This might suggest that the Turkish differential is smaller than Rodrik's estimates.

14. Turkey signed the subsidies code in February 1985.

15. Empirically, this was taken as the dollar value of Turkish exports deflated by the U.S. wholesale price index. An alternative specification in which the dollar value of exports was used without deflation yielded results that were very similar to those reported here. The data on PPP rates are given in Table 9, Chapter 4.

16. We were given a small book, published by the Turkish Foreign Trade Association (Turktrade), entitled "Turkish Foreign Trade Corporate Companies," which listed all foreign trade companies. There were thirty-two members in 1989. The description of the organization inside the front cover indicated that it anticipated that foreign trade companies would be responsible for over 60 percent of Turkey's exports in 1990.

17. Turktrade 1989.

18. In part because many of the FTCs were associated with large trading houses, it was not possible to keep meaningful track of the average split. Impressionistically, it appeared that the FTCs more often offered 3 percent and kept 2 percent than any other arrangement. FTCs became eligible for the additional incentives when their exports reached particular volumes. They therefore had a double incentive to attract business. On one hand, they could split a commission; on the other hand, without a sufficient volume of business, they would be ineligible for the additional incentives. Doubtless the sum offered the producer of the exportable varied depending on the producer's alternatives and on the existing level of exports of the FTC.

19. Etibank is an SEE that mines and exports numerous mineral products. Sümerbank is a large SEE producing primarily textile and apparel products. Taris is a Union of Agricultural Cooperative Societies, which is quasi–public sector and which handles marketing and exporting of figs, raisins, olive oil, and cotton. TDCI is an SEE producing iron ore and iron and

steel. Tekel is the SEE that has the monopoly on production and marketing of alcohol and tobacco. TMO is the SEE dealing with marketing of grains.

20. This claim received further support in July 1990 when the head of the Export Department at the Treasury announced that the law governing exports would be altered to conform to EC standards. He noted that the old law had been 300 pages long and the new law would be 4 pages long and stated that henceforth exporters would be required to file only a single document, instead of the eighteen previously required. *Financial Times,* July 11, 1990, p. 3.

21. It is not entirely clear why the lira appreciated in real terms in 1989. Earlier in the decade a clear commitment had been announced that the Central Bank would adjust the price of foreign exchange in such a way that the real return to exporters would not diminish. As measures were taken to move the lira closer to convertibility, however, market forces were increasingly permitted to operate in the foreign exchange market. In 1988 the Turkish current account balance was in surplus for the first time in many years. It is conceivable that market forces tended to lead to real appreciation and that the Central Bank was willing to permit this to happen. Alternatively, and perhaps more plausibly, the Central Bank may have been confronted with the unpleasant alternatives of purchasing foreign exchange (and thus increasing domestic credit at a time when inflation was proceeding at an already unacceptably high rate) or permitting the appreciation to occur. Yet a third explanation, and the one implicitly or explicitly believed by most respondents to the question, was that the authorities were deliberately delaying the nominal depreciation of the lira as an anti-inflationary measure.

22. See Data Appendix Table 15.

23. See, for example, Collins 1989, p. 14.

24. As indicated in Chapter 3, Turkish debt was rescheduled as a part of the 1980 reform package, and there is no question that rescheduling at that time was essential. The more critical question, from the viewpoint of ascertaining the relevance of Turkish experience for other countries, is whether Turkey received more new money in the early 1980s than other heavily indebted countries in comparable situations several years later did.

25. Turkish outstanding debt is estimated to have declined another $2 billion in 1989. *Financial Times,* March 6, 1990, p. 2. Changes in the dollar value of outstanding debt reflect both net borrowing and changes in the dollar exchange rate. Part of the change pre- and post-1985 thus reflects dollar appreciation until 1985 and depreciation in the next several years.

26. Anand and van Wijnbergen (1989) have developed a model in which they contrast the fiscal cost of borrowing domestically with the cost of borrowing abroad *given the size of the public sector deficit*. According to their analysis, external borrowing was cheaper than internal borrowing, and thus Turkey's ability to gain access to the international capital markets permitted less inflation than would otherwise have occurred. An alternative analysis would assume smaller public sector expenditures in the absence of additional foreign lending.

27. That this conjecture may have some validity is suggested by the sharp drop in private consumption expenditures as a percentage of GNP in 1985. See Data Appendix Table 5.

28. See next section for a discussion of the ways in which inflationary pressures may still pose a threat to the durability of the export orientation.

29. See Celasun 1989 for an analysis.

30. See Data Appendix Table 3.

31. See Celasun 1989 for a discussion.

32. See Data Appendix Table 6.

33. Estimates indicate that Turkey had a surplus on current account of $966 million in 1989, down from $1,596 million in 1988.

34. Along with other measures, the authorities further liberalized imports significantly at the end of February 1990.

Bibliography

Amelung, Torsten. 1988. "The Political Economy of Import Substitution and Subsequent Trade Liberalization: The Case of Turkey." Kiel Institute of World Economics, Working Paper no. 330. July.

Anand, Ritu, and Sweder van Wijnbergen. 1989. "Inflation and the Financing of Government Expenditure: An Introductory Analysis with an Application to Turkey." *World Bank Economic Review* 3, no. 1 (January): 17–38.

Balassa, Bela. 1985. "Outward Orientation and Exchange Rate Policy in Developing Countries: The Turkish Experience." Essay no. 10 in Bela Balassa, *Change and Challenge in the World Economy.* London: Macmillan Press.

Barkey, Henri. 1984. "Crises of the Turkish Political Economy: 1960–1980." In Ahmet Evin, ed., *Modern Turkey: Continuity and Change,* 47–63. Leverkusen, Germany: Leske und Budrich.

Baysan, Tercan, and Charles Blitzer. 1988a. "Turkey." Chap. 3 in *The Experience of New Zealand, Spain, and Turkey.* Vol. 6 of Liberalizing Foreign Trade, ed. Demetris Papageorgiou, Michael Michaely, and Armeane M. Choksi. London: Basil Blackwell, 1991.

———. 1988b. "Turkey's Trade Liberalization in the 1980s and Prospects for Its Sustainability." Paper presented at conference on "Turkey's Economic Development in the 1980s: Changing Strategies and Prospects for the Next Decade," Harvard University.

Bhagwati, Jagdish N. 1974. "On the Underinvoicing of Imports." In Jagdish N. Bhagwati, ed., *Illegal Transactions in International Trade,* 138–47. Vol. 1 of Studies in International Economics. Amsterdam: North-Holland Publishing Company.

Celasun, Merih. 1989. "Income Distribution and Employment Aspects of Turkey's Post-1980 Adjustment." *METU Studies in Development* 16, no. 3–4.

Celasun, Merih, and Dani Rodrik. 1987. "Debt, Adjustment, and Growth." Mimeo. November.

Collins, Susan M. 1989. "Debt, Policy, and Performance: An Introduction." In Jeffrey D. Sachs and Susan M. Collins, *Developing Country Debt and Economic Performance.* Vol. 3 of Country Studies—Indonesia, Korea, Philippines, Turkey. Chicago: University of Chicago Press.

Demircelik, A., and G. Sak. 1987. "Resource and Credit Costs in the Turkish Banking System, 1979–1986" (in Turkish). Capital Market Board, Ankara, Research Report no. 8/07.

Dervis, Kemal, Jaime de Melo, and Sherman Robinson. 1982. *General Equilibrium Models for Development Policy*, chaps. 10 and 11. Cambridge: Cambridge University Press.

Dervis, Kemal, and Sherman Robinson. 1980. "Structure of Income Inequality in Turkey." In Ergun Ozbundun and Aydin Ulusan, eds., *The Political Economy of Income Distribution in Turkey*, chap. 4, 83–122. New York: Holmes and Meier Publishers.

Heper, Metin. 1984. "Bureaucrats, Politicians, and Officers in Turkey: Dilemmas of a New Political Paradigm." In Ahmet Evin, ed., *Modern Turkey: Continuity and Change*, 64–83. Leverkusen, Germany: Leske und Budrich.

International Monetary Fund. *Annual Report on Exchange Arrangements and Exchange Restrictions.* Various issues.

Kim, Kwang Suk, and Michael Roemer. 1979. *Studies in the Modernization of the Republic of Korea: 1947–1975. Growth and Structural Transformation.* Cambridge, Mass.: Harvard University Press.

Kopits, George. 1987. *Structural Reform, Stabilization, and Growth in Turkey.* International Monetary Fund Occasional Paper 52. Washington, D.C. May.

Krueger, Anne O. 1974. *Foreign Trade Regimes and Economic Development: Turkey.* New York: Columbia University Press for National Bureau of Economic Research.

———. 1987. "The Importance of Economic Policy in Development: Contrasts between Korea and Turkey." In Henryk Kierzkowski, ed., *Protection and Competition in International Trade*, chap. 13, 172–203. Oxford: Basil Blackwell.

Krueger, Anne O., and Baran Tuncer. 1982. "Growth of Factor Productivity in Turkish Manufacturing Industries." *Journal of Development Economics* 11, no. 3 (December): 307–26.

Okyar, Osman. 1983. "Turkey and the IMF: A Review of Relations, 1978–82." In John Williamson, ed., *IMF Conditionality*, 533–61. Washington, D.C.: Institute for International Economics.

Organization for Economic Cooperation and Development. *OECD Economic Surveys. Turkey.* Paris. Various years.

Rodrik, Dani. 1988. "Some Policy Dilemmas in Turkish Macroeconomic Management." Kennedy School of Government Discussion Paper Series no. 173D. Harvard University. Mimeo. September. The estimates were separately printed as "Turkiye'nin Ihracat Patlamasinin Ne Kadari Hayali," in *Toplum ve Bilim,* 42 Yaz 1988, 133–36.

————. 1989. "Premature Liberalization, Incomplete Stabilization: The Özal Decade in Turkey." Kennedy School of Government. Mimeo. November.

Sachs, Jeffrey D. 1989. *Developing Country Debt and Economic Performance,* vol. 1. Chicago: University of Chicago Press for National Bureau of Economic Research.

Saraçoğlu, Rüşdü. 1987. "Economic Stabilization and Structural Adjustment: The Case of Turkey." In V. Corbo, M. Goldstein, and M. Khan, eds., *Growth-Oriented Adjustment Programs,* 119–43. Washington, D.C.: International Monetary Fund and World Bank.

Sturc, Ernest. 1968. "Stabilization Policies: Experience of Some European Countries in the 1950s." *International Monetary Fund Staff Papers,* July.

Turkish Foreign Trade Association (Turktrade). 1989. *Turkish Foreign Trade Companies.* Directory of members.

World Bank. *World Debt Tables.* Various issues.

Index

About the Authors

ANNE O. KRUEGER is currently Arts and Sciences Professor of Economics at Duke University and from 1982 to 1986 was vice president, economics and research, of the World Bank. She earlier taught at the University of Minnesota, Northwestern University, Monash University, the University of Paris, Australian National University, and a number of other institutions. She is the volume editor of *Development with Trade: LDCs and the International Economy* (ICS Press, 1988) and the author of many other books, articles, and chapters in multiauthor works.

OKAN H. AKTAN is professor in the Department of Economics at Hacettepe University, Ankara, Turkey. He holds a doctorate in economics from Oxford University and during the 1980s was awarded a Jean Monet fellowship, an ENKA award in economics, and a Ford Foundation fellowship. He has held several faculty appointments at Hacettepe University and has also taught in the Department of Economics at the University of Minnesota. He has written extensively on Turkish international economic relations.

ICEG Academic Advisory Board